Happy cooking!
Julie Dammento

Best Wishes
Rose Guarra

Bob Lendael

Menus for All Occasions

Also by Julie Dannenbaum:

Julie Dannenbaum's
Creative Cooking School

Menus for All Occasions

Julie Dannenbaum

Drawings by Regina Shekerjian

Saturday Review Press | E. P. Dutton & Co., Inc.
New York

Published simultaneously in Canada by
Clarke, Irwin & Company Limited, Toronto and Vancouver

Library of Congress Catalog Card Number: 73–76498
ISBN 0–8415–0275–7

Printed in the United States of America

Design by Lucy Fehr

For H.M.D., Jr.

The author wishes to thank her past and present assistants, namely Fritzie Grabosky, Claire Felix, Mary Hopkins, Jo Klein, Maxine Rogers, and especially Sandy Ainsworth who assisted me for five years. A special thanks to Kathryn Larson who assisted me in preparing this book.

Contents

Introduction   1

Methods and Techniques   5

Breakfasts and Brunches   9

Luncheons   39

Dinners   91

Buffets   181

Suppers   215

Cocktail Parties   227

Teas   243

Outdoor Entertaining   251

Basic Recipes   277

Index   291

Menus for All Occasions

Introduction

Let me tell you about entertaining as a way of life. I count my years in menus rather than days.

During the months that my cooking school is open, I "entertain" three, four, and sometimes five times during the week, preparing food each day to be served to from twenty-five to thirty-five students. (How fast my students learn to be critical, and how they keep me on my toes!) At home I invite guests over at least once a week, so I constantly put my teaching to practical tests. Or is it my social experience that makes my teaching more practical? Each side of my cooking life fuels the other. This is a collection of the best menus from both worlds, those special combinations I have found, from experience, to please. Sometimes you will wish to duplicate the menus exactly; at other times you may decide to substitute a salad, a plain vegetable, or fresh fruit for the richer counterparts I've suggested. And you may wish to vary menus because of your guests' known preferences. Always keep your options open in this way. My menu suggestions are just that—suggestions, ideas, starting points.

I've tried to steer clear of menus that are either tricky or cute. Every one of the recipes in this book, first and foremost, is *doable*. And because I never assume that a dish will *look* good just because it tastes good, I've emphasized throughout the garnishing and presentation of each dish. Many of the menus are introduced with notes on the preparation, timing, background, or special delights of the dishes represented, and in all I've aimed for the kind of step-by-step directions that instruct without either wearying or intimidating.

While it may sound dull, I can't overemphasize the importance of planning. Successful entertaining is part cooking, part list-making, and I recommend writing down on paper each stage of your party, from your marketing list and cooking schedule to your table appointments and seating arrangement. If possible, start planning three days ahead of serving time. With list in hand, you will be able to pace yourself through even a complicated party. Believe me, there is nothing more steadying when you're under stress than this reassurance that you have not forgotten anything. If you have help in the kitchen, be sure to leave them an equally explicit list before you join your guests.

The most important part of planning relates directly to the preparation of the food. With this in mind, I have included as many make-ahead dishes as possible, leaving only as many last-minute saucing, reheating, and unmolding steps as can be reasonably managed. A good number can be prepared several days ahead or even frozen. If you do this, remember to bring the dish to room temperature before either reheating it or continuing with the recipe.

The other best advice I can give you is to tell your butcher everything—take him into your confidence, and listen to his suggestions, too. Be suspicious of a butcher who only wants to sell you fillet of beef for a party. Almost everyone appreciates a simple meal, superbly cooked, so have the courage to produce one. Once when Dione Lucas was a guest, I was anxious to serve my most elegant recipes. She would have none of it; she informed me ahead of time that she was hungry for sauerkraut. What would you have done? I fixed choucroute garni, lentil salad, and steamed potatoes with caraway and melted butter. The recipes are in this book, along with one for the dessert I served on that most successful evening, a caramelized apple dish called Tart Tatin, which Dione loved. Dione, by the way, as well as other experts with whom I have studied—among them James Beard, Richard Olney, Ann Roe Robbins, Michael Field, and Simone Beck—have all greatly influenced my cooking and helped me to develop a style of my own.

My entertaining has changed since we sold our suburban house, patio and all, and moved into a large, five-story town house in center-city Philadelphia. It's a beautiful house, and the only structural work we did was in ripping out the kitchen—a dismal basement workroom—and redesigning it as a warm, low-ceilinged country-French-style kitchen. The overhead pipes were covered in weathered oak to create a beamed effect, and the rough white plaster walls set off the natural terra-cotta tile floor and the blue and gold Portuguese tiles framing the work counters, shelves, range, and cooktop. All the counter tops are chopping blocks, with a marble slab built in for pastry-making. I have no wall cabinets; instead there are floor-to-ceiling storage shelves at one end of the room. We eat and entertain at the other end, where I can seat eight at two round slate-topped tables. Guests love to eat in the kitchen, and I sometimes even throw black-tie dinners here.

In my dining room upstairs, which I use for more formal occasions, I finally have the table I've always wanted—a long walnut one perfectly sized for the room and seating twelve comfortably. It also unhooks to make three individual square tables, which I cover with pleated tablecloths to the floor—and suddenly the room has a more relaxed character. Guests remember a formal meal when you add a few flourishes. When I use the dining room, I write out the menus on white cards edged in gold. Wines are listed too, and I like to serve two or maybe three at a very formal dinner. On these evenings, we have cocktails in the library on the second floor and coffee in the drawing room on the first floor, for I have discovered that guests like to move around from one room or area to another, enjoying the contrast in settings.

It's certainly not necessary to have an excuse for a party, but I do think it heightens the mood if there's an occasion to celebrate, a person to recognize. I put my house to the test recently when Mme Simone Beck visited. Her new book, *Simca's Cuisine*, had just been published, and the list of Philadelphia food and press people that I wanted to meet her grew to 140! James Beard came in from New York, pleased to honor our friend, and the party was a glorious, milling, moving feast.

From simple to elegant, informal to formal, readers will, I hope, find a menu here for every occasion—from breakfast to lunch or dinner to midnight supper—for every season of the year. Many of the menus feature recipes from Alsace, the home of my maternal grandmother and a source of inspiration, in turn, for my mother's cooking. Alsace, lying on France's German border, is rich farming country, and its cuisine draws on the traditions of both countries to make full and delectable use of the variety of foods available—pork, goose, game, trout, goose livers for pâté, chestnuts for delicious purees, cabbage for sauerkraut, fresh berries and fruits for tarts and pies. I have also included a goodly number of American regional dishes, particularly those of the mid-Atlantic states. Perhaps the most dominant influence on my cooking, however, has been the various great cuisines of Europe. I travel twice a year to Europe searching for new ideas and new recipes for my school and party files. I visit food shops, hardware stores, flea markets, coffeehouses, and tea shops, as well as fine restaurants and country inns. Whenever I taste something I like, I pull out my notebook and write a description of it, together with an educated guess about what the actual recipe is. These notes are my starting points for experiments when I return to Philadelphia—inspiration for another series of lessons at my school, another round of dinner parties at home.

Methods and Techniques

Here are a few hints and pieces of information that I think you will find helpful—these techniques are used over and over in the recipes that follow.

All baking ingredients should be at room temperature unless "chilled" is specified.

Except in a few cake recipes that call for sifted flour, all flour in my recipes is measured as follows: before measuring, I stir or aerate the flour (which is stored in a canister) with a scoop or spoon, to loosen it; then I lightly scoop it into the measuring cup and level it off with a straight-edged knife. I'm careful not to pack it or shake it down into the cup. You'll see that flour is described in many recipes as "lightly spooned." When mixing dry ingredients (such as salt or baking powder) into the flour, it's usually sufficient just to stir them in. The recipe states when sifting is required.

When stirring flour and fat together (as when making a sauce), I always use a wooden spatula; then I switch to a whisk when liquid is added, to avoid lumps.

Some recipes call for a thickening agent such as cornstarch or potato starch. If you don't happen to have the one listed at hand, remember that potato starch (potato flour), cornstarch, and arrowroot are virtually interchangeable. Just substitute an equal amount of the thickener you do have.

Many herbs, such as tarragon and thyme, are sometimes available fresh but much more readily available, year-round, in their dried form. The measurements are therefore for dried herbs. If you have fresh, just remember that 1 tablespoon fresh equals 1 teaspoon dried. Of course, parsley, garlic, and dill in my recipes are *always* fresh.

I like to cook on high heat, in heavy pans, for many steps in my recipes—such as cooking onions or stirring flour into butter for a sauce base. This saves time. If, however, you have light-weight pans, or are nervous using high heat, use a lower flame or burner setting.

Reheating instructions may be varied to suit the needs of the menu. If you make up your own menu and find that a dish to be reheated at 350° is now paired with one to be baked at 375°, don't hesitate to change the directions. By the way, I nearly always bring food to room temperature before reheating, so do this unless the instructions tell you to put a refrigerated dish straight in the oven. Food at room temperature generally takes about 15 to 20 minutes in a 350° oven to reheat. It's a good idea, too, when cooking a recipe ahead, to undercook it slightly, allowing for the reheating.

Your freezer makes it possible to space out preparations for a dinner party or weekend guests, but I hope you'll use it like a checking account, not a long-term savings bank! I'm constantly putting food in and drawing it out; I believe in a fast turnover, nothing stored overlong. A 1-month limit is a good rule for all prepared items such as sauced main dishes, desserts, and breads. Quality goes only one way: down. Enjoy the good things you fix before they get tired.

If you wish to assemble ahead of time—and store in the refrigerator—a dessert decorated with whipped cream, be sure to whip the cream in a metal bowl, over ice, with a piano-wire balloon whisk. Cream beaten in the usual way with electric or rotary beaters, weeps. Confectioners' sugar (preferable to granulated) for sweetening should be added when the cream is mounding softly.

Breakfasts and Brunches

My favorite food memories from childhood begin at sunrise, when I would walk into my mother's kitchen, irresistibly drawn to the black coal stove where there'd always be a pot of soup simmering and, in wintertime, a heavy pan with the creamiest oatmeal ever. When my mother spooned it out, she pushed a lump of butter into it and sprinkled it with brown sugar; at the table, we poured on our own thick cream.

We always had fruit, fresh when it was ripe in the garden, but more often cooked. Whole baked pears, or sautéed cinnamon apples, or spicy-thick apple butter—the perfect complement to crisp-fried scrapple. A Sunday treat was double-dipped French toast with ginger sauce or maple syrup, and special breakfast bacon cut one inch thick and sautéed for half an hour until it was beautifully crisp.

9

Our cellar cold room was lined with jars of jelly and jam, the fruit and year of each identified by hand-lettered labels. We used it lavishly: rolled up in crêpes, or packed in crocks for everyone to help himself. Thanks to my mother's Alsatian background, we had plenty of breads and rolls to spread it on—and coffee cakes of all kinds and shapes besides.

When I think of inviting friends for early or late breakfast—or brunch, as the latter is almost always called nowadays—it's this yeasty-smelling, buttered-and-jellied cooked breakfast from my childhood that I remember: homey, heartwarming, hospitable, a wonderful way to entertain. It's a relaxed time of day: guests don't expect—or want!—elaborate, multicourse meals. You can devote yourself to one mainstay dish—and to bread-making. Service is usually informal; I often cook in front of my guests. Still, there's room for surprise in even a short menu, and many ways to depart from the bacon-and-eggs routine. Consider Onion Soup, Polenta Croquettes, Chicken Livers en Brochette, Ham Roulade, Roast Beef Hash. The menus in this chapter will suggest the range of dishes open to you at this most appealing hour.

Keep the drink service casual too. I usually have a pitcher of bloody Marys, bullshots, or screwdrivers ready to pour, as well as icy-cold fruit juices for nonimbibers. At late brunches I sometimes serve black velvets—that incomparably smooth mixture of stout and champagne. Wines, too, are always welcome, and of course there is nothing more festive and more refreshing than champagne when you have an occasion to celebrate—or even when you don't.

On chilly winter mornings you might consider leading off with steaming mugs of soup—my mother would have approved—and always, whatever the season, have plenty of freshly brewed coffee on hand, as well as tea, if anyone prefers it. It's fun to experiment with different kinds of coffee: espresso, cappuccino, Viennese coffee, or, for a very warm glow, Irish coffee, to name only a few.

And, whatever else is on your menu, add the indulgent extras: an assortment of home-baked rolls, breadsticks, coffee cakes, and doughnuts, plus pots of sweet butter and a generous selection of jams.

A Classic Continental Breakfast
for Any Number

Brioche and croissants
Assortment of jams, jellies, and conserves
Pot of unsalted butter
Café au lait

BRIOCHE

2 packages active dry yeast
½ cup warm water (105° to 115°)
4 cups lightly spooned flour

1½ cups butter
6 eggs
1 tablespoon sugar
1 teaspoon salt

Sprinkle yeast into warm water; stir until dissolved. Measure 1 cup of flour into a small bowl, add yeast mixture, stir to make a stiff dough, and knead until smooth. Form into a ball, cut a cross or X in the top with a knife (to help the dough rise), and drop the ball into a bowl of lukewarm water. The ball of yeast sponge should rise to the top of the water in about 7 minutes; if it doesn't, the yeast isn't working; throw it out and start over.

While yeast sponge is rising, whip butter until smooth and creamy (use the flat beater throughout recipe if you have a heavy-duty mixer) and set aside. In another bowl, beat together eggs, remaining 3 cups of flour, sugar, and salt. Use electric mixer and flat beater or beat by hand with a wooden spoon. Dough should become shiny, sticky, wet-looking, and very elastic. If it's very sticky and hard to get off the sides of the bowl, beat in another egg. (You'll develop a feel for brioche; don't expect to make it perfectly the first time.)

Remove yeast sponge from water, letting water run off. Add sponge and creamed butter to egg dough and beat until thoroughly mixed, using the flat beater or wooden spoon. Grease and lightly flour a large bowl. Place dough in bowl, cover with plastic wrap, and let rise in a warm place, free from drafts, for about 1 hour. The dough does not have to double in bulk, but indentations should remain when you press fingertip into dough. When it's risen, stir it down; re-cover with plastic wrap and refrigerate overnight. The next day, shape brioche according to the following directions, or as directed in other recipes in this book, and bake.

Note: You can freeze brioche dough for up to a month. When you are ready to use it, remove the freezer wrapping, place in a bowl, cover with plastic wrap, and refrigerate it overnight to defrost.

INDIVIDUAL BRIOCHE

Butter 30 individual 2-inch brioche molds (or use muffin pans or ovenproof custard cups). Turn refrigerated dough, which will be sticky, onto a lightly floured board and shape into a roll. Cut off small pieces of dough and shape to fill molds about ¾ full. To make the typical brioche knob or crown, cut a cross in the center of dough in each mold and open it up like flower petals. Brush opening with egg wash (1 egg yolk mixed with 1 tablespoon water). Form a smaller piece of dough with a pointy bottom and fit it into the opening. Cover brioche loosely with a cloth towel or plastic wrap and let rise away from drafts until doubled and puffing above the edge of the mold, about 1 hour. Brush with egg wash and bake in a preheated 375° oven for 15 to 20 minutes, or until nicely browned.

GIANT BRIOCHE

Butter a 2-quart charlotte mold (or you can use a round casserole). Turn refrigerated dough onto a lightly floured board. Shape ¾ of the dough into a ball and place it in the buttered mold. Cut a cross in the center of the dough and open it up like flower petals. Brush opening with egg wash. Shape remaining ¼ of dough with a pointy bottom and rounded top; fit the point into the opening. Cover brioche loosely with plastic wrap or a cloth towel and let rise away from drafts until doubled, about 1 hour. Brush with egg wash and bake in a preheated 375° oven for about 50 to 55 minutes, or until nicely browned and brioche begins to pull away from the sides of the mold. If it browns too fast, cover loosely with foil during baking

CROISSANTS

¾ cup butter
3 cups lightly spooned flour
¾ cup milk
¼ cup warm water (105° to
 115°)

1 package active dry yeast
3 tablespoons sugar
1 teaspoon salt
2 eggs
1 tablespoon cream

Work butter into ¼ cup of the flour until mixture is a smooth paste. Place between 2 sheets of waxed paper and roll out to 10 x 4-inch rectangle. Chill for 2 hours.

When butter mixture is chilled, scald milk and cool to lukewarm. Measure warm water into a large, warmed mixing bowl, sprinkle with yeast, and stir until dissolved. Add sugar, salt, 1 beaten egg, milk, and 1 cup flour, and beat until smooth with an electric mixer or wooden spoon. Stir in remaining flour and mix until completely blended.

Turn out dough onto a well-floured board and roll out to a 12-inch square. Carefully peel waxed paper from chilled butter mixture and place it over the center third of rolled dough. Fold both ends of dough over butter mixture into thirds (like a business letter). Give dough a quarter turn (folds will be on right and left), roll out again to a 12-inch square, and fold in thirds as before. Turn, roll, and fold dough 3 more times. (Rechill the dough if it softens while you are working with it. After 20 to 30 minutes in the refrigerator, it will be ready for you to continue with the recipe.) Wrap in waxed paper and refrigerate for 3 hours. (*Recipe can be prepared ahead to this point and held in refrigerator overnight or up to 12 hours.*)

To shape croissants, divide chilled dough into thirds. Take each third in turn, refrigerating remainder, and roll out to a 12-inch circle. Cut into 8 pie-shaped wedges. Brush point of each wedge with a mixture of 1 egg beaten with cream. Beginning at the wide end, roll up each wedge tightly and pinch point to seal. Place on a greased baking sheet with the point underneath and curve to form a crescent. Cover with plastic wrap or towel and let rise in a warm place free from drafts until almost doubled, about 30 to 45 minutes. Brush each croissant with egg-cream mixture and bake in a preheated 375° oven for about 12 to 15 minutes or until lightly browned. Makes 24 croissants. *Baked croissants may be frozen for up to one month. Bring to room temperature; warm if desired.*

CAFÉ AU LAIT

Make strong coffee. Heat (but do not boil) an equal amount of half-and-half. Pour them simultaneously into large breakfast cups and sweeten to taste.

A Country Breakfast for 6 to 8

Baked cinnamon apples
Breakfast bacon
Roesti potatoes
Easy coffee cake or Kugelhopf

BAKED CINNAMON APPLES

6 cups green apples, peeled, cored, and cut in eighths
1 cup sugar
2 teaspoons cinnamon
½ teaspoon freshly grated nutmeg

2 tablespoons apple brandy
Juice of 1 lemon
4 tablespoons melted butter
Sour cream, optional

Mix thoroughly apples, sugar, cinnamon, and nutmeg, using your hands. Put into a casserole dish and sprinkle with brandy, lemon juice, and melted butter. Cover and bake in a preheated 375° oven for 35 to 45 minutes, or until apples are soft. (*Apples can be cooked ahead and reheated.*) Serve hot or warm, with sour cream if you wish.

BREAKFAST BACON

Trim the rind from a 1-pound slab of bacon and cut it into slices 1 inch thick. Cook in an iron skillet over medium heat for about 30 minutes, turning occasionally. Do not pour off fat. Bacon will cook crisp all the way through. Drain on paper towels before serving.

ROESTI POTATOES

The trick is to keep the potatoes from sticking to the pan while they cook. You want to keep the potato cake "afloat" so you can turn it out, brown and crusty, on your serving plate. A non-stick pan helps.

6 large baking potatoes	2 teaspoons salt
½ cup butter	½ teaspoon freshly cracked
2 tablespoons vegetable oil	white pepper
or bacon fat	6 tablespoons melted butter

Put potatoes in a saucepan, cover with cold water, and bring to a boil; boil hard, uncovered, for about 10 minutes. Peel potatoes while still warm and grate them. Heat the ½ cup butter with the oil in a large skillet over high heat until foaming subsides, being careful not to let butter brown. Put about half of the grated potatoes into the skillet, pressing them down firmly with a spatula. Sprinkle with half the salt and pepper and drizzle with 4 tablespoons melted butter. Add remaining potatoes; press firmly with spatula. Shake the pan to make sure the potato cake moves freely; if it is sticking, use the spatula to push potatoes in from the edge of the pan. Drizzle with remaining 2 tablespoons butter and sprinkle with remaining salt and pepper. Cook over high heat for 5 minutes. Then press down hard on potatoes, using a flat lid just a bit smaller than skillet. Reduce heat to medium and cook, keeping the lid on, about 20 minutes or until potatoes are crusty on the bottom. Shake the skillet every few minutes to ensure that the potatoes stay afloat. Unmold on a round serving plate, crusty side up.

EASY COFFEE CAKE

This recipe makes enough yeast dough for 2 coffee cakes. You can fill and bake one cake, and store the dough for a second in the refrigerator for 5 to 6 days. Or you can freeze the dough, for up to one month, thawing it overnight in the refrigerator before using it. Or you can form the extra dough into small dinner rolls.

½ cup light cream
2 packages active dry yeast
1 cup butter
½ cup sugar
¼ cup sour cream
3 well-beaten eggs

1½ teaspoons salt
4 cups lightly spooned flour
   Filling (recipe follows)
1 egg white, slightly beaten
¼ cup slivered almonds

Heat cream to lukewarm; sprinkle with yeast and stir to dissolve. In a large bowl, cream butter and sugar together until fluffy. Add sour cream, eggs, and yeast mixture and beat very well until thoroughly blended (using an electric mixer if you wish). Mix salt with 1 cup of the flour and beat into yeast mixture. Add remaining flour gradually, mixing thoroughly. Shape the dough into a ball and put into a greased bowl, turning the ball to grease lightly all over; then cover dough with waxed paper and a towel and refrigerate overnight. The next day, divide dough in half. Refrigerate (or freeze) half for another occasion.

Place dough for 1 coffee cake on floured waxed paper. Sprinkle it lightly with flour and cover with a second sheet of waxed paper. Roll dough between sheets of waxed paper to make a 9 x 15-inch rectangle, ½ inch thick. If the paper begins sticking to the dough (lift the paper to check this), dust on a bit more flour. Peel off top sheet of waxed paper and, turning the dough upside down, carefully fit dough into a 9 x 5 x 3-inch bread pan, allowing it to drape over the sides of pan. Peel off second sheet of waxed paper. Spoon filling over dough in pan and fold dough over filling, pinching it to seal securely. Brush the top of the loaf with slightly beaten egg white and sprinkle with almonds. Place *at once* into a preheated 350° oven and bake for 1 hour. This loaf does not need to rise before going into the oven.

FILLING FOR 1 COFFEE CAKE

1½ cups cottage cheese
2 tablespoons flour
2 tablespoons light cream
3 egg yolks
¼ cup sugar

1 tablespoon melted butter
1 teaspoon vanilla extract
¼ cup raisins
2 egg whites
¼ teaspoon salt

Press the cottage cheese through a sieve. Add flour and cream and mix well. Beat egg yolks, beat in sugar and butter, and add to the cheese, along with vanilla and raisins. Beat egg whites with salt until stiff and fold into cheese mixture.

KUGELHOPF

½ cup milk
½ cup granulated sugar
1 teaspoon salt
¼ cup butter
¼ cup warm water (105° to 115°)
1 package active dry yeast
2 beaten eggs
2 cups lightly spooned flour

2 tablespoons fine bread crumbs
16 whole blanched almonds
½ cup raisins
½ teaspoon grated lemon peel
½ teaspoon freshly grated nutmeg
Confectioners' sugar

Scald the milk. Stir in sugar, salt, and butter and cool to luke-warm. Measure warm water into electric mixer bowl and sprinkle with yeast; stir until dissolved. Stir in the lukewarm milk mixture; add the beaten eggs and the flour and beat vigorously with electric mixer for about 5 minutes. Cover the bowl and let the dough rise in a warm place, free from drafts, until double in bulk, about 1 to 1½ hours.

Butter generously a 1½-quart Kugelhopf mold and sprinkle sides and bottom with bread crumbs. Arrange the almonds decoratively in bottom of mold. When dough has risen, stir it down, beating thoroughly. Beat in raisins, lemon peel, and nut-meg, and pour into the prepared mold. Let rise again in a warm place until double in bulk, about 1 hour. Bake in a preheated 350° oven for 50 to 60 minutes. Turn out to cool on a cake rack. To serve, sprinkle Kugelhopf with confectioners' sugar and poke a pleated paper doily, like a flag, into the hole in the center of the cake. *Baked Kugelhopf also freezes well.*

A Hearty Winter Breakfast for 6 to 8

Poached apples with meringue
Pennsylvania scrapple
Polenta croquettes
Popovers

If your family or guests enjoy appetite-building hikes on frosty mornings, here's the breakfast to welcome them home and warm them up. It's a mixture of things I like: poached apples, Pennsylvania Dutch scrapple—good with polenta, the Italian cornmeal—and crusty popovers with lots of butter. Some guests choose what they want; hungry ones eat it all!

To manage this menu with one oven, do half of it ahead of time. The apples can be fully prepared, scorched meringue and all, and held at room temperature ready to serve. You can also bake popovers ahead and reheat them; you can even freeze them and reheat them. Just be sure they're completely baked, so the shell is strong; they deflate if underbaked. Keep croquettes warm and reheat popovers while you fry the scrapple.

POACHED APPLES WITH MERINGUE

8 baking apples, Rome Beauty, Winesap, or Stayman	3 cups sugar
	2 cups water
⅓ cup Calvados	6 egg whites
½ cup mincemeat	¼ teaspoon cream of tartar

Peel and core the apples, but do not pierce through the bottom. Place them in a baking pan; do not let them touch each other. Put 1 teaspoon Calvados and 1 tablespoon mincemeat into each apple. In a saucepan, heat 2 cups sugar, the water, and remaining Calvados, stirring until sugar is dissolved and mixture boils. Pour around apples and cover the baking pan with aluminum foil. Place in a preheated 350° oven and poach apples until barely tender but not mushy, about 30 to 45 minutes. The time depends on the size and kind of apples. Remove apples to an ovenproof serving dish.

Boil down the syrup until thick enough to coat a spoon and ladle it over the apples. Beat egg whites and cream of tartar with electric mixer until foamy. Gradually beat in remaining 1 cup sugar, 1 tablespoon at a time. Continue beating until meringue looks thick and glossy, like marshmallow, and no longer feels grainy when you pinch it. Put meringue into a large pastry bag fitted with a star tube and pipe onto apples. You can cover the top only, or the entire apple, or make designs up and down the sides of the apple. Run apples under the broiler to set and scorch the meringue. *May be cooked ahead of time and served at room temperature.*

PENNSYLVANIA SCRAPPLE

Scrapple is the tasty product of German and Pennsylvania Dutch thriftiness. Wasting nothing at butchering time, we grind pork scraps and livers to mix with cornmeal and buckwheat flour, seasoning it well. The thinner you slice it the better, I think.

Cut 1 pound of scrapple into slices about ¼ inch thick, allowing 2 slices for each guest. Heat 2 tablespoons vegetable oil in a heavy skillet and sauté scrapple over fairly high heat for 3 to 5 minutes on each side. Do not let pieces touch each other. Scrapple should be crusty-brown, with a soft interior.

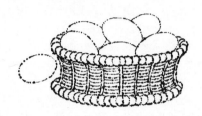

POLENTA

7½ cups water	2 teaspoons salt
2 cups quick-cooking polenta	½ teaspoon freshly cracked
½ cup butter	white pepper
¾ cup grated Parmesan cheese	¼ teaspoon freshly grated
2 tablespoons chopped	nutmeg
parsley	3 eggs
1 finely chopped clove garlic	

In a saucepan, bring water to a boil; add polenta gradually, in a thin stream, stirring. Stir continuously and cook over medium heat until it becomes so thick the spoon will stand upright—this will take about 5 minutes. Pour mixture into a big bowl and add butter, Parmesan cheese, parsley, garlic, salt, pepper, and nutmeg; blend them in. Beat the eggs and warm them with a bit of the polenta mixture; then stir eggs into polenta. Taste for seasoning.

Note: Semolina and yellow cornmeal are substitutes for polenta. If you can't find the quick-cooking variety, use the same amounts of regular polenta and water. It will take longer to cook it, however. When it thickens, set saucepan into a pan of boiling water and cook for another 30 to 35 minutes, over low heat, stirring occasionally.

POLENTA CROQUETTES

1 recipe Polenta (preceding
  recipe)
1 cup flour
2 beaten eggs

2 cups bread crumbs
  Fat for deep frying
½ recipe Tomato Sauce (see
  p. 64)

Spread polenta mixture in a baking tray or jelly-roll pan rinsed with cold water; smooth with a spatula and chill for at least ½ hour, or cover with plastic wrap and chill overnight. To form croquettes, take a good tablespoonful of the chilled mixture and, using the heel of your hand, very lightly shape it into a cork shape. Or cut mixture with a knife or with cutters to make squares, diamonds, or other shapes. Coat the shapes with flour, patting off excess; then dip in beaten egg and roll in crumbs. Chill again for at least ½ hour. Heat fat in saucepan or deep-fat fryer to 375° and fry croquettes, 2 or 3 at a time, for about 2 minutes or until nicely browned. Drain on paper towels and hold them in a 350° oven to keep warm while you fry remaining croquettes. Serve hot with Tomato Sauce.

Variation: Cut chilled mixture into squares or fancy shapes, then simply flour and sauté in butter, instead of deep-frying. Or place thinly sliced cheese (you can use any firm cheese, such as Cheddar or Swiss) and/or ham between 2 squares and bake in a preheated 350° oven for 15 to 20 minutes.

POPOVERS

Have all ingredients at room temperature before proceeding. Served with jam, popovers make an excellent dessertlike finale to this menu.

2 eggs
1 cup milk

1 cup lightly spooned flour
1 teaspoon salt

Beat the eggs with an egg beater for about 1 minute. Add milk and beat just until blended. Stir the flour and salt together in a mixing bowl. Make a well in the center and pour in the egg mixture, stirring with a wooden spoon until flour is dampened. Then beat (with egg beater) 1 minute longer. Place 8 ovenproof glass custard cups with narrow bottoms on a baking tray and grease them lightly. Half-fill each cup with batter. Place in a preheated 425° oven and bake for 30 minutes, or until puffed and brown. Turn heat down to 350° and continue baking for 15 to 20 minutes more, to dry out. (*Popovers may be baked ahead, removed from cups, and cooled or frozen. Reheat in a 350° oven for about 5 minutes; if frozen, bring to room temperature before reheating.*) Split popovers while hot and serve with unsalted butter and your favorite jam.

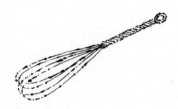

Breakfast for 4 for Weekend Guests

Baked pears with heavy cream
Double-dipped French toast with ginger sauce
Baked Canadian bacon
Panettone
Espresso coffee

BAKED PEARS WITH HEAVY CREAM

4 pears, half-ripe
½ cup sugar
2 teaspoons cinnamon
1 tablespoon butter
4 tablespoons light corn syrup

4 tablespoons melted butter
½ cup heavy cream, plus
   additional heavy cream,
   optional

Peel pears with a potato peeler and cut a slice off bottoms so they will stand upright. Do not core. Mix sugar and cinnamon and roll pears in mixture to coat well. Butter a baking dish and stand pears upright. Pour on any sugar mixture remaining. Drizzle each pear with 1 tablespoon corn syrup and 1 tablespoon melted butter. Cover pears with a tent of aluminum foil and bake them in a preheated 375° oven for 25 minutes, basting occasionally with pan juices. Remove foil, turn oven down to 350°, and continue baking until pears are tender-firm—test with point of knife at base of pear. Remove pears to serving dishes. Stir heavy cream into the juices in the baking dish and pour over pears. Serve warm, with additional heavy cream if you wish.

DOUBLE-DIPPED FRENCH TOAST

4 eggs
⅛ teaspoon salt
¼ cup sugar
1 cup milk
1 cup light cream
¼ teaspoon freshly grated
    nutmeg

4 slices day-old French bread,
    2½ inches thick
½ cup butter
Confectioners' sugar
Ginger Sauce (recipe follows)

Beat eggs, salt, sugar, milk, cream, and nutmeg together with a whisk or rotary beater. Dip bread into mixture, quickly, on both sides, and remove to a platter; let stand for 10 minutes. Dip again in egg mixture, turning bread so that it soaks up liquid all the way through. (*Recipe can be made ahead to this point.*)

Heat butter in a heavy skillet until foamy. Brown the bread for 3 to 5 minutes on each side, over medium heat. Shake confectioners' sugar over each piece before serving. Serve with Ginger Sauce.

GINGER SAUCE

1 cup light corn syrup
1 tablespoon grated lemon peel
3 tablespoons lemon juice

½ cup drained and finely
    chopped preserved ginger
    in syrup
½ cup finely chopped crystal-
    lized ginger, optional

Heat syrup with lemon peel and lemon juice over low heat 1 minute, just to blend. Add chopped preserved ginger and serve warm with French toast. Pass chopped crystallized ginger in a small bowl, if you wish.

BAKED CANADIAN BACON

Remove the casing from a piece of Canadian bacon weighing about 1½ pounds. Lay it on a rack in a baking pan and brush with 2 tablespoons melted butter. Pour hot water into pan to a depth of ¼ inch and place in a preheated 325° oven. Bake for about 30 minutes. To serve, slice it very, very thin.

PANETTONE

Panettone is a traditional Italian fruitcake—and a delicious, dessertlike finale to this menu.

1 package active dry yeast
¼ cup lukewarm milk
4 cups lightly spooned flour, about
¾ cup butter
½ cup sugar
3 beaten eggs
2 beaten egg yolks
1 teaspoon anise extract
1 teaspoon salt

½ cup raisins
¼ cup chopped candied orange peel
½ cup chopped citron
¼ cup chopped blanched almonds
Whole almonds or pine nuts, optional
Sugar, optional

Sprinkle yeast into lukewarm milk and stir to dissolve. Stir in ½ cup of the flour and let stand in a warm place until bubbly, about 1 hour. In electric mixer bowl, cream butter and sugar together. Add beaten eggs and egg yolks and the yeast mixture. Beat in anise, salt, and enough of remaining flour to make a dough that is soft but not too sticky. Turn dough out on a floured board and knead in fruits and chopped almonds; knead until dough is smooth and elastic, about 10 to 15 minutes. Place in a greased bowl, turning to grease top; cover and set in a warm place to rise until double in bulk, about 1 hour.

While dough rises, butter a 2-pound coffee can or Kugelhopf mold. Arrange whole almonds or pine nuts in bottom of mold, if you wish, and sprinkle with sugar. When dough has risen, punch it down and turn out on board; knead again for 3 to 5 minutes. Shape it into a ball and put it into coffee can, or shape it like a doughnut and place in Kugelhopf mold. Cover and let rise in a warm place until double in bulk, about 1 hour. Bake in a preheated 400° oven for 10 minutes; reduce oven temperature to 350° and bake 50 minutes longer. If top browns too fast, lay a piece of aluminum foil over it. Remove from pan and cool on cake rack.

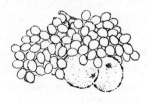

Brunch by the Fireplace
for 6

Glazed pineapple in kirsch
Roast beef hash
Danish pastry
Viennese coffee

When you expect guests to eat off their knees, serve fork food—hash is perfect. In front of the fire, this breakfast would be a leisurely one—fruit first, then hash, then pastry and coffee. Set it up buffet-style and let guests help themselves.

GLAZED PINEAPPLE IN KIRSCH

1 fresh pineapple
2 cups water
2 cups sugar
6 tablespoons light corn syrup
½ cup kirsch
2 tablespoons crystallized angelica, about, optional

Cut the top off the pineapple, trim it of damaged leaves, wash it, and set it aside, to garnish serving dish. Peel pineapple: stand it upright and with a serrated knife cut off the peel in strips from top to bottom. Remove eyes. (There's an easy way to do this: observe that the eyes are arranged in diagonal rows. With a sharp knife, cut diagonal grooves all around the pineapple and lift out the eyes in rows.) Slice the pineapple across, making thin slices (about ⅜ inch thick), and cut out the tough centers with a 1- to 1½-inch round cutter and reserve.

In a large skillet, bring water, sugar, and corn syrup to a boil, stirring until sugar dissolves. Add pineapple centers to syrup to help flavor it. Poach pineapple slices in boiling syrup over medium-high heat, a few at a time, until barely tender and a little translucent, about 7 minutes. Remove slices to serving dish. Keep syrup on high heat; when it is just shading to a pale caramel color, add kirsch and let it bubble for a minute. Pour syrup over pineapple slices, garnish with pineapple top placed at one end of serving dish and chopped crystallized angelica if you wish. Serve warm, cold, or at room temperature.

ROAST BEEF HASH

4 tablespoons butter
1 cup finely chopped onion
1 minced clove garlic
½ cup finely chopped green
  pepper
4 cups leftover roast beef,
  chopped
1 tablespoon Worcestershire
  sauce

2 teaspoons salt
½ teaspoon freshly cracked
  black pepper
1 cup finely diced raw potato
1 cup beef gravy *or* 1 cup beef
  stock (see p. 277) or
  chicken stock (see p. 278)
6 slices toast, optional

Heat butter in a heavy skillet and sauté onion, garlic, and green pepper over high heat until onion is transparent—do not let it brown. Add roast beef, Worcestershire sauce, salt, pepper, and potato. Pour on gravy or stock, cover, and cook over low heat until potatoes are tender, about 20 to 25 minutes. (*Recipe can be made ahead to this point; it can be frozen for up to one month if you wish. Bring to room temperature before reheating.*) Remove lid and cook for another 10 minutes to evaporate some of the liquid. (Consistency of hash will still be quite soft.) Serve with toast on the side if desired.

DANISH PASTRY

2 packages active dry yeast
½ cup warm water (105° to
  115°)
4 tablespoons butter, melted
  and cooled to lukewarm
5 tablespoons sugar
3 beaten eggs
½ cup lukewarm milk
1 teaspoon salt
1 teaspoon grated lemon peel
1 teaspoon vanilla extract

4½ cups lightly spooned flour
1 cup softened butter
1 egg yolk
1 tablespoon water
¾ cup raisins
1 tablespoon cinnamon
  Flaked toasted almonds
  Apricot Glaze (recipe
  follows)
  Vanilla Water Icing (recipe
  follows)

In a large warm mixing bowl, sprinkle yeast over warm water and stir to dissolve. Let rest 5 minutes. Then, with a wire whisk or electric mixer, beat in melted butter, sugar, eggs, milk, salt, lemon peel, and vanilla. Mix well. Beat in flour (use electric mixer or change from whisk to wooden spoon), to make a soft dough. Mix thoroughly—this dough is not kneaded. Cover the bowl with a towel and let dough rest in a warm place, free from drafts, to rise, for about 30 minutes.

Turn dough out onto a lightly floured board and roll it into a 10 x 20-inch rectangle. Mark dough lightly into 4 sections, each 10 x 5 inches. Dot the 2 center sections with ⅔ of softened butter. Fold 2 end sections over center sections and roll out with rolling pin. Dot half of dough with remaining butter and fold the other half over; roll out again with rolling pin. (*Note:* In these and subsequent foldings and rollings, turn dough so that you are rolling from open end to open end, not from fold to fold. Each "turn" consists of 2 foldings and rollings.)

Wrap dough in a damp towel and refrigerate for 30 minutes. Roll dough again into a 10 x 20-inch rectangle, fold end sections over center, roll out, fold in half, roll out again, wrap in towel, and refrigerate for another 30 minutes. Repeat rolling and folding once or twice more, letting dough rest 30 minutes in refrigerator after each "turn." After last turn, let dough rest overnight if possible.

To shape into twists, roll dough out ¼ inch thick into a 12 x 24-inch rectangle. Brush dough with egg wash (1 egg yolk mixed with 1 tablespoon water) and sprinkle half of it with raisins and cinnamon. Fold other half over and flatten very lightly with rolling pin. With a sharp knife, cut dough into strips about ¾ inch wide and 6 inches long. Twist ends of each strip in opposite directions and place 3 inches apart on baking sheets lined with baking parchment. Cover with a towel and let rise in a warm place, free from drafts, until almost double, about 20 to 30 minutes. Brush twists with additional egg wash and sprinkle with flaked toasted almonds. Bake in a preheated 400° oven for about 15 to 20 minutes, or until lightly browned. Remove and brush first with hot Apricot Glaze and then with Vanilla Water Icing.

APRICOT GLAZE

Heat ½ cup apricot jam with 1 tablespoon of water to boiling and push through a strainer. Any glaze left over may be stored in refrigerator.

VANILLA WATER ICING

Sift 2 cups confectioners' sugar into a bowl. Add 1 teaspoon vanilla extract and just enough boiling water to make a mixture of spreading consistency—it doesn't take much water, so be careful.

VIENNESE COFFEE

Coffee turns Viennese when it's topped with a big spoonful of *schlagobers*—whipped cream. Real Viennese whipped cream tastes sweet and fresh; to approximate it, add 1 tablespoon confectioners' sugar to 1 cup heavy cream when it's partly whipped; then whip fairly stiff. Coffee should be strong, and sweetened or not, as your guests prefer.

A Light Summer Brunch
for 4

Strawberries in fresh orange juice
Chicken livers en brochette
Sautéed mushrooms (see p. 284)
Brioche slices with mustard butter

Serve breakfast strawberries as they do in Madrid: pour fresh orange juice over them. The colors are good together and so is the taste. The berries will not need sugar. One pound of sautéed mushrooms will make generous servings for four.

CHICKEN LIVERS EN BROCHETTE

6 slices bacon	½ teaspoon freshly cracked
24 whole chicken livers	black pepper
¼ cup flour	½ cup melted butter
1 teaspoon salt	

Cut each piece of bacon into 5 pieces. Dry the chicken livers and roll them in flour. On 4 skewers, alternate chicken livers—

skewering them through fleshy lobes—with bacon pieces. Sprinkle with salt and pepper and place on a rack about 4 inches from broiler. Baste with the melted butter and turn frequently. Broil for a total of 6 minutes. Livers should be crisp and brown on the outside, still pink inside.

BRIOCHE SLICES WITH MUSTARD BUTTER

Cut very thin slices from giant brioche (see p. 12) and serve with mustard butter, made by beating 2 teaspoons Dijon mustard into ½ cup softened butter. The brioche will be easier to slice if you've chilled it in the refrigerator.

Breakfast for 8, the Morning after a Late Party

Bowl of fresh fruit
French onion soup, gratiné
Toasted French bread
Ice-cold beer or ale
Steaming cups of black coffee

French people don't eat onion soup before dinner—they eat it for breakfast or as an early-morning snack. You can trust their taste. It's a splendid way to revitalize your guests, and easy for you, too—the soup can be made ahead, ready for last-minute reheating and broiling. Offer both beer or ale and coffee.

BOWL OF FRESH FRUIT

Whenever fresh fruit is on your menu, make it your center-piece too. Arrange fruits in season in a beautiful bowl, striving for contrasts in colors and shapes: oranges, perfect pears, a few bananas, a bunch of black grapes, tangerines. Always provide fruit knives, as well as scissors to snip off bunchlets of grapes.

FRENCH ONION SOUP, GRATINÉ

Onion soup is only as good as the stock that goes into it. The stock simmers for 4 hours, but the onions for only ½ hour. Have extra toasted French bread for hungry guests and pass more Parmesan cheese separately, if you wish.

½ cup butter
8 cups sliced onions
1 tablespoon flour
2 quarts beef stock (see p. 277)
2 tablespoons brandy
  Meat glaze, optional (see
    p. 280)

Day-old French bread, at
  least ½ loaf
1 cup shredded Gruyère
  cheese
½ cup grated Parmesan cheese,
  plus more, optional

Melt butter in a large saucepan or kettle. Add onions and cook until golden, about 10 minutes—do not brown. Stir in flour. Pour on beef stock and brandy. Bring to a boil, reduce heat to simmer, half-cover the pan, and simmer for ½ hour. Taste for seasoning; add meat glaze if soup doesn't have the deep dark flavor you like.

Meanwhile, cut French bread in slices 1 inch thick and toast in a 300° oven for about 30 minutes. It should be completely dry and hard all the way through, like Melba toast.

To serve, fill broiler-resistant soup bowls half-full, sprinkle about 1 tablespoon of the shredded Gruyère on each, and broil for 2 to 3 minutes to melt cheese. This cheese layer will keep toast from sinking. Place 1 slice of toast in each bowl, cover with grated Parmesan and remaining Gruyère, and broil again until cheese melts, about 2 to 3 minutes.

Breakfast in Bed
for 2

Melon with port wine
Jelly crêpes
Sautéed Canadian bacon slices

Here's a happy way to keep house guests out of the kitchen while you're getting the luncheon menu under way. If the crêpes are prepared ahead, a child could also treat his or her parents to breakfast in bed with the Sunday paper.

MELON WITH PORT WINE

Serve ½ melon each (or 1 whole melon if cantaloupes are small). Cut in half (or cut off top, to make a lid) and scoop out seeds. In each melon half (or whole melon) put 2 teaspoons honey and fill to top with port wine. Cover with aluminum foil (or lid) and chill overnight. Serve *very cold*.

JELLY CRÊPES

½ recipe basic crêpes (see p. 285)
6 tablespoons melted butter

6 tablespoons jelly or jam
2 tablespoons confectioners' sugar

Count 2 large or 3 small crêpes for each serving. Brush the "wrong" (30-second) side of each crêpe generously with melted butter and spread with jelly or jam. Roll up and place in a buttered au gratin dish. Sprinkle with remaining butter. (*Recipe can be prepared ahead to this point.*) Place in a preheated 350° oven for about 15 minutes, or until heated through. Sift confectioners' sugar over crêpes just before serving.

SAUTÉED CANADIAN BACON SLICES

Cut 4 slices of Canadian bacon, ¼ inch thick, and remove casing. Heat 1 tablespoon butter in a skillet until hot and foamy; cook bacon over high heat about 2 minutes on each side.

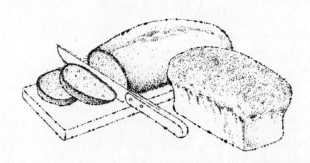

Holiday Brunch Buffet
for 16

Glazed fruit
Giant brioche stuffed with scrambled eggs
Individual ham rolls
Grilled tomatoes
Mushroom fritters
Assorted breads: croissants (see p. 13),
brioche (see p. 11), English muffins,
toasted French bread
Assorted jams

GLAZED FRUIT

Choose a cool time of the year to prepare and serve glazed fruit. The recipe doesn't work if it's hot and humid, and the fruit holds its hard, crackly glaze for only about 3 hours on the best of days. You cannot make it ahead and it should not be refrigerated. But it *is* good and worth trying—it looks spectacular!

48 pieces of fruit: tangerine
    sections, black and white
    grapes with stems left on
4½ cups (2 pounds) sugar

1 cup water
2 tablespoons light corn syrup
¼ teaspoon cream of tartar

Section tangerines and separate grapes, leaving stem on each grape and using care not to pierce skin of fruit. Mix sugar, water, corn syrup, and cream of tartar together in a saucepan and bring to a boil over high heat, stirring until sugar dissolves. Turn heat to medium and cook syrup to the hard-crack stage (300° to 320° on a candy thermometer). Remove pan from heat and immediately put it in a pan of warm water to stop the cooking. Using small tongs or tweezer, dip fruit in syrup and place on a greased platter or marble slab to set (this takes only a few minutes). Syrup is *hot,* so watch your fingers!

GIANT BRIOCHE STUFFED
WITH SCRAMBLED EGGS

2 giant brioche (see p. 12)
1 cup butter
32 eggs
¾ cup light cream

1½ teaspoons salt
¾ teaspoon freshly cracked
    white pepper

Cut tops off brioche, about a quarter of the way down. Scoop out interiors, leaving shells. (Save or freeze crumbs for another use—in place of bread crumbs.) Melt butter in a *big* saucepan; reserve ¼ cup of melted butter to brush insides of brioche shells. Beat eggs with cream, salt, and pepper and stir into hot butter in saucepan; set saucepan in a skillet filled with hot water. Cook the eggs, stirring constantly, over low heat, until they begin to set—this will take about 15 minutes. Eggs should be very creamy. Brush insides of brioche shells with reserved butter and divide the eggs between the 2 shells. Put brioche tops in place and serve immediately (or hold filled brioche in a 250° oven for 5 to 10 minutes if necessary).

INDIVIDUAL HAM ROLLS

1 pound ground ham
6 beaten eggs
1 cup bread crumbs
2 teaspoons tarragon
¼ cup chopped capers
1 teaspoon salt
½ teaspoon freshly cracked
    black pepper
1 tablespoon Dijon mustard

2 tablespoons finely chopped
    parsley
16 square pieces of boiled
    ham, approximately
    6 inches square and
    ⅛ inch thick
½ cup Madeira
¼ cup melted butter

Mix together ground ham, eggs, bread crumbs, tarragon, capers, salt, pepper, Dijon mustard, and parsley. Brush ham squares with ¼ cup Madeira and spoon ground ham mixture along one edge. Roll up and lay seam side down in a buttered baking dish. (*Recipe can be made ahead to this point.*) Place in a preheated 350° oven and bake for 30 minutes. Baste 3 times during baking with remaining Madeira and melted butter. Then turn oven to 250° and hold ham rolls, along with other foods, until serving time.

GRILLED TOMATOES

8 tomatoes

2 teaspoons salt

1 teaspoon freshly cracked
  black pepper

1 finely chopped clove garlic

1 tablespoon finely chopped
  shallots

1 tablespoon chopped parsley

8 teaspoons olive oil

Cut tomatoes in half. Put them on a broiler tray and sprinkle with salt, pepper, garlic, shallots, and parsley. Drizzle 1 teaspoon olive oil on each half. (*Recipe can be prepared ahead to this point.*) Broil for 6 to 8 minutes, or until bubbly. Keep warm in a low (250°) oven until ready to serve. *If you don't have a separate broiler, you can bake the tomatoes instead of broiling them—allow about 15 minutes in the 350° oven. Then hold in the 250° oven until serving time.*

MUSHROOM FRITTERS

32 large mushrooms

1 recipe beer batter (see
  p. 285)

Fat for deep frying

¼ cup chopped parsley

2 lemons cut in 8 wedges each

Clean mushrooms with paper towels dipped in acidulated water (1 quart water with 1 tablespoon lemon juice added) and wipe dry. Trim the stems but do not cut them off. Dip in beer batter, coating mushrooms completely. Fry them, a few at a time, in deep hot fat (375°) until golden, about 4 to 5 minutes. Remove with slotted spoon and drain on paper towels. (*Recipe may be made ahead to this point. To reheat, set cake racks on a baking sheet, cover with brown paper, lay mushrooms on the paper, and place in a 350° oven for several minutes.*) Keep warm in a 250° oven until ready to serve. Sprinkle with chopped parsley and serve with lemon wedges.

A Hunt Breakfast
for 10

Sliced oranges and grapefruit
Sautéed crab meat on Virginia ham
Hominy soufflé
Grilled tomatoes
Croissants (see p. 13) and carrot bread

Even if you don't have occasion to gallop through Eastern hunt country, this breakfast is a good ending for a morning ride, or after any strenuous early exercise. Fresh crab meat is easiest to obtain in the Chesapeake Bay region, but frozen or canned crab meat is widely available. If you're not familiar with hominy grits, try the soufflé. Hominy is the kernels of hulled dried white corn; when coarsely ground, it's called hominy grits, or grits for short. You cook it like other cooked cereals or grains, in boiling water, to make the base for the soufflé. In contrast with the somewhat heavy texture of the soufflé, the carrot bread is very light and delicate, almost cakelike—and marvelous served with soft butter.

SAUTÉED CRAB MEAT ON VIRGINIA HAM

½ cup butter
20 slices Virginia ham, cut very thin
3 pounds crab meat (preferably lump crab meat)

3 tablespoons lemon juice
1½ teaspoons salt
½ teaspoon freshly cracked white pepper
1 tablespoon freshly chopped parsley

Heat 2 tablespoons of the butter in a big skillet until hot and foaming. Sauté ham slices on both sides and line a large baking dish or 2 smaller au gratin dishes with the slices. Keep warm. Add remaining butter to skillet and heat to foaming. Add crab meat, lemon juice, salt, and pepper and toss over high heat until heated through, about 5 minutes. Pile in ham-lined baking dish and sprinkle with chopped parsley.

HOMINY SOUFFLÉ

4 cups water	2 cups milk
2 teaspoons salt	6 tablespoons butter
¾ cup hominy grits	8 eggs, separated

Bring water to a boil, add salt, and pour in hominy grits slowly, in a thin stream, stirring with a wooden spatula. Stir until water returns to a boil; then cook uncovered over very low heat for about 25 minutes, stirring occasionally. (Mixture will be very thick.) Let it cool. Meanwhile, heat milk and butter until butter melts and let cool. Combine cooled hominy and milk in a big mixing bowl and beat with a whisk until blended. Beat the egg yolks and blend them into the hominy mixture. (*May be prepared ahead to this point.*) Beat the egg whites stiff and fold them in. Pour into a buttered 8-cup soufflé dish and place in a pan with one inch of boiling water. Bake in a preheated 375° oven until very brown on top, about 45 minutes. This soufflé doesn't rise much, but it holds up quite well, and it has a heavier texture than other soufflés. Serve immediately.

GRILLED TOMATOES

See p. 33, but use 5 tomatoes (1 tomato half per serving) and adjust oil and seasonings.

CARROT BREAD

2 tablespoons vegetable oil	1 egg
¼ cup soft butter	1 cup lightly packed brown
¾ cup vegetable shortening	sugar
1¼ cups sifted flour	1 cup grated raw carrots
1 teaspoon baking soda	(about 2 large)
1 teaspoon baking powder	2 tablespoons orange juice
½ teaspoon salt	

Brush an 8-cup ring mold with oil and dust it with flour; set aside. Cream butter and shortening together in electric mixer bowl. Sift flour with baking soda, baking powder, and salt, add it and remaining ingredients to shortening mixture, and beat to mix well. Pour batter into prepared mold and bake in a preheated 350° oven for 45 to 60 minutes, or until bread tests done with a cake tester. Cool bread in mold on a cake rack for about 5 minutes. Then loosen edges with a small knife and turn it out on a serving plate.

A Champagne Breakfast
for 6

Fresh peaches with champagne
Ham roulade with mustard sour cream
Individual brioche (see p. 12)
Espresso coffee

FRESH PEACHES WITH CHAMPAGNE

6 ripe peaches
  Juice of ½ lemon

½ cup sugar
1 split champagne, chilled

Scald peaches in boiling water for about 10 seconds, peel, and leave whole. Sprinkle with lemon juice and sugar and put in the refrigerator to chill thoroughly. To serve, place 1 whole peach in each of 6 saucer champagne glasses and pour on champagne.

HAM ROULADE WITH MUSTARD SOUR CREAM

2 tablespoons vegetable oil
1 pound finely ground ham
6 eggs, separated
½ cup butter, melted and cooled
½ cup flour
½ teaspoon salt
½ teaspoon freshly cracked black pepper
2 tablespoons chopped parsley

2 teaspoons dried or 2 tablespoons chopped fresh tarragon
¼ cup dry Madeira

SAUCE:
1 cup sour cream
1 tablespoon Dijon mustard
1 teaspoon dried or 1 tablespoon chopped fresh tarragon

Brush a jelly-roll pan with vegetable oil, then line it with waxed paper, letting the paper extend 4 inches on each end. Brush the paper with vegetable oil and set aside. In a mixing bowl, mix together ham, egg yolks, melted butter, flour, salt, pepper, parsley, tarragon, and Madeira. Fold in egg whites, stiffly beaten. Spread in prepared pan and bake in a preheated 375° oven for 20 minutes. Turn out onto 2 overlapping sheets of waxed paper, peel off lining paper, and with the waxed paper to help, roll it up like a jelly roll and place on a serving platter. (*If made ahead to this point, reheat it in a 300° oven for 10 minutes. Just before serving, pour ½ cup sizzling hot butter over it.*) Serve with sour cream flavored with Dijon mustard and tarragon.

Luncheons

Since few men live close enough to their work to make it home for lunch, I think mainly of women when planning luncheon menus. I especially welcome more formal luncheons as a chance to show off. Why not use the arrival of a friend from out of town as an excuse for a party? Bring out your best china and embroidered placemats, have plenty of fresh flowers around, and serve something truly elegant—Chaudfroid Chicken followed by a dessert of Strawberry Barquettes, for instance. Another dazzler is Avocado with Crab Meat, which, when ready to be served to each guest, looks like a decorated Easter egg.

You'll have many an occasion, also, to entertain mixed groups—guests visiting for the weekend, for example, or maybe a crowd invited over on a Saturday to view network football. Depending on the degree of informality you wish, your choice of an entrée might range from Shrimp en Brochette or an unusual Polenta Ring filled with grilled mushrooms—an original of mine— to Hamburgers with Green Peppercorns, a selection of Danish open-face sandwiches, or a hearty kielbasa sausage baked in brioche.

Luncheons are an excellent time to practice new cooking techniques. The menus are simpler, with fewer courses, and thus fewer items to organize in the kitchen. If you've never prepared anything *en gelée,* by all means do so the next time it's your turn for the bridge foursome. Then you'll feel secure when you tackle a glamorous aspic for a large buffet.

Consider the occasion and try to make the food complement it if you can do this without being coy. It amuses me to make Butterfish en Papillote to honor a new bride, but it's a private joke since I'm the only one who knows I cut the baking parchment in heart shapes to wrap up the fish for baking. You could pay tribute to a bride more openly with Coeur à la Crème for dessert.

Almost never do I offer cocktails at lunch. A glass of sherry or Lillet seems just right at one o'clock, and we usually sit down for lunch at one-thirty.

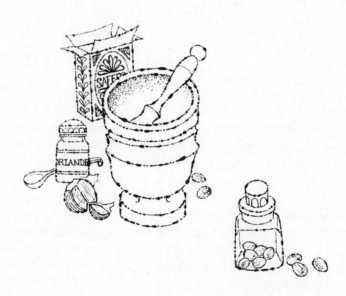

A Ladies' Luncheon
for 8

Eggs à la Princesse Caramon
Watercress and Belgian endive salad
Toasted Melba rounds
Apricot marzipan tart

EGGS À LA PRINCESSE CARAMON

12 hard-cooked eggs
12 tablespoons butter
4 tablespoons flour
1½ cups light cream
1 teaspoon salt
½ teaspoon freshly cracked white pepper
½ teaspoon finely chopped garlic
2 tablespoons finely chopped shallots

1½ cups finely chopped mushrooms
2 tablespoons chopped parsley
1 teaspoon dried or 1 tablespoon fresh tarragon
1 teaspoon dry mustard
1 cup heavy cream
½ cup shredded Gruyère cheese
4 tablespoons grated Parmesan cheese
2 tablespoons bread crumbs

Cut the eggs in half lengthwise, rub yolks through a very fine sieve into a mixing bowl, and set aside. Melt 3 tablespoons of the butter in a saucepan, stir in flour, and cook for 2 minutes over high heat, stirring with a wooden spatula; do not let it brown. Remove from heat, change to a whisk, and gradually add light cream, whisking vigorously. Return to heat and cook, stirring, until sauce thickens and comes to a boil. Lower heat and cook about 5 minutes. Season with salt and pepper.

Remove from heat and stir 4 tablespoons of the white sauce into sieved egg yolks. In a skillet, over high heat, melt 3 tablespoons butter and add garlic, shallots, and chopped mushrooms. Toss over high heat until mixture looks dry, about 5 to 10 minutes. Add to sieved egg yolks along with parsley, tarragon, and dry mustard. Beat in 4 tablespoons softened butter, and add more salt and pepper if needed. Stuff mixture into egg whites.

Thin out remaining white sauce with heavy cream, bring to

a boil, and stir in shredded Gruyère. Taste for seasoning. Spoon some of the sauce into an ovenproof serving dish. Arrange stuffed eggs on sauce and spoon more sauce over eggs, masking completely. Sprinkle with grated Parmesan and bread crumbs and drizzle with 2 tablespoons melted butter. (*Can be prepared to this point the day before, covered with plastic wrap, and refrigerated.*) When ready to serve, place in a preheated 350° oven and bake for 20 minutes.

WATERCRESS AND BELGIAN ENDIVE SALAD

2 bunches watercress	1 teaspoon salt
6 heads Belgian endive	½ teaspoon freshly cracked
2 tablespoons lemon juice	white pepper
5 tablespoons olive oil	

Trim stems from watercress. Trim root end of Belgian endive heads and remove any discolored leaves. With a chef's knife cut heads lengthwise into matchsticks. Dry thoroughly. (*May be prepared to this point the day before, wrapped in plastic wrap, and refrigerated.*) Just before serving, toss in a chilled salad bowl with a vinaigrette dressing made by beating together lemon juice, olive oil, salt, and pepper.

TOASTED MELBA ROUNDS

With a 2-inch cookie cutter, cut 24 rounds of very thinly sliced white bread. Put on a baking sheet and brush with ½ cup melted butter. Place in a preheated 350° oven for 15 minutes; turn oven down to 250° and bake 15 to 20 minutes longer, or until rounds are crispy and beautifully browned. You can bake these ahead of time and freeze them for up to 3 months—or freeze leftovers. Or make the day before and put in airtight container or plastic bag. Serve at room temperature, or reheat if desired.

APRICOT MARZIPAN TART

PASTRY:
2 cups lightly spooned flour
2 tablespoons sugar
¾ cup soft butter
2 egg yolks
1½ tablespoons ice water

FILLING:
½ cup unsalted butter
8 ounces almond paste
2 eggs
1 tablespoon flour
4 tablespoons brandy
1 28-ounce can apricot halves
¾ cup apricot preserves

Put flour in a bowl and stir in sugar. Blend in butter with your fingertips. Add egg yolks and water and mix with a pastry fork—dough will be sticky. Turn it out on a floured board and knead lightly. Wrap it in waxed paper and chill until firm enough to roll, about ½ hour. Roll between 2 sheets of waxed paper to make a round about ⅛ inch thick. Fit into a 10-inch flan ring or springform pan. Prick bottom and sides of pastry with a fork. Bake in a preheated 350° oven for 10 minutes.

While crust is baking, prepare filling. Cream butter and almond paste together, add eggs, and beat well with electric mixer, wire whisk, or wooden spatula. Blend in flour and 2 tablespoons brandy. Spread the almond mixture in the partly baked crust and return to oven, setting it on the lowest rack, to bake for another 45 minutes.

When tart comes out of the oven, drain apricot halves and arrange over almond filling. Heat apricot preserves with remaining 2 tablespoons brandy over medium heat until syrupy, about 5 minutes, stirring with wooden spatula; push through a sieve and brush generously over apricots and filling. Allow to cool and serve at room temperature.

An Elegant Luncheon
for 8

Cheese roll, four ways
Fish en croûte
Chinese carrots
Peaches in port

Both the cheese roll and the fish en croûte recipes are my own creations, and the carrots provide a delicious taste contrast to the fish.

CHEESE ROLL, FOUR WAYS

2 tablespoons butter	1 cup freshly grated Parmesan
2 tablespoons flour	cheese
1 cup milk	Filling or sauce
5 eggs, separated	Parsley or watercress for
	garnish

Brush an 11 x 17-inch jelly-roll pan with vegetable oil, line it with waxed paper, brush the paper with oil, and set aside. Melt the butter in a saucepan over medium-high heat and stir in flour. Cook, stirring with wooden spatula, for 2 minutes—do not let it brown. Remove from heat, change to a whisk, and add milk, whisking vigorously. Return to heat and cook, stirring, until mixture thickens and boils. Remove from heat and set aside to cool for 5 to 10 minutes. Beat egg yolks and beat them into the white sauce, to mix thoroughly. Beat egg whites until they form soft peaks. Stir one third of them into sauce; then fold in remainder. Lightly fold in grated Parmesan. Spread mixture in prepared jelly-roll pan and bake in a preheated 350° oven for 15 minutes.

Remove from oven and turn out onto 2 sheets of waxed paper, overlapping lengthwise. Serve either warm or cold, rolled up with 1 of these 4 fillings or sauces: (1) ¼ cup freshly grated Parmesan cheese sprinkled on rolled-up roll; (2) 1 recipe Mushroom Duxelles (see p. 283), as filling; (3) ¾ cup creamed butter mixed with ¾ cup chopped walnuts, as filling; (4) ½ recipe Tomato

Sauce (see p. 64), poured over rolled-up roll. Garnish with chopped parsley sprinkled over roll, if desired, or with a large bunch of watercress at one end of the platter.

FISH EN CROÛTE

1 recipe sour cream pastry (see p. 288)
8 brook trout, about ¾ to 1 pound each (or other small whole fish, such as butterfish, porgies, or small rockfish)
½ cup lemon juice, plus lemon juice to wash fish

1 tablespoon salt
1 teaspoon freshly cracked white pepper
½ cup butter
3 tablespoons melted butter
Lemon wedges for garnish

Prepare pastry and chill in the refrigerator for at least 1½ hours, or overnight. Scale and clean trout, or ask your fish seller to do it, being careful to leave heads and tails intact. Wash the fish in water acidulated with lemon juice (1 tablespoon to 1 quart), and dry them carefully. Remove the backbone of each fish by slitting the fish along the belly from head to tail and running a small sharp knife tight against the bone on each side. Use kitchen shears to snip through bone at head and tail and pull it out. Do not cut through the top (the back) of the fish. Sprinkle insides of fish with half the salt and pepper and inside each one put 1 tablespoon lemon juice and 1 tablespoon butter. Pinch the slit together—fish is gelatinous and it will hold without tying. Brush outside of fish with melted butter and sprinkle with remaining salt and pepper.

On a lightly floured board, roll chilled pastry into a rectangle about 15 by 12 inches and ⅛ inch thick. Cut it into 8 strips, 15 inches long and 1½ inches wide. Starting at the tail, on the underside, wind one strip of pastry around each fish. Do not overlap the pastry—the fish should show through the pastry spiral. Try to end near the head, on the underside. (*Recipe may be prepared to this point 1 or 2 hours before baking and held in refrigerator.*) Place fish on a buttered baking sheet and put into a preheated 375° oven to bake until pastry is golden brown and fish are done, about 15 to 20 minutes. Garnish with wedges of lemon.

CHINESE CARROTS

12 carrots
2 tablespoons vegetable oil
3 slices fresh ginger
1 teaspoon salt
½ cup chicken stock (see
    p. 278)

1 tablespoon soy sauce
1 tablespoon vinegar
½ teaspoon sugar
2 tablespoons chopped parsley

Peel carrots and cut them in diagonal slices about 1 inch thick. Or roll-cut carrots the way the Chinese do: lay carrot on a chopping board and make a diagonal cut, straight down, at wide end. Roll carrot a quarter turn (diagonal surface facing up) and make another diagonal cut straight down. Repeat until carrot is cut up. Each diagonal cut bisects the diagonal surface of previous cut.

Put carrots into saucepan, cover with cold water, and bring to a boil; boil 5 minutes; drain and set aside. In a skillet or wok, heat oil almost to smoking over high heat. Add ginger and stir for 1 minute; add carrots and stir-fry for about 3 minutes longer. Sprinkle with salt and pour on chicken stock mixed with soy sauce, vinegar, and sugar. Cover and cook, still over high heat, for about 10 minutes or until very tender. Garnish with chopped parsley.

PEACHES IN PORT

8 fresh peaches
2 cups sugar
   Grated peel and juice of 2
    lemons

½ teaspoon freshly grated
   nutmeg
2 cups port wine
1½ cups sour cream *or* 1 cup
   heavy cream, whipped

Scald peaches in boiling water for 10 seconds to loosen skins. Peel and put them whole in a baking dish. In a saucepan, mix together sugar, lemon peel and lemon juice, nutmeg, and port wine; bring to a boil, and pour over peaches. Cover peaches with aluminum foil and bake in a preheated 400° oven for 20 to 30 minutes, or until tender, basting 3 times during cooking. Serve warm or chilled, with sour cream or whipped cream.

Formal Summer Luncheon
for 12

Melon and prosciutto
Chaudfroid chicken
Salad of Bibb lettuce and cucumber
Strawberry barquettes

The French words "hot" and "cold" not only name but describe the method of preparation for this platter of cold chicken that looks as glamorous as Paris under lights. It's a three-step recipe, all done the day before your party: poach the chicken breasts; coat them with the chaudfroid white sauce; glaze them with aspic.

MELON AND PROSCIUTTO

Cut 3 large ripe cantaloupes (or other melon, such as Persian, Spanish, honeydew, or casaba) into thin slices, removing rind. Arrange 3 or 4 slices of melon on plates with 3 or 4 paper-thin slices of prosciutto ham (you will need about 1 pound). Season generously with freshly cracked black pepper and garnish with lime wedges, or lemon wedges.

CHAUDFROID CHICKEN

6 whole chicken breasts	3 egg whites
2 teaspoons salt	6 tablespoons vegetable oil
½ cup chopped celery	6 tablespoons flour
¾ cup chopped onion	1 cup milk
½ cup chopped carrot	½ teaspoon salt
7 cups chicken stock (use poaching liquid)	3 or 4 drops Tabasco sauce
	3 tablespoons light cream
9 tablespoons (9 envelopes) plus 1 teaspoon unflavored gelatine	Truffle or mushrooms, for garnish
1 cup dry white wine	1 can (400 grams) pâté de fois gras, chilled
2 tablespoons tomato paste	Watercress, for garnish
Pinch of salt	

Put chicken breasts in a deep kettle, cover with cold water, and add 2 teaspoons salt, celery, onion, and carrot. Bring to a boil over high heat, turn heat to simmer, and simmer 20 minutes only—do not overcook. Let chicken breasts cool in stock; this keeps them firm. When cool, peel off skin and, using a small knife and your fingers, carefully remove each side of the breast meat in one piece. Trim pieces so they look neat and lay them on cake racks set on a baking tray—the pieces should not touch. Refrigerate.

To make aspic, strain 6 cups of poaching liquid into saucepan; set over medium heat. Sprinkle 8 tablespoons of the gelatine into stock and stir to dissolve. Add wine, tomato paste, and pinch of salt. Beat egg whites to a froth and whisk them into the stock along with 3 eggshells. Bring to a boil, whisking constantly. Take off heat and let stand for 10 minutes. Line a strainer with 2 thicknesses of cheesecloth wrung out in cold water and pour aspic through it into a bowl. Let the liquid drain through without stirring or forcing it in any way. Pour the strained aspic into a baking tray and place it in the refrigerator to set (this takes about 1 to 2 hours).

To make the chaudfroid coating, heat vegetable oil in a saucepan. Stir in flour and cook, stirring with a wooden spatula, for 2 minutes—do not let it brown. Stir remaining gelatine into this *roux* and cook for 1 minute, to dissolve gelatine. Remove from heat, change to a whisk, and add 1 cup chicken stock and the milk all at once, whisking vigorously. Return to heat and cook, stirring, until sauce begins to thicken. Add salt and Tabasco. Set saucepan over ice and stir sauce until it is just to the point of setting; take it off ice. If necessary, thin it with a little of the light cream; it should be just fluid enough to coat or nap the chicken when spooned on. Remove chicken breasts—still on racks set on baking tray—from the refrigerator. Using a large spoon, coat each breast half with the chaudfroid sauce—one swoop of the spoon makes a smooth coat. Work fast, letting excess sauce run off chicken into tray. If the sauce in the pan sets while you're working, warm it; then stir it again over ice until it is of napping consistency. You can also warm and reuse the runover in the tray if you need it. Refrigerate the coated chicken breasts until set, about ½ to 1 hour.

Remove aspic from refrigerator. Scrape one third of it into a saucepan and set it over heat to melt. Turn out remaining aspic on a sheet of waxed paper on a chopping board and chop it into small cubes with a big chef's knife. Transfer the shimmery chopped aspic to a serving platter. Spread it out, making a bed of chopped aspic, and put the platter in the refrigerator.

When the chaudfroid is set, bring chicken from the refrigerator to decorate with a black truffle thinly sliced and cut in fancy shapes with tiny aspic cutters, or with a couple of mushrooms sliced thin from top to stem. Set the melted aspic over ice and stir until it's cool, thick, and syrupy, about 5 minutes. Dip truffle or mushroom slices in the aspic and place them on chicken breasts—the aspic "glue" sets immediately. Do not overdecorate! One large mushroom slice or 3 tiny truffle cutouts in a row will be ample. Finally, coat each decorated chicken breast with a spoonful of aspic—this gives the chicken a shine and also keeps the chaudfroid coating from drying out. Return chicken to refrigerator. Slice pâté de fois gras in pieces about the size of the chicken breasts. Arrange pâté on the platter of chopped aspic and place a chicken breast on top of each slice. Keep refrigerated until ready to serve. Garnish platter with watercress.

SALAD OF BIBB LETTUCE AND CUCUMBER

8 heads Bibb lettuce	2 tablespoons red wine vinegar
1 cucumber	1 teaspoon Dijon mustard
1 small onion, grated	1 teaspoon salt
6 tablespoons vegetable or olive oil	½ teaspoon freshly cracked black pepper

Wash, dry, and chill the lettuce, separating the leaves; place in a chilled salad bowl. Peel the cucumber and shave it lengthwise with a potato peeler; shave just the flesh—discard seeds. Add to salad bowl along with grated onion. Beat oil, vinegar, mustard, salt, and pepper together and pour over greens. Toss and serve immediately.

STRAWBERRY BARQUETTES

Barquettes are small boat-shaped tin molds, about 3½ inches long. You'll need a stack of them for baking the pastry boats—about 44 if you bake them all together, fewer if you bake in shifts.

2 cups lightly spooned flour
1 teaspoon salt
¾ cup chilled unsalted butter
¼ cup ice water
1 8-ounce jar currant jelly

2 tablespoons framboise or
kirsch
1 quart sliced strawberries,
about
Confectioners' sugar

Measure flour into a bowl and stir in salt. Cut chilled butter in chips and work it into the flour with pastry blender or fingertips until mixture resembles coarse cornmeal. Add ice water, only 2 tablespoons at first, more if needed, but no more than ¼ cup, and mix with a fork until you can press dough together to form a ball. Turn dough out on a lightly floured board. Using the heel of your hand, push the dough, bit by bit, against the board and away from you in short, quick smears. Work fast; you just want to smooth the dough a bit. Then form it into a ball, dust with flour, wrap in waxed paper, and refrigerate for at least 30 minutes.

On a lightly floured surface, roll out dough about ⅛ inch thick and fill barquette molds. (If you wish, you can work with half the dough at a time.) Line up the molds in 2 or 3 rows, fairly close together. Lay rolled-out pastry over the molds, gently push pastry down into each mold with your finger, and then roll over tops of molds with rolling pin to cut edges. Pinch pastry firmly into each mold. Stack one filled mold on top of another, 3 to a stack, place an empty mold on top, and press them all tightly together. Arrange the stacked molds on a baking sheet, lay a second baking sheet on top, and weight it with a brick. Bake in a preheated 375° oven until light brown, about 25 minutes. Remove from oven and let cool for a few minutes. Remove weight and carefully remove barquettes from molds. Cool. They'll keep for a week on the shelf, or you may wrap and freeze them. To store on shelf, package them in plastic bags or an airtight container. Crisp them in the oven when you take them out of storage. Makes 32 barquettes.

To fill barquettes, melt currant jelly with framboise or kirsch. Brush this glaze on the shells, fill with sliced fresh strawberries, carefully arranged, and brush berries with more glaze. (*Barquettes can be filled and glazed 2 hours ahead. Any remaining glaze can be kept in a jar in the refrigerator.*) Just before serving, sift confectioners' sugar over barquettes. Count 1 or 2 barquettes per serving.

A Light and Delicate
Luncheon for 6

Mushroom broth garnished with mushroom rounds
Cold spinach mousse, filled
with crab-meat salad
Green mayonnaise
Hot French finger rolls
Peaches with champagne (see p. 36)

MUSHROOM BROTH GARNISHED
WITH MUSHROOM ROUNDS

10 cups strong chicken stock
(see p. 278)
1½ cups finely chopped mushrooms, plus 4 whole
mushrooms for garnish

1 teaspoon salt
½ teaspoon freshly cracked
black pepper
2 egg whites

In a large saucepan, over high heat, bring chicken stock and
mushrooms to a boil; reduce heat to simmer, cover, and cook
½ hour. Strain and return broth to saucepan. Season with salt and
pepper. Beat egg whites until foamy, add to broth, to clarify it,
and whisk while you bring broth to a boil over high heat. Remove
from heat and let stand for 15 minutes. Strain through a sieve
lined with a double thickness of cheesecloth wrung out in cold
water, pouring carefully so as not to disturb coagulated egg
whites. Let consommé drip through by itself—do not push or
squeeze it. Taste for seasoning. (*Recipe can be made ahead to
this point.*) To serve, reheat it and garnish with very thin rounds
cut from fresh mushrooms.

COLD SPINACH MOUSSE

The various elements of this dish—spinach mousse, aspic-
coated eggs, crab-meat salad, and green mayonnaise—may all be
made the day before and unmolded and assembled an hour or so

before serving. The effect of the eggs nestled along the top of the spinach ring is truly beautiful. Incidentally, this is an original recipe, which I adapted from something like it that I had one time in Vienna.

2 tablespoons vegetable oil
3 10-ounce packages frozen
   chopped spinach
1 teaspoon salt
½ teaspoon freshly cracked
   black pepper
½ teaspoon freshly grated
   nutmeg
1 small onion
1 cup mayonnaise (see p. 283)

2 tablespoons (2 envelopes)
   unflavored gelatine
½ cup lemon juice
1 cup heavy cream
6 hard-cooked eggs
1½ cups aspic (see p. 280)
   Crab-meat Salad (recipe
   follows)
   Green Mayonnaise (recipe
   follows)

Oil a 6-cup ring mold and set aside. Cook spinach according to package directions. Drain well and squeeze out excess moisture. Chop with chef's knife as fine as possible. You should have about 1½ to 2 cups. Put it in a large bowl and season with salt, pepper, and nutmeg. Grate onion and add it to spinach along with mayonnaise. Soften gelatine in lemon juice; set mixture in a pan of hot water and stir to dissolve; add to spinach. Whip heavy cream until stiff and fold into spinach mixture; pour into prepared mold. Chill 2 hours.

To serve, unmold spinach ring on a serving plate. With the back of a spoon, make 6 depressions, equally spaced, on spinach ring. Place a hard-cooked egg, shelled and coated with aspic, in each. Fill center of ring with Crab-meat Salad. Serve with Green Mayonnaise.

CRAB-MEAT SALAD

1 pound lump crab meat,
   preferably fresh
1½ tablespoons drained capers
½ teaspoon salt

3 drops Tabasco sauce
2 tablespoons fresh chopped
   chives
½ cup mayonnaise (see p. 283)

Pick over crab meat to remove any bits of shell or filament. Mix all ingredients in a bowl, tossing with a fork to blend—do not mash.

GREEN MAYONNAISE

Drop 12 watercress leaves, 6 sprigs of parsley, and 12 spinach leaves into boiling water; blanch 1 minute. Drain and refresh with cold water. Drain well, squeeze dry, and chop with chef's knife until pureed. Stir into 1 recipe mayonnaise (see p. 283).

Formal Luncheon for 8

Mushroom flan
Butterfish en papillote with tartar sauce
Pea roulade
Raspberry ice with cassis

A formal luncheon is accomplished with greater ease if you have an extra pair of hands in the kitchen, moving things in and out of the oven—a teen-age daughter, perhaps, or hired help. But everything is prepared ahead, and you can manage this yourself if necessary. Glaze the flan just before you invite guests to the table, and put the fish in to bake while you eat the flan. When you take the fish out of the oven, put the pea roulade in to reheat; it will be ready by the time you've arranged the parchment packets of fish on your serving dish, ready for the dining room. Guests are ecstatic when you present food en papillote.

MUSHROOM FLAN

2 pounds mushrooms
½ cup butter
2 tablespoons chopped shallots
Juice of ½ lemon
¼ cup dry Madeira or dry sherry
1 tablespoon flour
1 teaspoon salt
½ teaspoon freshly cracked white pepper
2 cups heavy cream
1 wholly baked 9-inch pâte brisée shell (see p. 288)
2 tablespoons chopped parsley
¼ cup freshly grated Parmesan cheese

Roughly chop the mushrooms. Heat butter in a heavy skillet over high heat and cook shallots for 3 minutes, stirring—do not let them brown. Add chopped mushrooms and lemon juice. Cook, stirring, until mixture looks dry. Add Madeira and cook until it evaporates. Sprinkle flour, salt, and pepper over mushrooms and stir in. Add heavy cream and continue cooking until sauce is reduced and of napping consistency. Pour into baked tart shell and sprinkle with chopped parsley and Parmesan cheese. (*Tart may be made ahead to this point. It freezes well, too. Thaw in refrigerator before heating.*) Heat under a broiler until bubbly, about 3 to 5 minutes, or place in a preheated 350° oven for 15 minutes.

BUTTERFISH EN PAPILLOTE
WITH TARTAR SAUCE

8 butterfish, about ½ to ¾ pound each	2 tablespoons grated onion
Lemon juice to wash fish	2 teaspoons salt
8 pieces baking parchment	1 teaspoon freshly cracked black pepper
2 tablespoons melted butter	8 teaspoons tomato puree
8 thin slices ham	2 tablespoons finely chopped parsley
1 cup soft butter	
2 tablespoons anchovy paste	Tartar Sauce (recipe follows)

Clean fish—or ask your fish seller to do it—leaving head and tails intact. Wash them in acidulated water (1 tablespoon lemon juice to 1 quart water) and dry them. From baking parchment cut 8 wide hearts with a very slight dip in the center, large enough to enclose fish. Brush parchment with melted butter. Place 1 slice ham on right-hand half of each heart. Mix ½ cup of soft butter with anchovy paste and grated onion; spread on ham. Place fish on buttered ham and top with remaining butter (1 tablespoon per fish), salt and pepper, tomato puree (1 teaspoon per fish), and chopped parsley. Fold left half of parchment heart over fish, match edges, and fold them over together in 2 or 3 narrow folds, to lock fish inside. (*Recipe may be made ahead to this point and refrigerated, or frozen for up to 1 month. Bring to room temperature before baking.*) Place on baking tray and bake in a preheated 425° oven for 10 minutes or until parchment puffs.

TARTAR SAUCE

To 1 cup homemade mayonnaise (see p. 283), add 1 finely chopped small dill pickle, 2 tablespoons drained capers, and 2 tablespoons finely chopped parsley.

PEA ROULADE

2 10-ounce packages frozen peas
2 tablespoons butter
6 tablespoons flour
1 cup milk
3 eggs, separated
½ teaspoon salt

¼ teaspoon freshly cracked white pepper
½ teaspoon freshly grated nutmeg
1 cup sour cream
½ cup melted butter
2 tablespoons chopped parsley

Oil a 10 x 15-inch jelly-roll pan. Line it with waxed paper, leaving 3 inches overhanging each end. Oil the waxed paper. Flour it and bang out excess flour. Cook frozen peas according to package directions. Puree the drained cooked peas through a food mill, using the finest disk. Do not puree in blender. You should have a heaping cup of pea puree.

Melt 2 tablespoons butter over high heat and stir in flour with wooden spatula. This is a higher proportion of flour to butter than you generally use in making a *roux,* and it will lump. Keep stirring it and cook for 3 to 5 minutes to brown the flour. Mixture will look like brown sugar. Remove pan from heat and add milk a little at a time, stirring constantly. Lower heat to medium-high, return pan to heat, change to a whisk, and cook, whisking vigorously. Mixture will be very thick and perhaps still a little lumpy— don't worry about this. Remove sauce from heat; stir in pea puree, egg yolks, salt, pepper, and nutmeg. Beat egg whites until stiff peaks form; fold into pea mixture and spread in jelly-roll pan. Bake in a preheated 375° oven for 18 minutes.

Remove roll from oven and loosen it around the edges. Lay two strips of waxed paper on the counter, overlapping lengthwise. Turn roll out upside down on waxed paper; peel off the waxed paper liner. Let roll cool slightly. Spread it with sour cream, roll it up, and transfer it to serving platter with the aid of the waxed paper. Reheat it if necessary in a preheated 300° oven for a few minutes. Just before serving, pour sizzling hot melted butter over the roll and sprinkle with chopped parsley.

Note: 1 cup of mushroom duxelles (see p. 283) is an excellent filling that you might wish to try with other recipe combinations.

RASPBERRY ICE WITH CASSIS

1 quart fresh raspberries *or*
  2 10-ounce packages
  frozen raspberries
1 cup water
1 cup orange juice
  Juice of 1 lime or ½ lemon,
  for frozen berries only
1 teaspoon unflavored gelatine

3 tablespoons cold water
½ cup light corn syrup
¼ cup water
1 cup firmly packed light
  brown sugar
½ cup honey
1 to 2 tablespoons crème de
  cassis

Wash and drain fresh raspberries; put them in a saucepan with 1 cup water and the orange juice, bring to a boil, and simmer for 10 minutes. (If using frozen berries, no cooking is necessary. Instead thaw berries, drain, reserving juice, measure juice and add water to make 1 cup. Add orange juice and the lime or lemon juice.) Soak gelatine in 3 tablespoons cold water. Bring to a boil the corn syrup and remaining ¼ cup water and boil for 5 minutes; stir in gelatine mixture to dissolve. Add brown sugar and honey. Puree berries in electric blender and press them through a sieve to remove seeds. Combine with sugar-honey mixture and pour into refrigerator trays. When partly frozen, remove from trays and beat with rotary beater; return to freezer. Serve in parfait glasses with crème de cassis poured over.

An Elegant but Easy Lunch for 8

Shrimp en brochette
Risotto
Romaine salad
Coeur à la crème

The risotto in this menu is so delicious that it can stand on its own as a meal in itself. Here it is an excellent accompaniment to broiled shrimp. As served in Italy, the rice should remain slightly "hard to the bite."

SHRIMP EN BROCHETTE

2 pounds medium-size fresh or frozen raw shrimp	1 teaspoon freshly cracked black pepper
⅓ cup soy sauce	½ teaspoon ground ginger
½ cup dry white wine	1 cup sesame seeds

Peel, devein, and wash the shrimp. Mix together soy sauce, wine, pepper, and ginger; pour over shrimp and marinate for 2 to 3 hours in the refrigerator, turning shrimp about every half hour. Remove shrimp from marinade, roll in sesame seeds, and thread on skewers (not too tightly—leave a little space in between so that they cook properly). Broil 2 inches from heat, turning shrimp and basting with marinade, for a total of about 4 to 5 minutes. Serve at once.

RISOTTO

5 cups chicken stock (see p. 278) or veal stock (see p. 279)	1 teaspoon salt
6 tablespoons butter	½ teaspoon freshly cracked white pepper
1½ cups chopped onion	½ teaspoon saffron shreds, optional
1 teaspoon chopped garlic	½ cup melted butter
2 cups long-grain rice	2 tablespoons freshly grated Parmesan cheese
6 tablespoons dry white wine	

Bring stock to a boil and hold at a simmer. In another saucepan melt the butter and stir in onion and garlic; cook over high heat for a few minutes until onion is transparent; then reduce heat to simmer. Add the rice, stirring to coat well with butter. Add wine, stir, and cook over medium-high heat until wine is absorbed; add salt and pepper. Stir saffron (if desired) into 1 cup of hot stock, add to rice, stir, and cook over medium-high heat, stirring occasionally. As liquid is absorbed add more stock, 1 cup at a time, stirring only occasionally to keep rice from sticking, until rice is done and liquid very nearly absorbed (this will take about a half hour). Do not cover the pan. To test for doneness, taste a kernel of rice; it should be, like spaghetti, *al dente*—tender, but with a bite to it. And it should be a little wet—not the dry, separate kernels you want with steamed rice. To serve, mound the rice in a serving dish, pour melted butter over it, and sprinkle with grated Parmesan cheese.

ROMAINE SALAD

2 large heads romaine
2 cloves garlic
¼ cup olive oil

¾ cup ¼-inch bread cubes
French vinaigrette dressing
(see p. 282)
2 hard-cooked egg yolks, sieved

Wash romaine, shake off water, break into bite-size pieces, roll in towels, and crisp in refrigerator. Crush garlic cloves and heat with olive oil in a small skillet; add bread cubes and fry over medium heat until croutons are crisp, tossing or stirring with wooden spatula to ensure they crisp evenly. Cool slightly. When ready to serve, pour dressing over greens in a chilled salad bowl, add croutons and sieved egg yolks, and toss.

COEUR À LA CRÈME

For this recipe you will need about 10 individual coeur à la crème molds, approximately 3 inches long, 3 inches wide, and 1½ inches deep.

1 8-ounce package cream
 cheese
½ cup cottage cheese
½ cup confectioners' sugar
1½ teaspoons vanilla extract *or*
 seeds from ½-inch piece
 of vanilla bean

2 cups heavy cream
6 tablespoons currant jelly
1 tablespoon framboise
1 pint whole fresh straw-
 berries

Beat cream cheese with electric mixer until soft and fluffy. Add cottage cheese and continue to beat. Add sugar and vanilla and beat until smooth. In another bowl, whip cream until stiff. Fold whipped cream into the cream cheese mixture. Cut a strip of cheesecloth into 6-inch squares or pieces big enough to line heart-shaped coeur à la crème molds. Wring out cheesecloth in salted cold water and press into molds, letting edges hang over. Spoon the cream-cheese mixture into the molds and fold the cheesecloth over the top of the cream. Give molds a tap to allow mixture to settle. Set molds on cake racks set over baking sheets and put them in the refrigerator to drain overnight. A few hours before serving, prepare strawberries. Melt the currant jelly over high heat, stir in framboise, and pour over strawberries; let macerate. To serve, unmold coeur à la crème, remove cheesecloth, and place on dessert dishes. Spoon on berries and sauce.

A Celebration Luncheon for 12

Chicory salad
Chicken Périgourdine
Noodle ring
Macédoine of fruit
Sand tarts

Plan a celebration luncheon as a tribute to a retiring garden club president or to praise the chairman of a fund drive that went over the top. Maybe someone you know has published a book. Or you want to honor your best friend's out-of-town guest. All such occasions call for elegant food. Chicken Périgourdine, with two sauces, and garnished with truffles, couldn't be more exquisite. Lead up to this rich main course by serving a crisp salad first, California style.

CHICORY SALAD

Wash 4 heads of chicory (curly endive), shake off water, break into bite-size pieces, roll in towels, and crisp in refrigerator. Serve from a chilled salad bowl, tossed with French vinaigrette dressing (see p. 282).

CHICKEN PÉRIGOURDINE

8 whole chicken breasts	2 teaspoons lemon juice, plus
8 tablespoons butter	1 tablespoon to wash
¼ cup brandy	mushrooms
3 tablespoons flour	½ teaspoon salt
1½ cups chicken stock (see	¼ teaspoon freshly cracked
p. 278)	white pepper
½ cup light cream	1 teaspoon potato starch or
½ teaspoon salt	arrowroot, optional
¼ teaspoon freshly cracked	1 recipe Hollandaise Sauce
white pepper	(see p. 281)
¼ cup dry sherry	2 tablespoons chopped truffles
1 pound fresh mushrooms	

Skin and bone chicken breasts carefully and trim them into neat ovals. These are called suprêmes; you will have 16 of them, 2 from each whole breast. Heat 4 tablespoons butter in a large skillet and sauté chicken breasts a few at a time, over high heat, for 2 minutes on each side—just enough to stiffen them. Remove from skillet.

Heat brandy in a small pan just until warm, ignite it, and pour it flaming into the skillet. When flames die down, scrape up the brown bits. Add 2 tablespoons butter to skillet and stir in the flour with a wooden spatula. Cook, stirring, over high heat for 2 minutes to eliminate the raw flour taste. Take pan off heat, change to a whisk, and add chicken stock all at once, whisking vigorously. Return to heat and bring to a boil, whisking. Add cream, ½ teaspoon salt, ¼ teaspoon pepper, and the sherry. Return chicken breasts to skillet along with their juices, cover, and simmer chicken for 15 minutes.

Wipe mushrooms clean with a paper towel dipped in acidulated water (1 quart water mixed with 1 tablespoon lemon juice). Wipe dry and trim stems. Reserve 6 perfect mushrooms for fluting and slice remaining mushrooms. Heat remaining 2 tablespoons butter in another large skillet; when foaming subsides, add mushrooms (both sliced and whole fluted), sprinkling them with 2 teaspoons lemon juice, ½ teaspoon salt, and ¼ teaspoon pepper. Toss over high heat for about 3 minutes and set aside.

To serve, lift out chicken from sauce and arrange in a large au gratin dish. Add sliced mushrooms and their liquid to the sauce. Thicken sauce if you wish with 1 teaspoon potato starch or arrowroot dissolved in 1 tablespoon water. Spoon sauce over chicken;

be sure each piece of chicken has some sliced mushrooms on it. (*May be prepared ahead to this point, covered with plastic wrap, and refrigerated. Let stand 1 hour at room temperature and then reheat in a 375° oven for 15 minutes.*) With a large spoon, shake a ribbon of Hollandaise Sauce over the chicken, down the center of the platter. Sprinkle this ribbon with chopped truffles, and decorate the platter with the fluted mushrooms.

NOODLE RING

1 pound noodles, ¼ inch wide
1 tablespoon vegetable oil
3 cups milk
2 cups soft bread crumbs
½ cup plus 4 tablespoons softened butter, plus butter for mold
1 pound grated Cheddar cheese
6 eggs, beaten lightly
2 teaspoons salt
1 teaspoon freshly cracked white pepper

Cook noodles in 4 quarts of boiling salted water according to package directions, adding a little oil to the water so noodles won't stick together. While noodles cook, prepare cheese sauce. Bring milk to a boil, lower heat, add bread crumbs, and stir with a whisk. Beat in ½ cup softened butter and the cheese, and whisk over low heat until smooth. Pour a little of the hot sauce into the eggs, to warm them; then stir eggs into sauce. Heat through over medium heat, but do not boil. Stir in salt and pepper. When noodles are done (they should be tender, but firm to the bite), drain thoroughly and toss in a large bowl with remaining 4 tablespoons softened butter to keep them from sticking. Stir in cheese sauce and pour mixture into a heavily buttered 12-cup ring mold or soufflé dish. Set it in a *bain marie* (a water bath—water should be 1 inch deep and hot) and put it in a preheated 375° oven. Bake for 45 minutes. Remove from oven and let the mold stand in the hot water for 5 minutes, before turning it out onto a serving platter.

MACÉDOINE OF FRUIT

Fresh fruit macerated in a liqueur or liquor—kirsch, framboise, Scotch, bourbon, gin, Cognac, Grand Marnier, Cointreau, anything you want—will not taste raw if you sugar the fruit.

That's the trick. If fruit served to you in a restaurant has too strong a taste of liquor, sprinkle a bit of sugar on it and wait a few minutes. You'll enjoy it more.

3 red apples	1 quart jar fresh citrus fruit
2 Golden Delicious apples	½ cup sugar
2 pears	¾ cup liqueur or liquor
2 bananas	Juice of 1 lemon
½ cantaloupe	Fresh berries for garnish
Grapes, both green and	
purple, 1 small bunch of	
each	

Peel, core, and slice the apples and pears. Peel and slice bananas. Cut cantaloupe with melon baller. Seed grapes. Drain the jar of citrus fruit, removing the maraschino cherries. Place fruit in a large glass bowl, sprinkle with sugar, liqueur, and lemon juice, turning the fruit over in the liquid with big spoons. Cover bowl with plastic wrap and refrigerate for at least 2 hours. Decorate with fresh berries just before serving.

SAND TARTS

¾ cup unsalted butter	¼ teaspoon salt
1¼ cups plus 1 tablespoon	2½ cups lightly spooned flour
sugar	1 egg white, lightly beaten
1 egg	½ cup slivered or shaved
1 egg yolk	blanched almonds
1½ teaspoons vanilla extract	1 tablespoon cinnamon

Beat butter and 1¼ cups sugar in electric mixer bowl until light and fluffy. Beat in egg and egg yolk; add vanilla. Stir salt into flour and add to butter mixture, mixing well. Shape dough into a roll and refrigerate overnight in plastic wrap.

When ready to bake, divide dough in 4 pieces and roll out each piece ⅛ inch thick. (Keep remaining dough refrigerated until ready to roll.) Cut into crescent shapes with cookie cutter and place on buttered baking sheets. Or, if you don't want to roll dough, cut thin slices from roll, to make round cookies. Brush cookies with egg white and sprinkle with almonds and a mixture of cinnamon and 1 tablespoon sugar. Bake in a preheated 375° oven for 10 minutes or until lightly browned. Cool cookies on cake racks. Serve together with Macédoine of Fruit. Makes 3 dozen. Cookies will freeze.

A Pleasant and Inexpensive Luncheon for a Crowd of 12 to 16

Salami cornucopias on pumpernickel
Cheese croquettes with tomato sauce
Green pepper salad
Ginger roll

The next time it's your turn to entertain members of your pet committee, try this menu.

SALAMI CORNUCOPIAS ON PUMPERNICKEL

1 pound Italian salami, or any round, hard luncheon meat about 3 inches in diameter, thinly sliced
½ cup unsalted butter for filling, plus butter to form cornucopias
1 8-ounce can liver pâté
2 tablespoons brandy
½ teaspoon salt
½ teaspoon freshly cracked white pepper
Black olives or parsley, for garnish
Pumpernickel bread, thinly sliced

Remove rind from salami slices. Cut a slit from the edge of each slice to the center. Overlap cut edges to form a cone, pinching them together with a dab of butter. To make filling, cream butter with electric mixer; beat in pâté, brandy, and seasonings. Put mixture into a pastry bag fitted with a star tube and pipe into cornucopias. Decorate each with a bit of diced black olive or a small tuft of parsley, pressed into the filling, and place on small squares or rounds of pumpernickel.

CHEESE CROQUETTES WITH TOMATO SAUCE

¾ cup butter
2 cups lightly spooned flour
1 quart milk
1 pound grated cheese,
　　Cheddar, Swiss, or
　　Gruyère
1 teaspoon salt, about
½ teaspoon freshly cracked
　　white pepper

2 teaspoons Dijon mustard
4 egg yolks, lightly beaten
2 tablespoons chopped chives
3 beaten eggs
2 cups bread crumbs
　　Fat for deep frying
　　Tomato Sauce (recipe
　　　follows)

Melt the butter in a large saucepan over high heat and stir in 1 cup flour with wooden spatula. Cook, stirring, for 2 minutes; do not let it brown. Remove pan from heat, switch to a whisk, and add milk all at once, whisking vigorously. Return to heat and cook, still over high heat, whisking, until mixture comes to a boil; it will be very thick. Stir in cheese and whisk over heat until cheese melts and mixture is smooth. Add salt (but taste cheese mixture first—the cheese may be extra salty), pepper, and mustard and stir well. Stir a little of the sauce into the egg yolks, to warm them; then stir them into sauce. Stir in chives. Spread the mixture on a baking tray, cover with plastic wrap, and put in the refrigerator to chill for several hours, preferably overnight.

To form croquettes, pick up a good tablespoonful of the chilled mixture and, using the heel of your hand, very lightly shape it into a cork shape. Or cut shapes with cutters, if you wish. Coat the shapes with remaining 1 cup flour, patting off excess, then dip in beaten egg and roll in crumbs. Chill again for at least ½ hour. Heat 2 inches fat in saucepan or deep-fat fryer to 375° and fry croquettes, 2 or 3 at a time, for about 2 minutes or until nicely browned. Drain on paper towels and hold them in a 350° oven to keep warm while you fry remaining croquettes. Serve hot with Tomato Sauce.

TOMATO SAUCE

½ cup olive oil
4 cups chopped onions
4 finely chopped cloves garlic
2 28-ounce cans Italian-style
　　tomatoes

2 teaspoons salt
1 teaspoon freshly cracked
　　black pepper

Heat the olive oil in a large saucepan. Stir in onions and garlic and cook over high heat, stirring, until golden. Do not let burn. Add tomatoes, mashing them, and cook until mixture thickens, about 30 minutes. Stir frequently to prevent sauce from sticking.

GREEN PEPPER SALAD

5 cups very finely diced celery
3 green peppers, seeded and
   very finely diced
1 large, very finely diced,
   red onion
2 teaspoons salt

1 teaspoon freshly cracked
   black pepper
1 tablespoon Dijon mustard
2 tablespoons red wine vinegar
6 tablespoons vegetable oil
2 tablespoons chopped parsley

Combine diced vegetables in a serving bowl. Mix together salt, pepper, mustard, vinegar, and vegetable oil and pour over salad. Sprinkle with parsley and toss. Prepare ahead and marinate in refrigerator for at least 3 hours.

GINGER ROLL

2 tablespoons vegetable oil
3 eggs
½ cup sugar
¼ teaspoon salt
⅔ cup lightly spooned cake
   flour
2 teaspoons baking powder
1 teaspoon cinnamon
1 teaspoon ground ginger

1 teaspoon ground allspice
¼ cup dark molasses

FILLING:
1½ cups apple sauce
½ cup apricot jam
1 teaspoon grated lemon peel
2 tablespoons brandy

Brush a jelly-roll pan with vegetable oil, then line it with waxed paper, letting the paper extend 4 inches on each end. Brush the paper with vegetable oil and set aside. Beat eggs in mixing bowl with sugar and salt until mixture is very thick and holds its shape (this will take about 5 minutes). Sift together flour, baking powder, and spices; add to egg mixture and fold in very gently. Fold in molasses. Spread mixture in prepared jelly-roll pan and bake in a preheated 375° oven for 12 to 14 minutes. Remove from oven, dust surface of mixture with granulated sugar, and turn out upside down onto 2 overlapping sheets of waxed paper. Peel off lining paper and roll up like a jelly roll. Chill for at least 1 hour. Unroll carefully. Mix filling ingredients together and spread over roll; roll it up again and chill before serving. *Recipe may be fully prepared ahead; it also freezes well, for up to 1 month.*

Informal Lunch for 8

Hamburgers with green peppercorns
Red onion and black olive salad
Toasted French bread
Pears stuffed with Roquefort cheese

HAMBURGERS WITH GREEN PEPPERCORNS

Here is a new way of preparing hamburgers that elevates them to company food. Green peppercorns are unripe peppercorns and come mainly from Madagascar. I like the ones packed in water rather than in strong-tasting brine or vinegar.

⅓ cup green peppercorns	¼ cup red wine *or* 2 table-
2 chopped cloves garlic	spoons brandy
3 pounds ground beef	2 tablespoons chopped shallots
Salt, to taste	1 teaspoon Dijon mustard
6 tablespoons butter	1 cup heavy cream

Drain the peppercorns and, if packed in vinegar, rinse them. Put into a mortar with the garlic and crush lightly. Shape ground beef into 8 patties ¾ to 1 inch thick; use a light touch—don't compress the beef. Salt the patties and press the pepper-garlic mixture on both sides. Heat 4 tablespoons butter in a heavy skillet and for rare meat sauté patties over high heat 3 minutes on each side—don't let them touch. Warning: the pepper may spatter. Remove patties to serving platter, scraping up any peppercorns that have fallen off. Deglaze the pan with red wine, or with flaming brandy. Add remaining 2 tablespoons butter; stir in shallots, mustard, and heavy cream. Bring to a boil and shake pan over heat until sauce thickens slightly. Taste for seasoning, and pour over patties.

RED ONION AND BLACK OLIVE SALAD

5 red onions
1 cup finely chopped black
   olives
½ cup vegetable oil
2 tablespoons soy sauce
1 tablespoon dry sherry

1 tablespoon vinegar
½ teaspoon freshly cracked
   black pepper
2 tablespoons finely chopped
   parsley

Peel onions and slice very thin; put slices in a bowl and cover with ice water for 1 hour, until crisp. Drain and pat dry with paper towels. Place in salad bowl and sprinkle on chopped black olives. Combine oil, soy sauce, sherry, vinegar, and pepper. Pour over onions, sprinkle with chopped parsley, and refrigerate for about 3 hours; flavor improves as it marinates. Toss before serving.

PEARS STUFFED WITH ROQUEFORT CHEESE

8 ripe but firm pears
1 pound Roquefort cheese

1 cup unsalted butter

Wash pears; do not peel. Remove cores with apple corer from blossom end, leaving stems on. Cut a slice from bottoms, so pears will stand upright on dessert plates. Beat Roquefort cheese and butter together until very creamy. Put mixture in a pastry bag fitted with a small rose tube and fill cavities of pears. Decorate pears with a ribbon of the cheese-butter mixture, up one side and down the other. Refrigerate if not serving immediately, but remove from refrigerator 1 hour before serving.

A Robust Lunch
for 8 after Tennis or Golf

Olive butter, radishes
Kielbasa in brioche with assorted mustards
Onions stuffed with onions
Mostarda (mustard fruit from Cremona, Italy)
Assorted cheeses and crackers

This menu offers your palate some good contrasts—sweetness, tartness, and blandness—and a variety of textures. The dishes are by no means as strong-tasting as they may sound. Butter smooths out the flavors in the olive butter, making it lovely and subtle in combination with crisp radishes. Onions lose their bite when they're baked. Mostarda is a mixture of fruits—apricots, pineapple, pears, peaches, cherries—preserved in a very sweet, beautifully clear syrup. It contains mustard, but you won't detect it. It comes from Cremona and Italians serve it as a classic accompaniment to ham and tongue. Cheese stores today urge shoppers to sample; you can try their recommendations, or collect some Muenster, Cheddar, and Port Salut to serve with unsalted crackers for dessert.

OLIVE BUTTER

1 cup butter
1 1-pound can black olives, finely chopped
2 finely chopped cloves garlic
6 anchovy fillets, drained and chopped
½ teaspoon freshly cracked black pepper
1 teaspoon anisette, or any licorice-flavored liqueur
Salt, optional
Radishes
Pumpernickel bread

Cream butter with electric mixer. Add olives, garlic, anchovies, pepper, and anisette. Mix thoroughly, taste to see if it needs salt, and pack into a crock. Serve with plenty of whole radishes and small rounds of pumpernickel.

KIELBASA IN BRIOCHE
WITH ASSORTED MUSTARDS

2 pounds kielbasa
1 recipe brioche (see p. 11)
1 tablespoon Dijon mustard

1 egg yolk
Assorted mustards: Dijon,
   Düsseldorf, Creole

Put sausage in saucepan and cover with cold water; bring to a boil and boil quite rapidly for 10 minutes, to remove grease. Drain sausage, and when cool enough to handle, remove and discard the casing. Roll out brioche dough a little longer and wider than sausage. Spread with mustard. Wrap sausage in dough, pinching to seal seam and tucking in ends. Place seam side down on a baking tray and brush dough all over with egg yolk beaten with a tablespoon of cold water. Cut 3 gashes in top to let out steam. (*Recipe can be made ahead to this point, covered with plastic wrap, and refrigerated overnight.*) When ready to proceed, let sausage and brioche stand at room temperature for about 40 minutes to rise—brioche does not have to double. Place in a preheated 375° oven for 35 to 40 minutes or until crust is nicely browned. Serve warm, cut in 1-inch slices, with an assortment of mustards.

ONIONS STUFFED WITH ONIONS

8 medium-size onions, each
   about 2 inches in diameter
4 tablespoons butter or bacon
   fat
6 slices bacon, cooked and
   crumbled
2 tablespoons bread crumbs

2 tablespoons finely chopped
   parsley
½ teaspoon freshly cracked
   white pepper
½ cup chicken stock (see
   p. 278)

With a knife, cut out centers of onions, leaving a wall about ¼ inch thick. (Cut centers into 4 quarters and dig them out with a spoon.) Chop centers very finely. Heat butter or bacon fat in a skillet and cook chopped onion over high heat until transparent— do not brown. Stir in bacon; remove from heat and add bread crumbs, parsley, and pepper. Mix thoroughly. Stuff onion shells with mixture and place them in a buttered baking dish. (*Recipe can be prepared ahead to this point, or you can partially bake stuffed onions, undercooking them slightly and finishing them when you reheat.*) Pour on chicken stock, cover dish with foil, and place in a preheated 375° oven to bake until onions are barely tender, about 30 minutes.

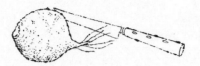

Summer Lunch for 4 Ladies and 8 Children

Deviled eggs
Cold barbecued chicken wings
Relishes, carrots, radishes, cucumbers,
pickles, and olives
Breadsticks
Alice Peterson's chocolate cheesecake

DEVILED EGGS

12 hard-cooked eggs
¾ cup unsalted butter
1 tablespoon Dijon mustard
  or 3 tablespoons tomato
  paste

1½ teaspoons salt
5 or 6 drops Tabasco sauce
  Parsley, for garnish

Peel hard-cooked eggs and split them lengthwise. Remove yolks and rub them through a fine sieve into a mixer bowl. Beat until creamy and smooth. Beat in butter, 1 tablespoonful at a time, and continue beating until extremely light and fluffy. Season with mustard or tomato paste, salt, and Tabasco. Put the egg yolk mixture into a pastry bag fitted with a star tube and pipe it into the reserved egg whites—there's enough filling to pile it high. Decorate with tiny sprigs of parsley.

COLD BARBECUED CHICKEN WINGS

Children adore chicken wings, and they are fairly inexpensive. When meaty (and they can be) they are fun to eat with one's fingers. They are also great for a picnic.

48 meaty chicken wings
1 12-ounce jar chili sauce
2 tablespoons Worcestershire
   sauce
½ cup cider vinegar
½ cup vegetable oil
½ cup firmly packed brown
   sugar
1 medium-size onion, grated
2 chopped cloves garlic
2 teaspoons salt
1 teaspoon freshly cracked
   black pepper

Lay chicken wings in a large roasting pan. Mix remaining ingredients together to make barbecue sauce and spread half of it over chicken. Bake in a preheated 375° oven for 30 minutes. Turn chicken wings over and spread with remaining barbecue sauce. Return to oven and bake for 30 minutes more, or until brown and tender. Run them under the broiler, if necessary, to brown. (*Recipe may be made ahead to this point.*) Cover and store in refrigerator, but bring to room temperature before serving.

ALICE PETERSON'S CHOCOLATE CHEESECAKE

This is the best chocolate cheesecake I have ever tasted. Alice Peterson was the food editor of the New York *Daily News* for years and was always expert at developing recipes. This one is a gem.

18 graham crackers
½ cup butter, plus butter to
   grease pan
¼ cup plus ⅔ cup sugar
2 8-ounce packages cream
   cheese
2 6-ounce packages semi-
   sweet chocolate bits
½ cup strong black coffee
4 eggs, separated
2 tablespoons dark rum
⅛ teaspoon salt
1 cup heavy cream
   Shaved chocolate or cocoa,
      for garnish

Crush graham crackers to make coarse crumbs (packaged crumbs are too fine). Melt ½ cup butter and stir it and ¼ cup sugar into crumbs; mixture should look like wet sand. Butter the sides of a 9-inch springform pan and press graham cracker mixture against bottom and sides of pan. Set aside.

Bring cream cheese to room temperature. Melt chocolate in coffee over low heat. In electric mixer bowl, beat egg yolks until sticky; add ⅔ cup sugar and beat until pale yellow and thickened. Gradually beat in cream cheese, a bit at a time, and beat until it looks like whipped butter. This takes 5 to 10 minutes, depending on your mixer; but you can't overbeat this cheese mixture. Beat in rum and salt.

In another bowl, beat egg whites until foamy; add remaining ⅓ cup sugar gradually, a tablespoonful at a time, and beat until glossy, but not stiff. Set aside. With mixer on low speed, beat the hot coffee-chocolate mixture into cheese mixture—batter will be thin. Then fold in egg whites and pour into prepared pan. Place on the middle shelf of a preheated 350° oven and bake 1 hour. Turn off oven and leave cake in the oven, door closed, until oven is cold. The cake will crack as it bakes, and sink as it cools—this is normal.

To serve, loosen cake from pan with a small knife; invert on serving plate and remove springform. Whip the heavy cream over ice; do not sweeten it. Pack into a pastry bag fitted with a star tube, and pipe rosettes of whipped cream all over the top. Decorate with shaved chocolate curls or with cocoa, sieved and sifted over cake with a teaspoon. Serve at room temperature. If there is any cake left over, store it in refrigerator.

A Refreshing Summer Lunch
for 6

Avocado with crab meat
Tomatoes with chives
Hot baking powder biscuits
Meringue cake with peaches

When you can serve something that everyone likes in a dramatic new way, your luncheon will be talked about. Here's a familiar dish—avocado stuffed with crab meat—that looks like a large, beautifully decorated Easter egg when it is assembled and ready to be served. Scoop the avocado halves out in one piece, pile the crab meat into the shells, and place the avocado meat over the salad, rounded side up; then decorate.

AVOCADO WITH CRAB MEAT

1 recipe crab-meat salad (see p. 52)	2 hard-cooked eggs
3 ripe avocados	2 tablespoons chopped parsley
3 tablespoons lime juice	¾ cup mayonnaise (see p. 283)
	Watercress, for garnish

Make crab-meat salad and refrigerate. Split the avocados (unpeeled) lengthwise, remove pits, and carefully pry the flesh out in one piece. To do this, ease the tip of a tablespoon between flesh and skin until you can lift the flesh out. Take care not to split the shells, and set them aside. As you remove each avocado half, sprinkle it immediately with lime juice to help keep it from darkening. Spoon crab-meat salad into the *shells;* place avocado halves over the crab meat, rounded side up—it will look like a whole avocado again. Peel hard-cooked eggs and chop the whites and sieve the yolks. Sprinkle avocados with whites first, then yolks, then chopped parsley. Put mayonnaise in a pastry bag fitted with a small star tube and pipe a ribbon of mayonnaise around the seam of each avocado, where flesh and shell meet. Add a mayonnaise rosette on top. Store avocados in refrigerator until ready to serve; they'll hold well for up to 2 hours. Garnish plates with watercress.

TOMATOES WITH CHIVES

3 large tomatoes	½ teaspoon freshly cracked black pepper
¼ cup finely chopped chives	3 tablespoons tarragon vinegar
1 teaspoon salt	2 teaspoons sugar

Scald tomatoes for 10 seconds in boiling water (or hold them, on a fork, in a gas flame until the skin splits). Peel and slice vertically, from stem to bottom. Arrange them, overlapping, on a long narrow platter. Sprinkle with chives, salt, pepper, vinegar, and sugar.

HOT BAKING POWDER BISCUITS

2 cups lightly spooned flour	1 teaspoon sugar
2 teaspoons baking powder	4 tablespoons butter
1 teaspoon salt	¾ cup milk

Put flour, baking powder, salt, and sugar in a bowl; stir to mix. Rub in the butter, using your fingers or a pastry blender, until the mixture looks like coarse cornmeal. Add milk and mix well to make a soft dough. Turn out on a lightly floured board and pat out ¾ inch thick. Cut biscuits with a 2-inch round cutter or cut in 2-inch squares with a sharp knife. Place on well-buttered baking tray and bake in a preheated 450° oven for about 12 minutes, or until biscuits are golden brown. Serve with a crock of butter. Makes 12 2-inch biscuits.

MERINGUE CAKE WITH PEACHES

½ cup butter	¼ cup chopped nuts, walnuts
1½ cups sugar	or pecans
4 eggs, separated	1 cup heavy cream
¼ cup milk	2 tablespoons confectioners'
½ teaspoon vanilla extract	sugar
1 cup lightly spooned flour	2 fresh peaches, peeled and
1¼ teaspoons baking powder	diced, or 4 canned peach
⅛ teaspoon salt	halves, diced

Grease 2 8-inch cake pans and line bottoms with waxed paper. Preheat oven to 350°. In electric mixer bowl, cream the butter, slowly add ½ cup of the sugar, and beat until light and fluffy. Beat in egg yolks, one at a time, then add milk and vanilla. Sift the flour and baking powder together and add to egg yolk mixture, beating slowly until mixed. Mixture will be thick. Stop the beater, scrape the sides of the bowl, and continue beating at least 2 minutes. Divide the batter between the 2 pans, smoothing the tops with a spatula.

In another bowl, beat the egg whites with salt until stiff. Add remaining 1 cup sugar, 1 tablespoon at a time, beating constantly. Continue to beat until mixture is like marshmallow and feels smooth when you pinch it. Spread meringue over cake batter in pans, and sprinkle *one* layer only with chopped nuts. Bake for 30 minutes. To assemble the cake, whip the heavy cream, sweeten it with confectioners' sugar, and fold in peaches. Place the un-nutted layer, meringue side down, on a serving plate. Spread with whipped cream and peaches. Place second layer, nut side up, on top. Chill in refrigerator before serving.

A Late Lunch
on a Wintry Day for 8

Hot oyster stew
Gougère
Black radish slices vinaigrette
Chocolate mousse

HOT OYSTER STEW

1 quart oysters	1 teaspoon freshly cracked
½ cup butter	white pepper
2 quarts half-and-half, scalded	Paprika
2 teaspoons salt	2 tablespoons finely chopped
	parsley

Heat oysters in their liquid over high heat until edges begin to curl, about 2 to 3 minutes. Add butter, cut in pieces, and scalded half-and-half, still piping hot. Season with salt and pepper and pour into heated tureen. Dust with paprika and sprinkle with chopped parsley. Don't boil or overcook this stew; if you do, the oysters will get rubbery.

GOUGÈRE

Imagine cream puff pastry, sharply flavored with cheese and baked in a ring until it's puffed, crusty, and golden brown. That's gougère, popular in Burgundy. It's good hot or cold, with a glass of Burgundy wine.

4 tablespoons butter
1 cup water
1 cup lightly spooned flour
4 eggs
1 tablespoon Dijon mustard
1 teaspoon salt

½ teaspoon freshly cracked
   white pepper
1½ cups grated Parmesan
   cheese
1 egg yolk
8 thin triangular slices of
   Gruyère cheese

To make *pâte à choux,* or cream puff paste, place the butter, cut in pieces, and the water in a saucepan and bring to a boil. As soon as butter melts, dump in flour all at once and stir vigorously. Beat the mixture over high heat until it leaves sides of pan and starts to film bottom, about 2 minutes. Remove pan from heat and beat in eggs, one at a time. Beat in each egg thoroughly before adding the next, and beat about 5 minutes more, until mixture is shiny, using the flat whip of an electric mixer if you have one. Beat in mustard, salt, pepper, and 1 cup of the grated Parmesan cheese. (*Recipe can be made ahead to this point.*)

Put mixture into a pastry bag fitted with a large (dime-size)` round tube. Grease baking sheets or line with baking parchment and draw 2 8-inch rings (if you can use an 8-inch cake pan as a guide). Pipe *pâte à choux* mixture in a circle just inside these rings. Brush tops but not sides of rings with egg wash (egg yolk beaten with 1 tablespoon cold water), balance 4 cheese triangles along the tops of each ring, and sprinkle with remaining Parmesan cheese. Bake in a preheated 450° oven for 15 minutes. Turn heat to 350° and bake 10 minutes, then to 325° and bake for another 20 minutes. Serve warm, cut in wedges.

BLACK RADISH SLICES VINAIGRETTE

Black radishes look like large black turnips—about the size of a fist; you can find them during the late fall and winter in gourmet or middle European markets. They're snowy white inside, with a fairly sharp taste. When you slice them paper-thin and put them into cold water, they ruffle. The black edges outline the ruffles and they really look fantastic—no one knows what they are.

Scrub 4 or 5 black radishes and slice them paper-thin on a vegetable cutter or mandoline. Soak them in cold water for about ½ hour. Put them in a chilled salad bowl, pour on French vinaigrette dressing (see p. 282), and toss. Let marinate 2 hours. Sprinkle with 2 tablespoons chopped parsley.

CHOCOLATE MOUSSE

½ pound dark sweet chocolate
5 tablespoons water *or* strong
    black coffee
5 eggs, separated
2 tablespoons orange liqueur,
    optional

Sweetened whipped cream,
    optional
Chocolate for garnish,
    optional

Cut chocolate into little pieces and melt in a saucepan, with water or coffee, over very low heat. Stir while melting, and don't let it get too hot. Beat egg whites until stiff but not dry. In another bowl, beat egg yolks to mix, then whisk chocolate into them. Beat in orange liqueur, if desired. Stir a spoonful of egg whites into chocolate mixture, to lighten it, then fold in remaining egg whites. Pour mousse into a crystal serving bowl, or into individual small white pots, and place in the refrigerator to chill, at least 2 hours, or overnight. Serve plain, or decorated with rosettes of sweetened whipped cream and garnished with a grating of chocolate.

A Holiday-Season Luncheon for 6

Passatelli soup
Ham roulade
Raw mushroom salad with a dressing of
sour cream, caraway, and chives
Steamed chocolate pudding with hard sauce

If you're looking for a new and unusual way to use up leftovers from a holiday ham, try this delicious ham roulade, which can be found on p. 36. Instead of the mustard sour cream, serve it with a lemon butter sauce (made by melting ½ cup butter, then adding the juice of ½ lemon and 1 tablespoon chopped parsley) or plain with Dijon mustard. The steamed pudding adds a further traditional holiday touch. The passatelli soup is adapted from a soup I had in Rome, and the ham roulade is one of my own original recipes.

PASSATELLI SOUP

2 eggs
4 to 6 tablespoons bread
    crumbs
1 tablespoon plus 1 teaspoon
    flour
6 tablespoons grated Parmesan
    cheese
6 tablespoons soft butter

2 tablespoons finely chopped
    parsley
½ teaspoon salt
½ teaspoon freshly cracked
    white pepper
¼ teaspoon freshly grated
    nutmeg
9 cups strong chicken stock
    (see p. 278)

Mix together in a bowl eggs, 3 tablespoons bread crumbs, flour, cheese, butter, parsley, salt, pepper, and nutmeg, working the mixture with a wooden spatula to form a stiff dough. Add more bread crumbs if necessary. (*Recipe may be made ahead to this point and refrigerated in covered container.*) Bring chicken stock to a boil. Put the cheese dough into a spaetzle machine or colander with large holes, hold it over boiling stock, and press dough through machine or colander so that it drops, in small bits, into stock. In 1 to 2 minutes, the tiny dumplings will rise to the surface; turn off heat and let stand for about 5 minutes before serving.

RAW MUSHROOM SALAD WITH A DRESSING OF SOUR CREAM, CARAWAY, AND CHIVES

1½ pounds very thinly sliced
    mushrooms
¾ cup sour cream
1 tablespoon caraway seeds

4 tablespoons chopped fresh
    chives
½ teaspoon salt
¼ teaspoon freshly cracked
    white pepper

Put sliced mushrooms in a bowl; mix together remaining ingredients and pour over mushrooms. Toss to coat mushrooms well and marinate for about 2 hours in the refrigerator. Taste for seasoning, and stir again just before serving.

STEAMED CHOCOLATE PUDDING
WITH HARD SAUCE

2 tablespoons butter to grease mold
6 ounces dark sweet chocolate
3 eggs
1½ cups sugar
3 tablespoons soft butter

3 tablespoons orange marmalade
3 cups lightly spooned flour
2 teaspoons baking powder
½ teaspoon salt
1½ cups heavy cream
Hard Sauce (recipe follows)

Heavily butter an 8-cup steamed pudding mold or 2-quart bowl. Melt chocolate over very low heat, stirring constantly with a wooden spatula, and set aside. Beat eggs in electric mixer bowl; add sugar gradually, beating until light and fluffy. Beat in cooled (but not set) chocolate, soft butter, and orange marmalade. Sift flour with baking powder and salt and beat into egg-sugar mixture alternately with cream, about one third at a time. Pour batter into mold; it should be about ¾ inch from top of mold. (If you have extra batter, put in custard cup, cover, and steam like the big pudding.) Fasten lid tightly (or cover the 2-quart bowl with cloth and then aluminum foil, tied tightly with string) and stand mold on a rack in a large pot filled halfway up sides of mold with boiling water. Cover pot and steam the pudding in boiling water on top of the stove for 2 hours. Replenish boiling water as necessary. (*Recipe may be made ahead to this point. Leave the pudding in the mold and reheat in boiling water. Or steam it for 1½ hours and reheat for ½ hour.*) Turn pudding out onto a platter and serve with hard sauce.

HARD SAUCE

Cream ½ cup butter in mixing bowl and gradually add 1 cup confectioners' sugar. Beat in 1 teaspoon lemon juice and 2 tablespoons rum, brandy, sherry, or more lemon juice. Beat until fluffy.

Danish Open-face Sandwich
Luncheon for 12

Assorted Danish open-face sandwiches
Ice-cold beer
Brandy curls

ASSORTED DANISH OPEN-FACE SANDWICHES

Danish open-face sandwiches are a delicious and eye-pleasing departure from the usual. Really try to stretch your imagination in decorating them! They always taste best if assembled just before serving.

No matter what combination of ingredients you select, first butter the bread thoroughly with a thin layer of softened butter. This will prevent the bread from getting soggy. Be sure to have on hand ample mayonnaise (see p. 283), mustard mayonnaise (mayonnaise flavored to taste with Dijon mustard), and whipped cream cheese to spread or pipe (from pastry bags fitted with small star tubes) onto sandwiches. For garnish, make tomato and cucumber "riders": cut the vegetables into thin slices, make a cut from the edge to the center of each slice, grasp the resulting ends, and pull them apart, twisting the slice as you pull. Make orange or lemon riders in the same way.

Several sandwich suggestions follow the ingredients list. Count 2 sandwiches per person.

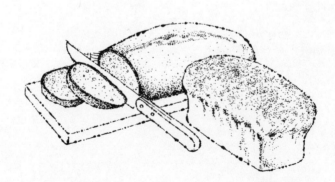

1 loaf Danish rye bread, thinly
sliced
1 loaf pumpernickel, thinly
sliced
Butter
Mayonnaise
Dijon mustard
Cream cheese
Danish liver pâté
Bacon strips, crisply fried
Hard-cooked egg, sliced
Scrambled egg
Cooked chicken, sliced
Rare roast beef, sliced
Steak Tartare (see p. 221)
Boiled ham, sliced
Danish salami, sliced
Tiny canned shrimp
Pickled herring

Smoked salmon
Danish blue cheese
Coleslaw
Potato salad
Tomatoes, sliced
Cucumbers, sliced
Raw mushrooms, sliced
Onion rings
Lettuce leaves
Watercress sprigs
Gherkins
Sweet pickles
Capers
Orange slices
Lemon slices
Cooked prunes
Black olives, sliced
Parsley, chopped and in sprigs
Black caviar
Chives, chopped

SANDWICH SUGGESTIONS

1. Lettuce, liver pâté, a few slices of raw mushroom, a sweet pickle, and a piece of crisply fried bacon, all topped with a tomato rider.

2. Lettuce, 4 overlapping slices hard-cooked egg on 1 side of the bread, overlapping tomato slices on the other side, mayonnaise piped down the center, and a dab of black caviar for garnish.

3. Three slices of ham, rolled up, topped with mustard mayonnaise, an orange rider, 2 cooked prunes, and a small sprig of parsley.

4. Ham slices topped with a rider made by sandwiching a slice of cucumber between 2 slices of tomato. Stand the rider on a ribbon of cream cheese sprinkled with chopped chives.

5. Lettuce and sliced chicken, topped with a rosette of mayonnaise, 2 cucumber riders, and a sprig of watercress.

6. Two slices roast beef topped with coleslaw nested in a bit of lettuce. Decorate with tomato rider and a gherkin thinly sliced at one end and spread to look like a fan.

7. Lettuce, overlapping slices of salami, onion rings, and a sprig of parsley.

8. Tiny shrimp, lined up in rows, with mayonnaise piped down the center, garnished with a bit of lettuce, a lemon rider, and chopped parsley.

9. Lettuce, pickled herring, and overlapping onion rings, garnished on one corner with tomato sliver and sprig of parsley.

10. Lettuce and overlapping thin slices of Danish blue cheese, garnished with a row of sliced black olives.

11. Steak tartare, decorated in a crisscross pattern with back of knife, garnished with pickles and/or capers.

12. Smoked salmon, plain with freshly cracked black pepper or topped with a diagonal stripe of scrambled egg.

13. Two slices roast beef topped with potato salad, garnished with watercress and tomato rider.

BRANDY CURLS

1¼ cups lightly spooned flour	4 tablespoons brandy
⅔ cup sugar	1 cup heavy cream
1 tablespoon ground ginger	2 tablespoons confectioners'
¼ teaspoon salt	sugar
½ cup molasses	3 tablespoons chopped crystal-
½ cup butter	lized ginger

Sift flour, sugar, ginger, and salt together. In a saucepan, bring molasses and butter to a boil over medium-high heat. Remove from heat and gradually stir in dry ingredients. Return to medium-high heat, stirring until blended. Remove from heat and stir in 3 tablespoons brandy. Drop batter by half teaspoonfuls on a greased baking sheet, 3 inches apart. Bake only 6 cookies at one time, in a preheated 300° oven, for 8 minutes, or until they stop bubbling. Cool 1 minute. Quickly remove each cookie with a spatula and drape it over a wood dowel or small rolling pin so that it will harden in a curl. Or roll it at once around the handle of a wooden spoon to make a scroll. When cool, store curls in an air-tight container or plastic bags. When ready to serve, whip cream, adding confectioners' sugar, chopped ginger, and remaining 1 tablespoon brandy. Put cream in a pastry bag fitted with a star tube and pipe it into cookie curls. Or fill with vanilla ice cream. Recipe makes 50 curls.

A Country-Kitchen Luncheon
for 6

Polenta ring mold with
sautéed fluted mushroom caps
Braised celery
Oranges Grand Marnier

POLENTA RING MOLD WITH
SAUTÉED FLUTED MUSHROOM CAPS

½ pound thinly sliced
    prosciutto ham
1 recipe polenta (see p. 19)
8 ounces mozzarella cheese,
    diced

½ recipe Tomato Sauce (see
    p. 64) or 1 recipe Pesto
    (see p. 202)
1 pound Sautéed Fluted Mush-
    room Caps (see p. 284)

Brush an 8-cup ring mold with vegetable oil and line it with overlapping slices of prosciutto ham, letting slices overhang rim of mold. Spoon half the polenta mixture into the prepared mold and bang the mold to settle it. Spread with diced mozzarella. Spoon on remaining polenta and bang the mold again. Fold ham ends over top. (*Recipe can be made ahead to this point.*) Set mold in a pan of hot water, with the water three-quarters of the way up the mold, and bake in a preheated 350° oven for 25 minutes. You can hold this dish in the water bath (oven turned off) for up to 2 hours, or let it cool and reheat it in the water bath. Before unmolding, take mold out of the water bath and let stand for 5 minutes. Then run a knife around the edge to loosen it and turn it out on a serving dish. Serve with Tomato Sauce or Pesto. Fill center or ring with Sautéed Fluted Mushrooms.

BRAISED CELERY

3 heads celery
2 teaspoons salt
3 tablespoons chopped shallots
1 cup beef stock (see p. 277)
3 tablespoons butter

½ teaspoon freshly cracked
    black pepper
2 tablespoons freshly chopped
    parsley

Cut off tops and trim roots of celery to make from each head a heart about 6 to 8 inches long; cut them in half lengthwise and put them in a saucepan. Cover with cold water, add 1 teaspoon salt, and parboil 10 minutes. Drain and place in an ovenproof serving dish. Scatter shallots over celery, pour on beef stock, dot with butter, and sprinkle with remaining 1 teaspoon salt and the pepper. Lay a piece of buttered waxed paper or aluminum foil over the celery and bake in a preheated 350° oven until celery is barely tender, from 30 to 45 minutes. (*Recipe can be made ahead and reheated.*) Sprinkle with chopped parsley before serving.

ORANGES GRAND MARNIER

Peel 6 oranges, removing all the white membrane. Slice them crosswise in very thin slices, sprinkle with about 2 tablespoons sugar and ½ cup Grand Marnier (or other orange liqueur), and let macerate for 30 minutes or so.

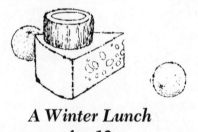

A Winter Lunch
for 12

Radishes with olive butter
Black bean soup with garnishes
Onion pie
Fruit and cheese

RADISHES WITH OLIVE BUTTER

Scrub 3 or 4 black radishes—available in the fall and winter from gourmet and middle European markets—and slice them paper-thin on a vegetable cutter or mandoline. Soak them in cold water for about ½ hour. Scrub and trim 2 bunches of red and white radishes, but leave stems on. Serve with olive butter (see p. 68).

BLACK BEAN SOUP WITH GARNISHES

1½ pounds dry black beans
2 quarts chicken stock
      (see p. 278)
1 2-pound smoked pork
      shoulder butt *or* leftover
      ham bone with meat
      clinging to it
1½ cups diced onions
1 cup diced carrots
1 cup diced celery
2 teaspoons finely chopped
      garlic
1 tablespoon salt, more if
      needed

1 teaspoon freshly cracked
      black pepper
½ cup dry sherry or Madeira

GARNISHES:
1 cup finely diced green
      pepper
1 cup finely diced onion
1 cup cooked rice
2 thinly sliced lemons
1 cup sour cream
1 cup chopped ham

Rinse beans well, cover with cold water, and let stand overnight. Drain beans, put them in a kettle, and cover with chicken stock. Add pork butt or ham bone, onions, carrots, celery, garlic, salt, and pepper. Bring to a boil over high heat, cover kettle, turn heat to simmer, and cook until beans are tender, about 3 to 4 hours. Remove half the beans from the soup and puree them in blender or food mill, using the fine disk; return to soup. Add sherry or Madeira, taste for seasoning, and serve hot. Pass garnishes in individual bowls. This soup is better if made the day before, and it will freeze for up to 1 month.

ONION PIE

1 pound yellow onions, plus 1
      large yellow onion
2 tablespoons bacon fat
2 eggs
2 egg yolks
2 teaspoons Dijon mustard
½ cup grated Parmesan cheese

1¼ cups light cream, scalded
1 10-inch partly baked pâte
      brisée shell (see p. 288)
Flour
1 recipe beer batter (see
      p. 285)
Fat for deep frying

Slice 1 pound onions and cook them slowly in bacon fat, stirring, until they are limp, about 5 minutes. Drain on paper towels. Beat together lightly eggs, egg yolks, mustard, and Parmesan cheese. Stir in onions and add hot scalded cream slowly, stirring, so as not to curdle eggs. Pour into partly baked pâte brisée shell and bake in a preheated 350° oven for 25 minutes, or until custard tests done. (*Recipe can be made ahead to this point and reheated; it will also freeze.*)

While pie is baking, prepare garnish: Slice remaining large onion ¼ inch thick, separate into rings, and dust with flour. Dip rings into beer batter and deep-fry in 2 inches of hot fat (375°). Overlap them around edge of pie.

A Light, Easy-to-Prepare Lunch for 4

Sautéed bay scallops
Mixed yellow and green beans,
with shallots and butter
Tomato salad
Dessert omelette

SAUTÉED BAY SCALLOPS

1½ pounds bay scallops	1 teaspoon salt
½ cup flour	½ teaspoon freshly cracked
½ cup butter	white pepper
Juice of ½ lemon	2 tablespoons chopped parsley

Dry scallops well and roll in flour. Heat butter in a skillet; when it's foaming, add scallops and shake them over heat for 3 to 4 minutes—do not overcook. Sprinkle with lemon juice, salt, pepper, and parsley and give them another shake. Serve at once.

MIXED YELLOW AND GREEN BEANS, WITH SHALLOTS AND BUTTER

¾ pound yellow wax beans	3 tablespoons finely chopped
¾ pound green beans	shallots
1 tablespoon salt	1 teaspoon salt
4 tablespoons butter	½ teaspoon freshly cracked
	black pepper

Tip and tail the beans and put them in water to cover with 1 tablespoon salt. Bring them to a boil and boil gently for 7 minutes only. Drain; then refresh them in cold water. (*May be cooked in advance to this point and refrigerated.*) When ready to serve, heat butter in a small pan and sauté the shallots over high heat for a minute or two. Set aside. Put the beans in a skillet and shake them over high heat until they are completely dry. Dress them with butter and shallots and season with 1 teaspoon salt and the pepper.

TOMATO SALAD

4 medium-size tomatoes
1 large red onion
1 recipe French vinaigrette dressing (see p. 282)

2 tablespoons finely chopped capers
2 tablespoons finely chopped parsley

Peel tomatoes, first dropping them in boiling water for 10 seconds to loosen skins, and slice. Peel and slice onion very thinly. Layer tomato and onion in a salad bowl, sprinkling each layer with vinaigrette. Sprinkle capers and parsley over salad and let stand in a cool place (not the refrigerator) until ready to serve.

DESSERT OMELETTE

4 tablespoons sugar
4 egg yolks
1 tablespoon vanilla extract *or* liqueur such as Cointreau or Grand Marnier

5 egg whites
2 tablespoons confectioners' sugar

In electric mixer bowl, beat together sugar and egg yolks until very thick, about 5 minutes. Beat in flavoring. (*May be prepared ahead to this point.*) In another bowl, beat egg whites until very stiff. Fold ⅓ of the egg whites into egg yolk mixture to lighten it. Then lightly and quickly fold in remaining egg whites. Mound ⅓ of omelette mixture in an ovenproof serving dish. Put remaining mixture into a large pastry bag fitted with a large star tube, and pipe it in swirls up and down and around the sides of the base mound. Sift confectioners' sugar over the omelette and place it in a preheated 375° oven to bake until set, about 7 minutes.

A Low-Calorie Lunch
for 4

Consommé Normande (see p. 119)
Sautéed crab meat
Lemon-dressed lettuce
Fruit and champagne

An elegant lunch for those watching their weight. The Consommé Normande is an extremely delicate and successful light soup, and the crunchiness of the lettuce is just right with the crab.

SAUTÉED CRAB MEAT

If you cannot find fresh crab meat, use frozen; canned crab meat is the third choice.

1 pound lump crab meat,
    preferably fresh
2 tablespoons butter
1 tablespoon lemon juice

½ teaspoon salt
¼ teaspoon freshly cracked
    white pepper
1 tablespoon chopped parsley

Pick over crab meat to remove any bits of shell or filament. Heat butter in a skillet; when it's foaming, add crab meat and sprinkle with lemon juice, salt, and pepper. Toss over high heat about 5 minutes or until heated through. Serve immediately, sprinkled with chopped parsley.

LEMON-DRESSED LETTUCE

Wash leaves from 2 small heads of tender lettuce, roll in towels, and chill. When ready to serve, toss with the juice of 1 lemon, ½ teaspoon salt, and ¼ teaspoon freshly cracked black pepper.

FRUIT AND CHAMPAGNE

3 or 4 ripe peaches or
    nectarines
1 pint raspberries or straw-
    berries
2 tablespoons Curaçao or
    Cointreau

2 tablespoons honey
1 pint orange, lemon, or
    raspberry ice
1 large bottle champagne

Peel and slice the peaches or nectarines; wash and drain the berries and place all in a bowl. Drizzle with liqueur and honey. When ready to serve, spoon fruit ice into goblets, fill with fruit, and flood with champagne. You'll have enough champagne left for 4 glasses, too.

Summer Lunch at Tables under a Shade Tree for 8

Chaudfroid chicken on cold capered rice
Fava beans with coarse salt
Raspberries with chilled framboise

Because it's spectacular—and completely do-ahead—chaudfroid chicken is always worth a repeat. In this version, skip the pâté and arrange the decorated chicken breasts on a bed of cold capered rice instead of chopped aspic. Fava beans are crisp and different; eat them with your fingers, like radishes. Dip the raspberries with your fingers, too. Under a shade tree, this meal is like a picnic.

CHAUDFROID CHICKEN
ON COLD CAPERED RICE

Follow directions for Chaudfroid Chicken (see p. 47), allowing ½ chicken breast per person (4 whole breasts). You'll need only enough aspic to coat the chicken breasts, so make aspic from 2 cups chicken stock, 4 teaspoons unflavored gelatine, 2 teaspoons tomato paste, and a tiny pinch of salt; clarify with 1 egg white.

COLD CAPERED RICE

1 cup long-grain rice
1 teaspoon salt
½ teaspoon freshly cracked
    black pepper
¼ cup olive oil

2 tablespoons wine vinegar
2 teaspoons Dijon mustard
¼ cup drained capers
2 tablespoons chopped parsley

Put rice, salt, pepper, and 2 cups of water in a small heavy pan with a tight-fitting lid. Bring to a boil, cover, reduce heat, and simmer, covered, for 20 minutes. Put cooked rice in a bowl and add oil, vinegar, mustard, capers, and parsley. Toss to mix, and chill. Spread on serving platter and arrange chaudfroid chicken breasts on top.

FAVA BEANS WITH COARSE SALT

Shell fresh young fava beans (sometimes called broad beans), allowing 6 to 8 beans per person, and serve them raw, with a dish of coarse salt on the side to dip them in.

RASPBERRIES WITH CHILLED FRAMBOISE

Heap fresh raspberries—¾ cup for each serving—on individual plates garnished with leaves. (Use any beautiful green leaves you can find, such as maple, magnolia, or grape; if you have none in your yard, get some from the florist.) Serve with icy-cold framboise and confectioners' sugar on the side; guests dip the berries into the framboise and then the sugar.

Dinners

If you wish to give a successful dinner party, build the guest list with as much care as you plan the menu. The invitation "come to dinner" means "come for the evening." If you spend hours ahead of time perfecting the food, you deserve a reward: hours of good conversation. Make sure you get it by mixing in new friends with old. Always the same group means always the same talk, and that can be as boring as always serving roast beef. A surprisingly good conversation starter—or "picker-upper"—for people meeting each other for the first time is the food they are eating. With this in mind, I plan food guests can talk about—at least one dish in the menu that's unfamiliar or unusual.

A cardinal rule in planning any dinner party, whether it is an informal or formal occasion, is to be realistic about what you can do given the time you have at your disposal, the work space in your kitchen, the refrigerator and freezer storage available, whether or not you have two ovens, whether you will be hiring help for the evening, and—not least—your talent as a cook. Always plan a menu you can manage, so that you will be relaxed and at ease when your guests arrive.

Three or possibly four courses for dinner are ample, as is a one-vegetable accompaniment to the meat if you are also serving a salad. Add formality to your dinner by serving the salad as a separate course after the main course. Never follow a rich first or main course with a too rich dessert. Be serene about cutting down on food, knowing that most hostesses tend to serve too much. A shorter menu, with each dish perfectly prepared, is the better showcase for your talents. Knowledgeable guests with chic palates appreciate this.

Think your menu through to be certain that a good part of it is truly make-ahead and that there are only as many last-minute saucing, reheating, or unmolding steps as you can handle. Read the recipes in advance from beginning to end, check your cupboards for supplies, and complete your shopping list.

The season of the year is usually my starting point for menu-thinking. Strawberries ripened in Pennsylvania's warm June sun just taste better to me than California's December crop airlifted east, miracle though that may be. You'll see I've indulged this personal prejudice by labeling many of the menus in this chapter as particularly suited to either summer or winter. Others I have designated as formal or informal in the kinds of dishes offered and their manner of presentation.

No matter what the season or occasion, though, I hope you will approach the menus here in a spirit of openness. They are not intended to be rigid fiats, but suggestions inviting your active participation. If a given menu seems too rich for the guests you have in mind, make a substitution: a green salad for a creamed vegetable, a fruit compote for a chocolate mousse. Relax—and experiment. It's half the fun!

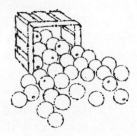

A Potluck Dinner
for 4

Chicken pie
Leeks vinaigrette
Hot chocolate mint soufflé

CHICKEN PIE

1 recipe sour cream pastry
  (see p. 288)
3 pounds chicken pieces
2 cups chicken stock (see
  p. 278)
⅓ cup chopped carrot
¾ cup chopped onion
½ cup chopped celery
6 hard-cooked eggs
½ pound thickly sliced mushrooms

4 tablespoons butter
4 tablespoons flour
1 cup light cream
¼ cup heavy cream
2 tablespoons chopped parsley
1 teaspoon salt
½ teaspoon freshly cracked
  white pepper
1 egg, lightly beaten

Make pastry and put it in the refrigerator to chill for at least 1½ hours. In a saucepan, cover chicken pieces with chicken stock, add carrot, onion, and celery, and bring to a boil over high heat. Reduce heat to simmer and simmer, covered, for 25 minutes. Cool chicken in stock. When chicken is cool enough to handle, remove skin and bones, reserving stock to make sauce. Cut chicken in large pieces and put it in a bowl with hard-cooked eggs, cut in half lengthwise, and mushrooms. Set aside.

Boil reserved chicken stock to reduce it to 1 cup, and make sauce: melt butter in a saucepan, stir in flour with a wooden spatula, and cook, stirring, over high heat for 2 minutes; do not let it brown. Take pan off heat, change to a whisk, and add strained chicken stock and light cream all at once, whisking vigorously. Return pan to high heat and cook, stirring with whisk, until sauce comes to a boil and thickens. Thin it with heavy cream as necessary—the sauce should be of coating consistency. Add chopped parsley, salt, and pepper and carefully fold sauce into the chicken-egg-mushroom mixture. Pour into a 9-inch pie pan and set it in the refrigerator to chill, for at least ½ hour.

When chicken has chilled, roll out pastry on a lightly floured board, about ½ inch thick. Brush the rim of the pie pan with beaten egg and lay crust over chicken, pressing edge to rim. Trim neatly. Cut 2 slits in center of crust. Cut pastry trimmings into leaves or flower shapes to decorate top. Brush the crust with egg, add decorations and brush them with egg, too. (*Recipe may be prepared ahead to this point. Omit hard-cooked eggs if you plan to freeze it—it can be frozen for up to 1 month.*) Put the pie pan on a baking sheet and bake in a preheated 375° oven for 40 minutes. Be sure that the crust, which is thick, is baked through.

LEEKS VINAIGRETTE

12 leeks	1 recipe French vinaigrette
2 cups water	dressing (see p. 282)
1 tablespoon salt	2 tablespoons chopped chives, for garnish

Cut the roots and tops off the leeks, leaving about 1 inch of green, split lengthwise, and hold under running water, separating the layers, to wash thoroughly. Put them in a saucepan, cover with salted water, and cook, uncovered, over medium heat until barely tender, about 15 minutes. Drain them in a sieve and rinse under cold water. Leave them in the sieve to dry and put in refrigerator to chill slightly, about 15 minutes. Make vinaigrette, arrange leeks in a serving dish, cover with vinaigrette, sprinkle with chopped chives, and chill until ready to serve.

HOT CHOCOLATE MINT SOUFFLÉ

Butter and sugar to coat soufflé dish	¼ cup white crème de menthe
	4 egg yolks
6 ounces dark sweet chocolate	4 tablespoons sugar, plus sugar to sprinkle on top
1¼ cups light cream	
3 tablespoons butter	6 egg whites
4 tablespoons flour	Pinch of salt
1 tablespoon vanilla extract *or* seeds scraped from 1 inch of vanilla bean	Confectioners' sugar

Butter a 6-cup soufflé dish and sprinkle with sugar on bottom and sides, knocking out excess. Melt chocolate in cream over medium-high heat, stirring occasionally. In another pan, melt butter, stir in flour, and cook, stirring, for 2 minutes—do not let it brown. Remove from heat and add chocolate-cream mixture. Return to medium-high heat and stir until smooth and thick. Remove from heat and let cool slightly. Add vanilla and crème de menthe. In a large bowl, beat egg yolks with sugar until light and fluffy. Add chocolate mixture and blend thoroughly. (*Recipe can be made ahead to this point.*) Beat egg whites with a pinch of salt until stiff. Fold into chocolate mixture. Pour into prepared soufflé dish and sprinkle top with sugar. Bake in a preheated 375° oven until firm, about 20 minutes. Sift confectioners' sugar over soufflé and serve at once.

An Autumn Dinner for 6, with an Alsatian Touch

Rack of pork
Red cabbage
Mashed potatoes and celeriac
Apple chausson with sour cream

When fall shades into winter, I get hungry for the hearty Alsatian cooking I grew up with. This menu borrows from both the German and French traditions of the border province of Alsace—pork and red cabbage, fruit turnover. The celeriac and potatoes make a wonderful companion to pork.

RACK OF PORK

Notice that the pork roast is carved as a saddle—that means that, instead of cutting between the bones, you carve the meat in long strips. An interesting twist to serving pork.

1 center-cut pork loin roast containing 8 rib chops, about 6 to 7 pounds
1 tablespoon salt
1 teaspoon freshly cracked black pepper
2 slivered cloves garlic
1 piece bacon rind, 5 x 8 inches

Trim gristle and fat from roast to expose about 2 inches of the rib bones. Rub meat all over with salt and pepper. Poke slivers of garlic into the meat by inserting the point of a small knife in the fatty side and using the knife blade as a slide to push slivers into holes. Cut bacon rind into strips ½ inch wide and 5 inches long, tie each in a loop, and arrange them in the pan around the roast (which should be spine side down). Roast for 25 minutes per pound in a preheated 325° oven, or until meat thermometer registers 170°. Remove roast to carving board and keep warm; let rest 15 minutes before carving. Drain the bacon loops on paper towels and ring them over the bones. Carve the meat parallel to the spine in long thin slices, using a ham slicer if you have one. Turn it to cut loose the tenderloin (fillet section) and carve it in long thin slices, too.

RED CABBAGE

1 large red cabbage	1 teaspoon salt
3 tablespoons butter	½ teaspoon freshly cracked
1 cup finely chopped onions	black pepper
½ cup dry red wine	1 teaspoon cornstarch
2 tablespoons brown sugar	

Trim cabbage of any bruised leaves and shred it very thin, using a large chef's knife (do not grate it). Soak cabbage in cold water for 5 minutes. Heat butter in a large saucepan and cook onions over high heat until limp, about 5 minutes. Drain cabbage and add to onions. Mix wine, brown sugar, salt, and pepper and pour over cabbage. Cover pan tightly and cook slowly over low heat until cabbage is tender, 30 to 45 minutes. (Young cabbage will take less time.) Drain cabbage and place in serving dish, reserving ½ cup liquid. Dissolve cornstarch in 1 tablespoon cold water, stir into cabbage liquid, and cook until it thickens. Pour over cabbage and mix lightly together. *This recipe can be made entirely ahead and reheated.*

MASHED POTATOES AND CELERIAC

1 pound celeriac
4 medium-size potatoes
3 teaspoons salt
¾ cup heated heavy cream,
plus more if needed

6 tablespoons soft butter
1 teaspoon freshly cracked
white pepper
2 tablespoons chopped parsley

Peel and cube celeriac and potatoes and put them into 2 saucepans to cook separately. Cover each with cold water seasoned with 1 teaspoon salt, and bring to a boil. Reduce heat, cover pans, and simmer until tender, about 20 minutes. Drain. Put both through a potato ricer or food mill—mixing them together if you wish—and beat in cream, butter, pepper, and remaining teaspoon salt. Beat until fluffy, adding more cream if necessary. Keep warm by placing serving dish in a pan of simmering water. Sprinkle with parsley just before serving.

APPLE CHAUSSON

CRUST:
3½ cups lightly spooned flour
2 tablespoons sugar
1 teaspoon salt
1 cup chilled butter
3 lightly beaten egg yolks
Ice water, if necessary

½ cup butter
¼ cup Calvados, brandy, or
rum
1 teaspoon cinnamon, optional
¼ teaspoon grated nutmeg,
optional

FILLING:
8 large, or 10 small, Winesap
(or Greenings, Cortland,
or McIntosh) apples,
peeled, cored, and cut in
eighths
¾ to 1 cup sugar
Grated peel of 1 orange
Juice of 1 orange

1 egg yolk
1 tablespoon water
Confectioners' sugar
Sour cream or whipped
cream, optional
2 tablespoons Calvados,
brandy, or rum, optional

To make crust, stir flour with sugar and salt, cut the 1 cup chilled butter in chips, and toss with flour. Add 3 lightly beaten egg yolks and work with pastry blender or fingertips until mixture is granular. Press together; if mixture remains granular, add just enough ice water to make it hold. Turn dough out onto a lightly floured board and, using the heel of your hand, push the dough, bit by bit, against the board and away from you in short, quick smears. Work fast. Scrape up the dough, shape it into a ball, dust with flour, wrap in waxed paper, and refrigerate for at least 30 minutes.

Cook apple slices, sugar, orange peel, orange juice, and the ½ cup butter in a saucepan over high heat, covered, for 10 minutes, stirring mixture often to be sure it doesn't burn. Uncover and cook 10 minutes more, or until juice evaporates and mixture looks like a thick puree. Stir in Calvados and cinnamon or nutmeg if desired; chill for at least ½ hour, or overnight, in refrigerator.

Roll out pastry ⅛ inch thick and place on baking tray. Pile chilled apple mixture on one half of the circle of pastry and turn the other half over the filling. Roll edges back on themselves and press with a fork to seal. Cut 3 long 3-inch gashes across the top of the turnover. Brush dough with egg yolk mixed with water. Chill 20 minutes or longer. (*Recipe can be made ahead to this point; it may be frozen for up to 1 month; defrost for 24 hours in refrigerator.*) Bake in a preheated 375° oven until pastry is nicely browned, about 30 minutes. Serve warm, dusted with confectioners' sugar and topped with sour cream or with whipped cream, sweetened and flavored with Calvados.

A Relaxed Sunday Night Dinner for 6

Cream of mushroom soup
Roast chicken with tarragon butter
Cauliflower and black olive salad
Swedish almond cake

Here is a pleasant way to end an active weekend, or redeem an uninspired one.

CREAM OF MUSHROOM SOUP

1 pound mushrooms	1 teaspoon salt
4 cups chicken stock (see p. 278)	½ teaspoon freshly cracked white pepper
¾ cup finely chopped onion	2 tablespoons dry sherry or dry Madeira
7 tablespoons butter	
6 tablespoons flour	1 tablespoon lemon juice
3 cups light cream	1 tablespoon chopped parsley
1 cup heavy cream	

Reserve 6 mushroom caps, and chop the rest, including stems. Put the chopped mushrooms into a saucepan with chicken stock and chopped onion, bring to a boil, lower to simmer, cover, and cook for 30 minutes. In another pan, melt 6 tablespoons of the butter and stir in flour. Cook, stirring with a wooden spatula, over high heat for 2 minutes—do not let it brown. Remove from heat, change to a whisk, and add the light cream, whisking vigorously. Return to high heat and cook, stirring, until mixture is thick. Stir in heavy cream and the mushroom mixture. Season with salt and pepper. (*Recipe can be made ahead to this point.*) When ready to serve, reheat soup, adding dry sherry. Slice the reserved mushroom caps and sauté quickly in remaining 1 tablespoon butter, adding the lemon juice. Garnish soup bowls with sliced mushrooms and sprinkle with chopped parsley.

ROAST CHICKEN WITH TARRAGON BUTTER

Follow directions for Roast Capon or Turkey (see p. 147) substituting a 4- to 5-pound roasting chicken for the capon, and decreasing butter to ½ cup, tarragon and parsley to 2 teaspoons each. Omit truffle. Figure 20 minutes per pound total roasting time, or 1 hour 40 minutes for a 5-pound bird. Preheat oven to 475° and roast for 30 minutes, basting every 15 minutes with red wine and pan juices. Reduce heat to 425° and roast 50 to 70 minutes longer; continue basting. Garnish the serving platter with a bunch of watercress.

CAULIFLOWER AND BLACK OLIVE SALAD

1 head cauliflower
12 large or 24 small black
   olives, pitted
2 tablespoons chopped
   shallots
1 2-ounce can flat anchovy
   fillets, drained and
   chopped

2 tablespoons capers, drained
2 tablespoons chopped parsley
2 tablespoons red wine vinegar
4 to 5 tablespoons olive oil
   Freshly grated white pepper

Trim cauliflower and cut into flowerets. Put into a saucepan, cover with cold water, and bring to a boil. Reduce heat to simmer and simmer 15 minutes. Drain flowerets and drop them into cold water to stop the cooking. Drain again and place in a salad bowl. Add olives, shallots, anchovies, capers, parsley, vinegar, olive oil, and pepper and mix gently. Cover with plastic wrap and refrigerate overnight. Serve at room temperature.

SWEDISH ALMOND CAKE

½ cup butter, plus butter to
   grease cake pan
1 cup plus 1 tablespoon
   lightly spooned flour
1½ teaspoons baking powder
⅛ teaspoon salt
2 eggs
1 cup sugar

1 teaspoon vanilla extract
¼ cup cream, light or heavy

TOPPING:

4 tablespoons butter
⅓ cup slivered almonds
3 tablespoons sugar
2 tablespoons flour
1 tablespoon cream

Melt butter and set aside to cool. Butter an 8-inch round pan heavily and set aside. Sift flour after measuring with the baking powder and salt; set aside. Beat eggs with electric mixer; add sugar gradually and beat until thick and lemony. Add vanilla; then add flour alternately with cream and beat just to mix. Do not overbeat. Pour in the cooled melted butter and blend with a spatula. Pour into cake pan and place on the middle shelf of a preheated 350° oven to bake for 30 minutes (or 5 minutes longer if cake moves slightly in the center when you give it a little push). While cake bakes, prepare topping. Mix topping ingredients in a small saucepan and cook over high heat until sugar dissolves.

Remove cake from oven, raise oven temperature to 375°, spread topping over cake, and return to oven for about 10 minutes, or until it sizzles and browns—look at it after 5 minutes. The cake sinks when you add topping. *Cake may be prepared ahead, and it may also be frozen.*

An Informal Dinner
for 8

Asparagus soup
London broil
Roesti potatoes (see p. 15)
Braised fennel
Lemon tart

ASPARAGUS SOUP

¾ cup butter
4 cups finely chopped onions
6 medium-size potatoes, diced
3 pounds asparagus, cut up in
 2-inch pieces
4 cups chicken stock (see
 p. 278)

2 teaspoons salt
1 teaspoon freshly cracked
 white pepper
2 cups light cream
¼ teaspoon freshly grated
 nutmeg

Heat ½ cup butter in a large saucepan and cook onions over high heat until they are wilted, about 5 minutes. Stir in potatoes and asparagus, reserving tips. Pour on chicken stock and water, if needed, to cover vegetables. Season with salt and pepper, bring to a boil, cover, reduce heat to simmer, and cook until vegetables are tender, about 20 minutes. Put mixture through a food mill, using the finest disk. (*Soup can be prepared ahead to this point.*) Add light cream, nutmeg, and reserved asparagus tips and bring to a boil. Pour into heated tureen and float remaining ¼ cup butter, cut in chips, on the top.

LONDON BROIL

The cut of beef I use as "London broil" is the top 2 inches cut from the top of the round. It weighs up to 4½ pounds. It should be at least 1½ inches thick, and it must be prime quality.

1 London broil, 3½ to 4 pounds	1 teaspoon thyme
1 cup olive oil	¼ cup brown sugar
½ cup red wine vinegar	2 tablespoons chili sauce
Juice of 2 limes	2 mashed cloves garlic
1 teaspoon oregano	3 tablespoons soy sauce

Marinate the London broil for 24 hours in a marinade made from the remaining ingredients, turning it frequently. Heat the broiler or prepare a bed of coals. Adjust broiler rack to place meat 2 inches from heat in an oven broiler, or 2 to 3 inches from coals. For rare beef—and London broil should always be served rare—count 10 minutes total broiling time per inch thickness of meat. Thus, if your meat is 1½ inches thick, broil 7½ minutes on each side; if it's 2 inches thick, broil 10 minutes on each side. Carve the meat into *thin* slices, cutting across the grain and on a diagonal.

BRAISED FENNEL

4 heads fennel	1 teaspoon salt
1 tablespoon salt	½ teaspoon freshly cracked
4 tablespoons butter	white pepper
2 cups chicken stock (see	1 teaspoon potato starch,
p. 278)	optional
1 tablespoon sugar	1 tablespoon water, optional
Juice of 1 lemon	

Cut tops from fennel, pull off the feathery leaves, and chop and set them aside. Cut fennel heads or bulbs in half, discard hard outside pieces, put the heads in a saucepan, cover with cold water, add 1 tablespoon salt, and bring to a boil. Boil, uncovered, over high heat, for 15 minutes. Drain. Place fennel in a big skillet and add butter, chicken stock, sugar, lemon juice, 1 teaspoon salt, and pepper. Bring to a boil, then reduce heat and simmer, covered, for 20 to 45 minutes, or until fennel is tender—test it with the point of a small knife. Shake the pan a time or two, so fennel doesn't glaze. When fennel is done, remove to serving dish.

Thicken broth in pan by boiling to reduce it, or stir in potato starch dissolved in cold water. Pour sauce over fennel and sprinkle with chopped fennel leaves. *Recipe can be made ahead and reheated in the oven.*

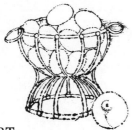

LEMON TART

PASTRY:
2½ cups lightly spooned flour
½ cup sugar
¼ teaspoon salt
10 tablespoons butter
1 egg
1 tablespoon water

FILLING:
4 lemons
1½ cups sugar
5 lightly beaten eggs

½ cup plus 1 tablespoon
softened butter
2 tablespoons light rum

MERINGUE:
2 egg whites
¼ teaspoon cream of tartar
¼ teaspoon salt
2 tablespoons sugar
1 tablespoon confectioners'
sugar

To make pastry, combine flour, sugar, and salt in a bowl. Cut in butter until mixture looks like coarse crumbs. Beat egg with water, add to flour mixture, and toss to blend. Gather dough into a ball, dust with flour, wrap in waxed paper, and chill for 30 minutes. Roll it out and fit it into a 9-inch flan ring or pie pan.

To prepare filling, grind the lemons, including rinds, in a food chopper or grinder. Combine with sugar, eggs, butter, and rum, and blend well. Pour into the pastry shell and bake in a preheated 375° oven for about 30 to 35 minutes or until set. Cool on a rack before adding meringue.

To make meringue, beat egg whites until foamy; add cream of tartar and salt and beat until they hold soft peaks. Beat in sugar and confectioners' sugar a spoonful at a time and continue beating until meringue is very glossy and smooth, not grainy, when you pinch it. Spread over lemon filling and bake in a 350° oven about 10 minutes or until meringue peaks are lightly browned. Serve warm or cooled, as desired.

A Duckling Dinner
for 6

Broiled duckling
Brown rice pilaf with pine nuts
Braised onions and carrots
Salzburger Nockerln

For a different approach to duck, try broiling small 3-pound ducklings. They're tender and not so fatty when done this way. I don't recommend broiling larger ducks, though—it takes too long.

BROILED DUCKLING

3 3-pound ducklings
3 tablespoons salt
3 teaspoons freshly cracked
    black pepper
1 cup apricot jam
¼ cup lemon juice
2 tablespoons butter
2 tablespoons brandy
2 cups basic brown sauce
    (see p. 281)

1 tablespoon vinegar
½ teaspoon meat glaze (see
    p. 280)
1 20-ounce can whole water-
    packed marrons, drained
1 20-ounce can apricot halves,
    drained
2 tablespoons chopped parsley

With poultry shears cut the necks off and the backbones out of the ducklings. Spread them flat for broiling, skin side down, with wings tucked under, or cut each duckling into 4 to 6 pieces, separating legs from breast and cutting breast pieces in half. Place ducklings on broiler rack, skin side down. Broil 3 inches from heat for 20 minutes. Turn, sprinkle with salt and pepper, and brush with apricot jam thinned with lemon juice. Broil 10 minutes longer or until done—test duckling for doneness by pricking it; juices should run clear.

To make sauce, melt butter in skillet and quickly sauté duckling livers until they are browned on the outside but still pink inside. Warm brandy in a little pan, ignite it, and pour it over livers. Remove livers, scrape up brown bits in pan, and stir in brown sauce. Chop livers and return to sauce along with their juices. Stir in vinegar and meat glaze. Add marrons and the apricot halves, dried on paper towels, reduce heat, and heat through. Taste for seasoning. (*The sauce can be made ahead, but do not broil duckling until ready to serve.*) Arrange duckling on serving platter and pour sauce over it. Sprinkle with chopped parsley.

BROWN RICE PILAF WITH PINE NUTS

4 tablespoons butter
¾ cup finely chopped onion
½ cup pine nuts
1½ cups brown rice
4½ cups chicken stock (see p. 278)

1½ teaspoons salt
½ teaspoon freshly cracked black pepper
2 tablespoons chopped parsley

In a heavy flameproof casserole with a tight-fitting lid, melt butter and stir in onion, cooking over high heat until it is wilted, about 3 minutes. Stir in pine nuts and cook until they take on a little color, about 2 minutes. Add brown rice and stir to coat well with butter. Pour on chicken stock, add salt and pepper, and bring to a boil. Turn heat to simmer, cover casserole, and set timer for 30 to 35 minutes. Do not lift lid until timer sounds. Fluff rice with 2 forks; if liquid is not absorbed and the rice tender, cover and cook for 5 to 10 minutes longer. (*Rice can be cooked ahead and reheated—to reheat, pour 2 tablespoons melted butter over it, cover, and set over low heat.*) To serve, fluff with forks and sprinkle with chopped parsley.

BRAISED ONIONS AND CARROTS

24 small white onions
24 diagonally cut carrot pieces (see p. 46)
4 tablespoons butter
4 tablespoons lard, melted pork fat, or oil

1 teaspoon salt
½ teaspoon freshly cracked black pepper
1 tablespoon chopped parsley

Peel onions—cutting a cross in the root end of each—and parboil for 10 minutes. Parboil carrots for 5 minutes. Melt butter and lard in a shallow baking dish and add drained vegetables, rolling them around to coat well with fat. Season with salt and pepper and bake, uncovered, on the bottom shelf of a preheated 375° oven until browned and tender-crisp, about 1 hour. Baste occasionally or stir with spoon. (*Recipe can be cooked ahead to this point and reheated.*) Sprinkle with parsley to serve.

SALZBURGER NOCKERLN

Butter and sugar to coat baking dish
6 eggs, separated
1 tablespoon flour
1 teaspoon freshly grated lemon peel *or* 1 teaspoon vanilla extract *or* 1 tablespoon rum
½ teaspoon cream of tartar
4 tablespoons sugar
Strawberry Sauce (recipe follows)

Heavily butter an oval baking or au gratin dish and sprinkle with sugar; knock out excess sugar and set aside. In a bowl, beat egg yolks lightly, add flour and lemon peel or flavoring, and set aside. Beat egg whites in mixer bowl until they start to foam. Add cream of tartar and, while continuing to beat, gradually add sugar, 1 tablespoon at a time. Beat until stiff and shiny, almost like meringue. Pour yolk mixture over whites and fold in very lightly. Heap in baking dish, making 3 mounds—this is the traditional way to shape a Salzburg soufflé. Bake in a preheated 425° oven for 10 to 12 minutes, or until puffed and lightly brown. Serve at once—it deflates as fast as any soufflé. Pass Strawberry Sauce.

STRAWBERRY SAUCE

6 tablespoons butter
½ cup sugar
¼ cup framboise or kirsch
1 quart strawberries, washed, dried, and hulled, or about 3 8-ounce packages frozen strawberries

Melt butter in a skillet. Add sugar, liqueur, and strawberries and shake over high heat for about 5 minutes. Berries do not cook—they just get heated through.

An Informal Dinner
for 6

Turkey-breast and ham paupiettes
Cauliflower covered with broccoli puree
Marinated cucumber balls
Meringue bananas

You can get a whole turkey breast where poultry parts are sold, but you may have to order it in advance. (Sometimes I slice one *very* thin and use it like veal to fool guests.) Cauliflower, masked by a pale-green broccoli puree, is an unusual and interesting accompaniment, and the crunchy marinated cucumber balls provide a good texture contrast.

TURKEY-BREAST AND HAM PAUPIETTES

6 thin slices raw turkey breast
   meat
4 tablespoons melted butter
1 teaspoon salt
½ teaspoon freshly cracked
   white pepper
6 slices prosciutto ham
½ cup flour
2 beaten eggs

1 cup fine bread crumbs
   Fat for deep frying
1½ cups Velouté Sauce,
   optional (see p. 280)
3 tablespoons Mushroom
   Duxelles, optional (see
   p. 283)

Place turkey slices between 2 sheets of waxed paper, pound flat, then trim each slice to approximately equal size. Brush with melted butter and season with salt and pepper. Lay a slice of ham on each and roll up loosely, fastening ends with toothpicks. Roll in flour, dip into beaten egg, and roll in bread crumbs; chill paupiettes for at least 5 minutes. (*May be prepared ahead to this point or deep-fried in advance and reheated. Reheat paupiettes, in an au gratin dish and brushed with butter, in a 350° oven for 10 to 15 minutes.*) In a deep saucepan, heat 3 inches of fat—I prefer solid vegetable shortening—to 375° and fry paupiettes, 3 at a time, for about 8 minutes. Drain on paper towels and keep warm in low oven. Serve plain or with Velouté Sauce into which you've stirred Mushroom Duxelles.

Variation: If you do not wish to deep-fry the paupiettes, place them in a buttered au gratin dish, brush generously with melted butter, sprinkle with 2 to 3 tablespoons grated Parmesan cheese, and bake in a preheated 350° oven for about 15 minutes, basting frequently with melted butter.

CAULIFLOWER COVERED WITH BROCCOLI PUREE

1 head cauliflower	Salt
¼ cup milk	Freshly cracked white
1 slice bread	pepper
½ cup melted butter	Broccoli Puree (recipe
¼ cup freshly grated Parmesan	follows)
cheese	2 tablespoons chopped parsley

Trim cauliflower, leaving head whole. Place in a saucepan and add water almost to cover, milk (to keep cauliflower white), and bread (to mask odor). Boil, uncovered, over high heat until almost done, then cover and simmer until cauliflower is tender, about 30 to 45 minutes total. Drain cauliflower and place on a serving platter. Pour melted butter over cauliflower and sprinkle with cheese, salt, and pepper. Nap with Broccoli Puree and reheat, if necessary, in a 350° oven. Just before serving, sprinkle with chopped parsley.

BROCCOLI PUREE

2 10-ounce packages frozen	¼ teaspoon freshly grated
broccoli	nutmeg
2 tablespoons butter	6 tablespoons heavy cream or
2 tablespoons flour	sour cream
1 teaspoon salt	3 tablespoons melted butter
½ teaspooon freshly cracked	
white pepper	

Cook broccoli according to package directions. Drain and puree through a food mill, using the finest disk. Melt butter in a saucepan, stir in flour, and cook, stirring, over high heat until the *roux* is nicely browned. Add pureed broccoli and beat over high heat with a wooden spatula. Add salt, pepper, and nutmeg. Thin the mixture with enough heavy cream or sour cream to make a smooth puree that will mask the cauliflower. (*Recipe may be made ahead to this point and held over hot water for up to ½ hour.*) Stir in melted butter and pour over cauliflower.

MARINATED CUCUMBER BALLS

Peel 6 medium-size cucumbers with a potato peeler and cut into balls with a melon baller. Marinate in 1 recipe French vinaigrette dressing (see p. 282) for an hour or so. Sprinkle with 2 tablespoons chopped parsley.

MERINGUE BANANAS

8 bananas, ripe but firm	2 tablespoons melted butter
3 tablespoons butter	5 egg whites
12 tablespoons sugar	¼ teaspoon cream of tartar
2 tablespoons rum	

Peel bananas and cut them in half lengthwise. Melt 3 tablespoons butter in a large skillet, add bananas, sprinkle with 2 tablespoons sugar, and sauté gently over high heat for 2 minutes, turning once. Remove pan from heat. Warm rum in a little pan, ignite it, and pour it over bananas, shaking pan until flames die. Arrange bananas in a buttered ovenproof serving dish—each 2 halves close together, cut side up. Score the surface of the bananas with a table knife, making crosswise cuts about 1 inch apart.

Make meringue as follows: beat egg whites in large bowl of electric mixer. When they start to foam, add cream of tartar, and continue beating until soft peaks form. Add remaining 10 tablespoons sugar, 1 tablespoon at a time, beating constantly, and continue beating until meringue looks like marshmallow. Pinch it; it's ready when it no longer feels grainy. Fit a large pastry bag with a star tube and fill it with the meringue. Pipe meringue over bananas, covering each pair of halves completely. (*Recipe may be made 1 hour ahead to this point.*) Place bananas in a preheated 400° oven and bake until meringue is set and lightly browned, about 10 minutes. Serve hot or cold.

A Formal Dinner for 8
on a Winter's Evening

Caviar barquettes
Crown of lamb, Béarnaise
Brown rice pilaf with almond slivers
Celeriac sticks
Bibb lettuce salad
Cold Grand Marnier soufflé

CAVIAR BARQUETTES

1 recipe barquettes (see p. 49)
8 ounces red and/or black
   caviar

½ cup sour cream
Parsley sprigs, for garnish

Prepare barquettes or unfreeze and crisp them in the oven. Fill with caviar and top with a dot of sour cream, with a little parsley sprig placed on the sour cream. Allow 4 per person with drinks—if cocktail hour is prolonged—or 2 per person as a first course.

CROWN OF LAMB, BÉARNAISE

Crown of lamb is most elegant when served to pink perfection. Too often it is cooked to death and has no lamb taste. Europeans generally eat lamb rare or pink, and I suspect that many Americans who think they don't like lamb would like it better if they tried it this way.

Ask your butcher to prepare a crown of lamb for you by tying or sewing 2 rib roasts or racks together in a crown shape. Rub the meat all over with 1 tablespoon coarse salt and 1 teaspoon freshly cracked black pepper. If you like a garlic seasoning, cut 2 cloves into slivers and insert by sticking a knife point into meat here and there and, using knife blade as a slide, poking sliver into meat. Put ball of aluminum foil in center of meat so it will keep its shape while roasting, cover ends of rib bones with foil, stand crown upright in pan, and roast in a preheated 425° oven for 1 hour, no more. This will yield a very rare piece of meat. If you prefer lamb medium-rare, roast for 70 miutes. Fill center of crown with brown rice pilaf (recipe follows). Remove foil from bone ends and cover with paper frills. Serve with Béarnaise Sauce (see p. 282).

BROWN RICE PILAF WITH ALMOND SLIVERS

Following recipe for Brown Rice Pilaf with Pine Nuts on page 105, substituting ½ cup slivered almonds for pine nuts. If desired, add ½ cup light raisins soaked in ¼ cup dry sherry along with the almonds.

CELERIAC STICKS

4 large celeriac	½ teaspoon freshly cracked
4 teaspoons salt	white pepper
Juice of ½ lemon	½ cup melted butter
	2 tablespoons chopped parsley

Peel the celeriac and cut them into julienne strips about the size of kitchen matches. Drop them into a saucepan of cold water to cover. Add 3 teaspoons of the salt and the lemon juice and bring to a boil on high heat. Turn heat to medium, cover pan, and cook until barely tender, about 20 minutes. Drain. Return celeriac to pan, add the remaining teaspoon of salt, the pepper, and melted butter. Shake over high heat for 2 minutes. Sprinkle with chopped parsley.

BIBB LETTUCE SALAD

4 heads Bibb lettuce	French vinaigrette dressing
1 large tomato, peeled and	(see p. 282)
seeded	1 tablespoon chopped parsley

Wash lettuce, trim, and roll in towels to chill thoroughly. Cut tomato into slivers, place in a chilled salad bowl with lettuce and parsley, and toss with vinaigrette dressing to taste just before serving. Serve as a separate course.

COLD GRAND MARNIER SOUFFLÉ

An original recipe, and an unbelievably elegant dessert. To facilitate its preparation, assemble and ready all ingredients ahead of time. While the soufflé may be prepared the night before, the garnishing is better done nearer the serving time. Put orange slices on no more than 2 hours ahead, or sugar will dissolve. The whipped cream rosettes may be piped on the night before only if cream is beaten over ice—otherwise it will weep.

Grated peel of 2 oranges and 1 lemon	6 eggs, separated
¾ cup orange juice	2 cups sugar
¼ cup lemon juice	½ teaspoon salt
2 tablespoons (2 envelopes) unflavored gelatine	2½ cups heavy cream
	1 orange, for garnish
¼ cup Grand Marnier	1 egg white
	¼ cup crystallized sugar

Make a waxed paper collar for a 6-cup soufflé dish by folding paper in half, lengthwise, brushing inside edge with vegetable oil, and tying it around the top of the dish so that it extends 4 to 5 inches above it. Set aside. Grate oranges and lemon and squeeze juice. Sprinkle gelatine into ½ cup of the orange juice and set aside. In a saucepan, put the grated peel, remaining ¼ cup orange juice, lemon juice, Grand Marnier, 6 egg yolks, 1¼ cups of the sugar, and the salt. Beat until fluffy; then stir over low heat until the mixture coats the back of a spoon. Remove from heat and stir in the softened gelatine–orange juice mixture, stirring until gelatine dissolves. Place in the refrigerator to cool until the mixture mounds slightly when dropped from a spoon, about 20 minutes.

Meanwhile, beat egg whites to soft peaks. Beat in remaining ¾ cup sugar, 1 tablespoon at a time, and beat until stiff and glossy. Beat 2 cups of the heavy cream until it mounds nicely, but isn't too stiff. Fold egg whites and then whipped cream into egg yolk custard and pour into prepared dish—work quickly, the cold whipped cream makes it set up quickly. Place in refrigerator to chill. Mixture sets quickly, but the flavor is better if you chill it overnight.

Prepare garnish: Use a lemon stripper to cut grooves in orange, ¼ inch apart. Slice orange crosswise; edges will look fluted. Dip slices in beaten egg white and then in crystallized sugar. Whip remaining ½ cup heavy cream and put it into a pastry bag fitted with a rose tube. Pipe rosettes around edge of soufflé, and overlap the sugared orange slices in a ring just inside the whipped cream. Remove the collar carefully just before serving.

A Rich and Delicious Formal Dinner for 8

Poached trout with Hollandaise sauce
Roast sirloin strip with maître d'hôtel butter
Endive à la crème
Chinese carrots (see p. 46)
White asparagus vinaigrette
Riz à l'impératrice

POACHED TROUT WITH HOLLANDAISE SAUCE

The secret of this really delicate recipe lies in undercooking rather than overcooking the trout. To keep the fish you cook first warm while simmering the rest, hold them in an oven at low heat. Or cook the fish ahead, keep them in the cooled court bouillon, and then reheat slightly. In this case, be very careful to under-cook the fish in the beginning.

8 small trout, less than 1
    pound each
1 recipe court bouillon (see
    p. 279)
¼ cup melted butter

1 lemon
1 bunch watercress
1 recipe Hollandaise Sauce
    (see p. 281)

Buy trout cleaned and degutted but not split, and with heads and tails intact. Handle them as little as possible as they are very fragile. Do not wash them: the slime with which they're covered gives them a blue color when you cook them—like European blue trout. Tie fish in crescent shape: push a trussing needle threaded with string through the body just above the tail and through the eye sockets; pull tight and knot. Leave the string end long enough to help you later to remove trout from the pot. (*Fish may be prepared ahead to this point and refrigerated.*)

Drop fish 2 at a time into simmering (not boiling) court bouillon. Set timer. For each inch thickness of fish (measured through the middle), poach 7 minutes. For example, for trout ¾ inch thick, poach 5 minutes only. Remove fish from poaching liquid and arrange on serving dish. Keep warm while you poach remaining fish. Remove strings—fish will stay in crescent shape. Brush with melted butter. With a small knife make zigzag cuts around center of lemon, pull halves apart, and nest them in the watercress. Serve with Hollandaise Sauce, passed separately.

ROAST SIRLOIN STRIP

This is an excellent roast, very expensive, but you have no waste. A 10-pound sirloin strip will leave you with leftovers, and it's good cold. Bring meat to room temperature. Rub all over with 1 tablespoon coarse salt and 1 teaspoon freshly cracked black pepper. Put it on a rack in a shallow pan and roast it in a pre-heated 350° oven for 10 minutes per pound, or until it registers 125° on a meat thermometer. (This timing is for rare meat; for medium-rare, roast for 12 minutes per pound, and for medium, 15 minutes per pound.) Remove from oven and let it stand for 15 to 20 minutes to set the juices. Carve into thin slices and serve with a ball of Maître d'Hôtel Butter on top of each slice.

MAÎTRE D'HÔTEL BUTTER

In electric mixer bowl, cream ½ cup butter. Beat in 1 table-spoon lemon juice, ½ teaspoon salt, ¼ teaspoon freshly cracked black pepper, 1 tablespoon chopped parsley, and—if you wish— 1 teaspoon finely chopped shallot and ¼ teaspoon finely chopped garlic. *Prepare butter ahead and store in refrigerator.*

ENDIVE À LA CRÈME

12 heads Belgian endive	1 tablespoon sugar
2 quarts boiling water	¾ cup chicken stock (see
½ teaspoon salt	p. 278)
1 slice bread	6 tablespoons heavy cream
6 tablespoons butter	2 tablespoons chopped parsley

Count on 1 or 2 heads of endive per person. Trim stem ends. Drop into boiling salted water, along with the bread, and boil 7 minutes. (The bread helps draw out the bitter taste of endive.) Melt butter in a large skillet over high heat; add sugar and chicken stock. Place parboiled endive heads in skillet, side by side, cover, and cook over high heat for 10 minutes. Reduce heat to simmer, turn endive heads over, re-cover, and cook for 20 minutes longer, or until endive heads are tender and a glaze forms in the bottom of the pan. Watch them carefully; do not let them burn. Arrange endive heads in a serving dish. Pour cream into pan juices and bring to a boil, stirring and scraping up brown bits. Boil 1 minute. Pour sauce over endive and sprinkle with chopped parsley. *Recipe can be done ahead and reheated.*

WHITE ASPARAGUS VINAIGRETTE

Use only the very best canned white asparagus available. Rinse and dry stalks, dress with French vinaigrette dressing (see p. 282), and sprinkle with chopped parsley. Count 3 stalks for each person.

RIZ À L'IMPÉRATRICE

1 cup long-grain rice
4½ cups light cream, plus more if necessary
2 inches vanilla bean, or 1 tablespoon vanilla extract
8 egg yolks
1 cup sugar
2 tablespoons (2 envelopes) unflavored gelatine

½ cup water
2 tablespoons lemon juice
2 cups heavy cream
4 tablespoons confectioners' sugar
½ cup finely chopped mixed candied fruits soaked in rum or fresh strawberries, or fresh raspberries

In a saucepan, stir rice into 3 cups light cream, add a 1-inch piece of vanilla bean, slit and scraped, or 1½ teaspoons vanilla extract, and cook very slowly over low heat until rice is soft, about 20 to 30 minutes. Stir constantly with a wooden spatula—don't rush it. Add more cream if necessary. In a bowl, beat egg yolks, add sugar gradually, and beat until light and fluffy. Blend into mixture the remaining 1½ cups light cream and a 1-inch piece of vanilla bean, slit and scraped, or remaining 1½ teaspoons vanilla. Transfer the mixture to a nonaluminum pan—or place bowl in a pan of simmering water—and stir over low heat until custard thickens. In a cup, soften gelatine in water and lemon juice, set cup in a pan of hot water, and stir until gelatine dissolves. Stir dissolved gelatine into custard and strain the mixture. Stir. rice into strained custard—first removing vanilla beans; place bowl over a bowl of ice, and stir until it thickens, or chill in refrigerator, stirring occasionally. Whip the heavy cream over ice until it thickens, then sweeten with confectioners' sugar. Fold it slowly, a spoonful at a time, into the custard-rice mixture, stir in candied fruits or berries, and pile high in a crystal bowl. *Recipe can be prepared a day ahead, covered with plastic wrap, and refrigerated.*

A Formal Dinner
for 6

Oysters Rockefeller
Lamb noisettes with veal mousse
Soufflé potatoes
Watercress and Belgian endive salad
Glazed pineapple with kirsch

Ideally, formal service means extra hands in the kitchen, and certainly this dinner party will go more smoothly if the hostess has help. But if you intend to manage it alone, here are some do-ahead changes to make in the recipes . . . or in the menu.

Both oysters and potatoes are best if prepared no more than 2 hours ahead, so you may want to substitute Pommes Parisienne (see p. 255) for the Soufflé Potatoes. In fact, Soufflé Potatoes are rather tricky and only accomplished cooks should try them. The potatoes can be deep-fried 2 hours ahead and held in the kitchen near the oven; they should not be held *in* the oven. Better to serve them at room temperature, if necessary. The Lamb Noisettes with Veal Mousse may be completely done ahead as follows: cut baking time from 20 to 15 minutes; refrigerate; then bring to room temperature before reheating in a 350° oven for 5 to 10 minutes, while you eat oysters. You will find the recipe for Watercress and Belgian Endive Salad on p. 42 and for Glazed Pineapple with Kirsch on p. 24.

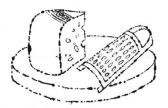

OYSTERS ROCKEFELLER

3 dozen oysters on half shell
½ package (10 ounces) frozen
   chopped spinach
½ cup chopped parsley
½ cup chopped scallions
½ cup chopped Boston lettuce
1 clove garlic
   Clam juice, if necessary
½ cup butter
1 cup bread crumbs

1 tablespoon Worcestershire
   sauce
1 teaspoon anchovy paste
4 drops Tabasco sauce
1½ tablespoons Pernod
½ teaspoon salt
¼ cup freshly grated
   Parmesan cheese
   Melted butter
   Rock salt

Open oysters or have them opened for you—open them as close to serving time as possible and never more than 2 hours before serving—and reserve oyster juice. Put thawed spinach, parsley, scallions, lettuce, and garlic in a blender with about 2 tablespoons oyster juice, or clam juice, if there is not enough oyster juice, and blend thoroughly. Cream butter in a bowl, blend in ¾ cup of the bread crumbs, and combine it with spinach puree. Add Worcestershire sauce, anchovy paste, Tabasco, Pernod, and salt. Mix thoroughly. Drain any excess liquid still remaining from oysters, add it to sauce, and cover each oyster with a spoonful of the sauce. Sprinkle with Parmesan cheese and remaining ¼ cup of bread crumbs and drizzle with melted butter. (*Recipe may be prepared ahead to this point and refrigerated. Bring to room temperature before baking.*)

Twenty minutes before you are ready to bake oysters, spread an ovenproof serving dish with a layer of rock salt and place it in a preheated 450° oven to heat the salt. Place oysters in their half shells on the hot rock salt and return pan to oven to bake for about 20 minutes, or until oysters are lightly browned. Do not overcook.

LAMB NOISETTES WITH VEAL MOUSSE

4 slices bacon
8 loin lamb chops, 1½ inches
   thick
2 teaspoons salt
1 teaspoon freshly cracked
   black pepper
2 tablespoons butter
½ pound veal, ground twice
2 egg whites
½ cup light cream
1 teaspoon salt

½ teaspoon freshly cracked
   black pepper
½ teaspoon chopped garlic
6 tablespoons brandy
½ cup melted butter
1 cup basic brown sauce
   (see p. 281)
Black truffle cutouts or
   sautéed fluted mushroom
   caps (see p. 284), for
   garnish
Watercress, for garnish

Blanch the bacon slices: put them in a saucepan, cover with cold water, bring to a boil, and boil 1 minute. Drain. Bone the lamb chops, sprinkle them generously with 2 teaspoons salt and 1 teaspoon pepper, and wrap a piece of blanched bacon around the edge of each, tying it on with string. Melt 2 tablespoons butter in a heavy skillet and sauté noisettes over high heat on one side only, for 2 minutes only, just to brown them. Place noisettes, browned side down, in a baking pan.

Make veal mousse as follows. Put veal into electric mixer bowl—using the flat whip if you have a heavy-duty mixer—gradually add egg whites, and beat thoroughly, or place bowl over ice and beat with a wooden spatula. Gradually beat in cream. Add 1 teaspoon salt, ½ teaspoon pepper, garlic, and 2 tablespoons brandy, and beat thoroughly. Mound or "dome up" veal mixture on each lamb noisette. If veal mixture is too soft to dome up, put it in the refrigerator to stiffen. Drizzle veal-topped noisettes with 4 tablespoons melted butter. Add remaining butter and brandy to baking pan, to use for basting. (*May be prepared ahead to this point.*) Place noisettes in preheated 350° oven and bake for 20 minutes, basting frequently with the butter-brandy mixture. Remove from baking pan and arrange on a warm platter. Pour off excess fat from pan, leaving 1 tablespoonful. Add basic brown sauce to pan and bring to a boil, scraping up brown bits. Spoon sauce over platter. Garnish each chop with a truffle cutout (see p. 49 for instructions) or sautéed fluted mushroom cap. *Can be made ahead to this point, but bake for only 15 minutes to allow for reheating. May be refrigerated; then bring to room tempera-*

ture and reheat in a 350° oven for 5 to 10 minutes. Garnish platter with watercress.

SOUFFLÉ POTATOES

Count 9 Idaho potatoes for 6 people—some of them won't puff in the hot fat, so you need some reserves. Peel potatoes and slice them lengthwise or diagonally on a vegetable cutter or mandoline, so that they are elongated oval in shape and the thickness of a fifty-cent piece. Cover with cold water and soak for 15 minutes. Drain and dry well. Heat vegetable shortening in 2 saucepans (2 inches deep in each), one pan to 300° and the second to 450°. Drop 2 to 3 potato slices at a time into the 300° fat and fry for 2½ minutes. Remove with slotted spoon and drop into 450° fat. They should puff up—the centers will be hollow. This takes about 2 to 3 minutes. Remove when puffed and crisp, drain on paper towels, and salt and serve immediately.

Note: You can do the initial 300° frying of the potato slices earlier in the day, draining them on paper towels and refrigerating. Bring to room temperature before second frying. Give them the 450° plunge just before serving. Keep checking temperature of fat and don't overload the pans. Hold slices at room temperature or near (but not in) oven when they are fried.

A Winter Dinner
for 6

Consommé Normande
Chicken suprêmes with champagne sauce
Spinach timbales
Watercress salad
Coffee praline ice cream

CONSOMMÉ NORMANDE

6 cups strong chicken stock
   (see p. 278)
1 egg white

6 tablespoons Calvados
2 tablespoons freshly grated
   apple

Heat chicken stock. Beat egg white until foamy and add to stock, to clarify it, whisking while you bring the stock to a boil. Remove from heat and let stand for 15 minutes. Strain broth through a sieve lined with a double thickness of cheesecloth wrung out in cold water, pouring carefully so as not to disturb the coagulated egg white. Let consommé drip through by itself. Taste for seasoning. (*Recipe may be made ahead to this point.*) When ready to serve, reheat consommé, stir in Calvados, and garnish each bowl with 1 teaspoon grated apple.

CHICKEN SUPRÊMES
WITH CHAMPAGNE SAUCE

6 whole chicken breasts
6 tablespoons brandy
  Mushroom-ham stuffing
  (recipe follows)
5 to 6 tablespoons butter
1 teaspoon finely chopped
  garlic
2 tablespoons finely chopped
  shallots
3 tablespoons flour
½ teaspoon meat glaze (see
  p. 280)
2 tablespoons chopped truffle

2 teaspoons tarragon
1 cup champagne *or* dry white
  wine *or* dry vermouth
½ cup chicken stock (see
  p. 278)
½ cup heavy cream
¼ teaspoon freshly cracked
  white pepper
2 tablespoons freshly grated
  Parmesan cheese
  Chopped parsley
1 bunch watercress

Bone and skin chicken breasts carefully and trim into neat ovals. You will have 12 suprêmes, 2 from each breast. Cut a pocket in each suprême from the thicker side. Brush pockets with 4 tablespoons of brandy and put about 1 tablespoon stuffing in each pocket. Pinch to seal. Heat 3 to 4 tablespoons butter in a heavy skillet and sauté chicken over high heat—to stiffen it, the meat should not brown—3 minutes on each side. Cook it under a flat lid, pressed down with a 2- to 3-pound weight to help keep stuffing from coming out. Remove chicken and set aside.

Deglaze skillet over medium-high heat with remaining 2 tablespoons brandy and scrape up any brown bits. Add remaining 2 tablespoons butter and stir in garlic and shallots. Cook for a minute or two over high heat. Stir in flour and cook for 2 minutes. Add meat glaze, chopped truffle, tarragon, champagne, chicken stock, and heavy cream. Whisk and cook over medium-high heat until sauce thickens and is smooth. Season with pepper and Parmesan cheese. Return chicken and chicken juices to skillet and baste with sauce. (*May be prepared ahead to this point, covered with plastic wrap, and refrigerated or frozen. Bring to room temperature before final cooking.*) Cover and simmer chicken for 10 to 15 minutes—do not overcook. Arrange chicken on serving platter, pour sauce over it, and sprinkle with chopped parsley. Arrange a bunch of watercress at one end of platter.

MUSHROOM-HAM STUFFING

Sauté ½ pound sliced mushrooms and 4 thin slices of boiled ham, cut in dice, in 2 tablespoons butter. Sprinkle with 2 tablespoons lemon juice and season with ½ teaspoon salt and ¼ teaspoon freshly cracked black pepper.

SPINACH TIMBALES

Vegetable oil to oil molds
2 10-ounce packages frozen
   chopped spinach
3 eggs
1 egg yolk
¼ cup grated onion
½ chopped clove garlic
2 teaspoons salt

½ teaspoon freshly cracked
   black pepper
½ teaspoon freshly grated
   nutmeg
2 cups milk
4 tablespoons grated Parmesan
   cheese, optional

Brush 10 *oeuf en gelée* molds, or one 6-cup ring mold, with vegetable oil. Cook spinach according to package directions. Drain it in a sieve and, when cooled, squeeze it in your hands to press out all excess moisture. Lay it on a chopping board and chop very fine, even though it has been previously chopped. Put it in a bowl and stir in eggs, egg yolk, onion, garlic, salt, pepper, nutmeg, and milk. Add grated Parmesan cheese if desired. Fill molds almost to the top with spinach mixture and set them in a pan of very hot water. Place in a preheated 350° oven and bake about 35 minutes or until custard tests done. It will begin to pull away from sides of mold, and a knife inserted in custard will come out clean. (*Timbales may be baked ahead to this point and reheated in the water bath—but cut original cooking time by 5 minutes.*) Remove molds from hot water bath and let stand for a few minutes. Then run a knife around the edges and unmold. Serve immediately.

WATERCRESS SALAD

Wash 3 bunches of watercress, remove stems, roll in towels, and chill. When ready to serve, toss with 1 tablespoon chopped shallots and French vinaigrette dressing (see p. 282).

COFFEE PRALINE ICE CREAM

Churned ice cream is always a treat. When I was a child, my father and uncles took turns cranking our hand-operated freezer; now people who value ice cream own an electric freezer. Of course, you can still-freeze ice cream in refrigerator trays if you whip the cream lightly, but the texture of churned ice cream is better. This is definitely a make-ahead recipe; after churning, the ice cream should be ripened for a few hours before you serve it. For a 1-gallon ice-cream freezer, you'll need about 20 pounds of ice and about 6 cups of rock salt.

If you do not wish to make your own ice cream, buy rich vanilla ice cream, serve in individual dishes, and sprinkle the powdered praline over.

¾ cup sugar
¼ teaspoon cream of
   tartar
⅓ cup cold water
3 egg yolks
1½ cups heavy cream

2 tablespoons coffee essence,
   or 2 tablespoons instant
   coffee dissolved in 1 tablespoon boiling water
1 cup praline powder (recipe
   follows)

Combine sugar, cream of tartar, and water in a small saucepan. Stir over heat until sugar dissolves, then cook until syrup spins a thread (230° on candy thermometer). When syrup is almost ready, beat egg yolks well with electric mixer. Slowly add the hot syrup, in a thin stream, beating constantly. Continue beating until mixture is cold and thick. Blend in heavy cream and flavor with coffee essence.

Chill the ice-cream mixture and pour it in the freezer can— from two-thirds to three-quarters full, to leave room for expansion. Put the can in the freezer and adjust the dasher and cover; follow manufacturer's directions if using an electric freezer. Pack the freezer with ice mixed with rock salt—3 parts ice to 1 part salt. If using a hand-operated freezer, turn the dasher slowly until enough ice melts to form a brine; then turn the handle fast and steadily, adding more ice and salt to maintain the ice level. When ice cream is partly frozen, add praline powder (or other fruits or flavorings)—clear ice and salt away from the cover before you open the can! Continue freezing until the machine begins to labor. Again clear away ice below cover line and open the can to remove the dasher. To ripen ice cream, pack it down into the can, cover can with foil, plug the opening in the cover, and put it back on. Pack more ice and salt as needed around the can to fill freezer, and cover entire freezer with heavy cloth or newspapers.

Note: Melting ice will drain from the freezer—the whole process of making ice cream is an outdoor or in-the-sink job.

PRALINE POWDER

In a heavy skillet over medium heat, stir and melt 1½ cups sugar with 1 cup almonds (blanched or unblanched) and ¼ teaspoon cream of tartar. Stir continuously with wooden spatula until mixture turns a dark caramel color, about 15 minutes. Remove from heat, immediately pour onto a buttered baking sheet, and let it harden. When hard, break it into pieces and pulverize it in a blender or pound it to powder with a mallet. *It may be made ahead and stored on the shelf in an airtight jar, for up to a month.*

An Elegant Summer Dinner
for 6

Glazed poached trout on aspic
Rack of veal, Béarnaise
Sautéed fluted mushroom caps
Green salad with Roquefort cheese
Peaches in port

This menu presents fine ingredients in a simple classic style. The sauces and garnishes lend distinction, yet the dinner remains light and perfect for summertime. Allow about 4 mushrooms per person (the basic recipe is on p. 284) and, if you wish, pass fresh French bread for guests to nibble on. The recipe for Peaches in Port is on p. 46.

GLAZED POACHED TROUT ON ASPIC

You can, if you wish, poach the trout, decorate it, and arrange it on aspic the day before serving it. Cover it with plastic wrap and refrigerate until you're ready to bring it to the table. When you prepare the aspic, use the court bouillon from poaching trout instead of chicken broth.

6 small trout, poached in crescent shape (see p. 113)	1 recipe aspic (see p. 279) Sprigs of fresh dill 1 sliced truffle 1 hard-cooked egg

Remove skin and strings from poached trout and place fish on cake racks set on a tray or shallow pan. Put in refrigerator to chill for at least ½ hour. Melt aspic and then stir it over a bowl of ice. It should be syrupy, on the point of setting, when you work with it; if it begins to set, remelt it and stir it again over ice. Use a pastry brush to brush the first coat of aspic on chilled trout; return to refrigerator until aspic sets, about ½ hour. Spoon on a second, thicker coat of aspic and chill until set.

Decorate each fish by dipping decorations in aspic and placing them on fish. Put a dill sprig on the head. Use hors d'oeuvre cutters to cut fancy shapes from thin slices of truffle and place 1 cutout on back of each fish. Cut eyes from hard-cooked egg white. Mix egg yolk with a bit of mustard or cream and put in a tiny paper cone or pastry bag to pipe on eyebrows. Spoon a third coat of aspic over fish to set decorations. Chill extra, runover aspic until it sets, chop it on waxed paper with a chef's knife, and spread it on a serving platter. Arrange glazed trout on bed of aspic and refrigerate until serving time.

RACK OF VEAL, BÉARNAISE

Fat adds both tenderness and flavor to meat. Since veal is a very dry meat, it is often enhanced, as here, when barded, or covered with a thin sheet of fat that serves to baste meat as it roasts. Barding fat is available from most butchers.

1 rack of veal, about 8 chops
   Fresh pork fat for barding
2 teaspoons coarse salt

1 teaspoon freshly cracked
   white pepper
Béarnaise Sauce (see p. 282)

Have the butcher trim the rack, or trim it yourself, so that about 2 inches of bone are exposed on each chop. The chine bone, or backbone, should be removed, to make rack easier to carve into chops. Tie the barding fat onto the back of the rack. (*Veal may be prepared ahead to this point.*) Stand fat side up in roasting pan and roast in a preheated 350° oven 25 minutes per pound or until meat thermometer registers 170°. (Veal should not be pink.) Remove barding fat, sprinkle meat with salt and pepper, and let it rest for 10 to 15 minutes before carving between the bones. Serve with Béarnaise Sauce, passed separately.

GREEN SALAD WITH ROQUEFORT CHEESE

Serve this unusual salad-and-cheese as a separate course after the veal—it's well worth such formal attention! I first encountered it at the home of a friend, returned from Europe after eleven years, and I've served it many times myself. Guests are invariably enchanted.

¾ pound Roquefort cheese
¼ cup unsalted butter
3 or 4 heads Bibb lettuce,
   yielding 36 to 42 leaves

1 recipe French vinaigrette
   dressing (see p. 282)
2 tablespoons chopped parsley

Beat Roquefort cheese and butter together until very creamy. Pack into a medium-size pastry bag fitted with a star tube and pipe a pointy mound of cheese into the center of each individual salad plate. Poke the stems of 6 or 7 Bibb lettuce leaves into each cheese mound—it should look like a small head of lettuce. Spoon 2 tablespoons vinaigrette over each salad and sprinkle with chopped parsley.

Formal Summer Dinner
for 8

Cold tomato and dill soup
Glazed Cornish hens or squabs
Straw potatoes
Celery Victor
Raspberry tart

Each course in this joyful menu has its own assertive taste. First
the dill, quite subtle. Then the sweet glaze on the birds, contrasted
with salty straw potatoes and crisp-cooked celery garnished with
anchovy and pimento. The sweet ending is a glorious fresh raspberry tart.

COLD TOMATO AND DILL SOUP

½ cup butter
1 tablespoon chopped garlic
1½ cups chopped onions
8 tomatoes, plus 4 for garnish
¼ cup flour
1 teaspoon salt
½ teaspoon freshly cracked
    white pepper

4 cups chicken stock (see
    p. 278)
1 tablespoon tomato paste
1 cup light cream
½ cup heavy cream
3 tablespoons chopped fresh
    dill

Melt butter in a large saucepan, add garlic and onions, and
stir over high heat until onions are transparent. Do not let them
brown. Slice (but do not peel) 8 tomatoes and add to onion mixture. Continue stirring over high heat and smooth in the flour.
Add salt, pepper, and chicken stock, and bring it to a boil. Stir in
tomato paste, then cover and simmer for about 30 minutes. Peel
remaining tomatoes for garnish: quarter them, remove seeds and
pulp and add to soup kettle, and cut tomato flesh in shreds; set
aside. Puree the soup through a food mill, using the fine disk, or
in the blender; then push the puree through a sieve to strain out
all the seeds. Taste for seasoning and chill thoroughly. (*Recipe
can be made to this point and refrigerated or frozen.*) When ready

to serve, stir in light cream. Lightly whip the heavy cream, just past the foaming stage, and fold it into the soup. Garnish each serving with tomato shreds and sprinkle with fresh chopped dill.

GLAZED CORNISH HENS OR SQUABS

8 12- to 15-ounce Cornish hens or small squabs
4 tablespoons butter, more if needed
2 teaspoons salt

1 teaspoon freshly cracked black pepper
1 8-ounce jar currant jelly, melted

Wash birds, dry thoroughly, and truss. Heat butter in a large skillet and thoroughly brown the birds all over, not letting them touch each other; take plenty of time to do this, at least 20 minutes. If necessary, brown birds a few at a time, adding more butter if needed. Put in roasting pan and season with salt and pepper. Roast in preheated 375° oven, uncovered, for about 30 minutes, basting every 5 minutes with melted currant jelly. Birds should be brown and shiny at the end of cooking time. If not, boost oven temperature to 450° for the last 5 to 10 minutes. They're good served hot, warm, or cold, and they can be frozen without losing their glaze. *May be fully prepared ahead and put in oven to warm through.*

STRAW POTATOES

4 large Idaho potatoes
Fat for deep frying

1 tablespoon salt

Peel potatoes and slice as thin as possible with a vegetable slicer or mandoline. Stack 3 or 4 slices at a time on cutting board and cut them, thinner than matchsticks, hair-thin if possible, with your chef's knife. Put in cold water immediately and let them soak for 15 minutes. Drain them and dry thoroughly. In a saucepan, heat 3 inches vegetable shortening to 375° and fry potatoes a handful at a time, until they turn straw color. Remove with a slotted spoon and drain on paper towels. Spread them on a baking sheet. (*Can be done ahead to this point, and they freeze well. Bring to room temperature before reheating.*) Just before serving, run potato sticks into a moderate oven to warm through and crisp (may be reheated in oven with Cornish hens). Sprinkle with salt and serve hot.

CELERY VICTOR

1 bunch celery	2 tablespoons red wine vinegar
2 cups chicken stock (see p. 278)	½ cup olive oil
1 teaspoon coarse salt	1 2-ounce can flat anchovy fillets, drained
½ teaspoon freshly cracked white pepper	1 pimento, sliced
	2 tablespoons chopped parsley

Slice or dice the celery, put it in a saucepan, and cover with chicken stock. Cook over high heat until barely tender, about 15 to 20 minutes. Don't overcook. Drain celery, put in a bowl, cover and refrigerate. (*Can be made the day before.*) Strain the stock and save it for consommé—it's quite flavorful. When ready to serve, make vinaigrette dressing: Beat salt, pepper, vinegar, and oil together in a small bowl with a fork, or shake in a small jar, pour over celery, decorate with anchovy fillets and sliced pimento, and sprinkle with parsley.

RASPBERRY TART

2 to 4 large, or 4 to 8 small, macaroons	1 wholly baked 9-inch pâte brisée shell (see p. 288)
⅓ cup flour	2 tablespoons dry bread crumbs, if needed
¾ cup sugar	
Pinch of salt	1 quart fresh raspberries, or 2 10-ounce packages frozen whole raspberries
2 eggs	
2 egg yolks	
2 cups scalded milk	½ cup currant jelly
1 tablespoon kirsch	1 tablespoon cassis syrup Confectioners' sugar

Unwrap macaroons to let dry overnight and chop them up; you should have about 2 cups. Set aside. To make pastry cream, put flour, sugar, and salt into a nonaluminum saucepan. Mix in 1 egg and 1 egg yolk with a wooden spatula, then add remaining egg and egg yolk, mixing well. Change to a whisk and pour scalded milk into egg mixture, whisking constantly. Set over medium-high heat and stir with whisk until custard thickens to consistency of thick mayonnaise. This mixture burns easily, so watch it carefully. Remove from heat, stir in kirsch, and let cool. Stir it now and then as it cools, or cool it quickly by stirring over ice. (*Pastry cream may be made 1 day ahead, covered closely with plastic wrap, and refrigerated.*) If you want to assemble whole tart in advance—but not more than 2 hours in advance—sprinkle shell with bread crumbs to help prevent pastry from getting soggy. (Bread crumbs are not necessary if tart is not prepared in advance.) Stir macaroon crumbs into cooled pastry cream, and fill pastry shell. Arrange raspberries on filling, around the edge in neat rows, stem side down, and piled up in the middle of the tart. Melt currant jelly, stir in cassis, and dab over berries with a pastry brush to glaze. Just before serving, sift confectioners' sugar around the edge of the tart.

Formal Dinner for 6 on the Terrace

Cold truffled lobster halves, vinaigrette
Roast lamb with soubise
Roman asparagus
Platter of crisp raw vegetables (cherry tomatoes,
fava beans, celery sticks, carrot curls, etc.)
Fresh pear tart

COLD TRUFFLED LOBSTER HALVES, VINAIGRETTE

3 live lobsters, about 1¼ pounds each
1 recipe court bouillon (see p. 279)

18 slices truffle
1 recipe French vinaigrette dressing (see p. 282)

Drop live lobsters into boiling court bouillon and boil until they turn red, about 6 to 10 minutes. Let lobsters cool in the broth to room temperature, about 1 hour. Remove and split them down the center back, discarding the sac between the eyes and the spinal cord. Carefully remove the one large piece of meat from each half—keeping it whole—turn it over, and put it back into the half shell so the red, rounded side is now up. Make 3 slits in the meat of each half lobster and insert a slice of truffle in each slit. Spoon vinaigrette over the lobster halves and let marinate for at least 1 hour before serving. (*Recipe may be done ahead to this point, covered with plastic wrap, and refrigerated. Bring to room temperature before serving.*) Serve lobster halves accompanied by the claws and individual bowls of extra vinaigrette on the side, for dipping claw meat into. The claws should be already cracked for easy handling.

ROAST LAMB WITH SOUBISE

If you've never made soubise, you should know that it is quite bland despite being an onion-based sauce—it's just enough to give lamb or veal a lift. This version is thickened with potatoes; sometimes rice, or rice-and-potato is the thickener.

1 7-pound leg of lamb, boned	1 thinly sliced medium-size baking potato
2 cloves garlic	
Coarse salt	2 tablespoons flour
Freshly cracked black pepper	½ cup light cream
½ cup plus 2 tablespoons butter	2 egg yolks
1 teaspoon salt	¼ cup chopped parsley
½ teaspoon freshly cracked white pepper	¼ cup dry red wine
	¼ cup dry bread crumbs
3 thinly sliced onions	¼ cup melted butter

Trim excess fat from lamb—leave no more than ¼ inch on it. Cut garlic cloves into slivers. With a small sharp knife, make little slits all over the meat and, using the knife blade as a slide, push the garlic slivers into the meat. Tie the leg at intervals with butcher's cord to re-form it; it should look like a roll of lamb. Rub it with coarse salt and pepper, set on rack in roasting pan, and roast in a preheated 350° oven 12 to 15 minutes per pound for pink lamb.

To make soubise, melt ½ cup butter in a heavy saucepan; stir in salt and pepper, onions, and potato, and cover and cook over medium-high heat for 20 to 30 minutes or until vegetables are soft. Stir occasionally during cooking, so onions won't burn. When vegetables are soft, puree the mixture in a blender or put it through a food mill, using the fine blade. In another saucepan, melt 2 tablespoons butter, stir in the flour, and cook it, stirring with a wooden spatula, over high heat for 2 minutes. Remove from heat, change to a whisk, and add light cream, whisking vigorously. Return to high heat, and cook, stirring, until mixture is really thick. Beat egg yolks with a fork. Stir a little of the sauce into the yolks to warm them; then stir yolks, onion-potato puree, and chopped parsley into the sauce and taste for seasoning.

When lamb is done, let it rest on a carving board while you deglaze roasting pan. Pour off all but 1 tablespoon fat; pour in wine and set pan over heat for a minute while you scrape up the brown bits. Pour this liquid into a large au gratin serving dish. Carve the lamb into slices about ¼ inch thick and pour its juices into serving dish. Spread lamb slices with the soubise and arrange them, overlapping, in the serving dish. Sprinkle with bread crumbs and drizzle with melted butter. (*Recipe can be made ahead to this point. Cool in refrigerator, uncovered, for ½ hour or longer; then cover with plastic wrap and refrigerate. Bring to room temperature before reheating.*) When ready to serve, preheat oven to 400° and heat lamb. If you overcooked lamb when you roasted it, reheat it for 10 to 15 minutes. If lamb was too pink when you carved it, reheat it for 20 to 25 minutes.

ROMAN ASPARAGUS

2 pounds very thin fresh
   asparagus
½ cup melted butter
   Juice of 1 lemon

½ cup freshly grated Parmesan
   cheese, plus more if
   needed
   Freshly cracked white
     pepper
   Salt, if necessary

It's not necessary to peel thin asparagus, but check to see if there's sand under scales, and trim the ends. Place asparagus in a big skillet and add water almost to cover. Bring to a boil, reduce heat, and simmer until asparagus is tender-crisp, only a few minutes. Do not cover pan; do not add salt to water. Drain cooked asparagus and spread on a towel to dry. Brush a serving dish with butter; arrange asparagus in a thin layer; pour on melted butter and lemon juice and sprinkle with Parmesan cheese. You may need more than ½ cup cheese to cover asparagus. Sprinkle with pepper and a tiny bit of salt if cheese is not salty. (*Can be made ahead to this point.*) Bake in a preheated 400° oven for 10 minutes.

FRESH PEAR TART

6 fresh pears
2 cups sugar
2 cups water
1 8-ounce jar currant jelly
1 wholly baked 9-inch pâte
   brisée shell (see p. 288)
1½ cups heavy cream

2 tablespoons confectioners'
   sugar, plus more for
   sifting
2 tablespoons kirsch
12 strawberries
¼ cup chopped almonds

Peel, cut in half, and core pears and poach them in a syrup of sugar and water until barely tender, about 15 to 20 minutes. Melt the currant jelly and spread half of it over the bottom of the tart shell. Whip the cream, sweetening it with confectioners' sugar and kirsch, and spread over the currant glaze. Drain pear halves and arrange them, cored side up, on the whipped cream. Glaze the strawberries with remaining currant jelly and place a strawberry on each pear half. Sprinkle entire tart with chopped almonds. (*May be assembled 2 hours ahead.*) Just before serving, sift a little confectioners' sugar around the rim of the tart.

A Summer Dinner
for 8

Seafood mélange
Veal birds with brown sauce
French-fried zucchini
Berries with cold zabaglione

SEAFOOD MÉLANGE

1 pound shrimp, fresh or
   frozen
1 pound crab meat, fresh,
   frozen, or canned
5 tablespoons butter
¼ cup dry sherry or Madeira
3 tablespoons flour
1½ cups milk
1 cup light cream

1 egg yolk
½ teaspoon salt
¼ teaspoon freshly cracked
   white pepper
4 tablespoons freshly grated
   Parmesan cheese
½ cup bread crumbs
½ cup softened butter

If shrimp are frozen, put them in water to cover, bring to a boil and turn off heat. Let cool. Shell and devein shrimp and chop in large pieces. Pick over crab meat. Melt 2 tablespoons butter in a heavy skillet, add shrimp and crab meat, and toss over high heat to mix, trying to avoid shredding crab meat. Add sherry and cook until wine evaporates, about 3 to 5 minutes. Set aside. In a sauce-pan, melt remaining 3 tablespoons butter, stir in flour, and cook, stirring with a wooden spatula, over high heat for 2 minutes. Do not let it brown. Remove from heat, change to a whisk, and add milk, whisking vigorously. Add cream. Return to medium-high heat and cook, stirring, until sauce thickens. Stir a little of the hot sauce into the egg yolk, to warm it; then stir yolk into sauce. Bring it to the boiling point (but do not boil) and remove from heat. Add seafood, season with salt and pepper, and pour into an au gratin dish, or into individual scallop shells or ramekins. Sprinkle with cheese and bread crumbs and dot with butter. (*Can be made ahead to this point, covered with plastic wrap, and refrigerated. Bring to room temperature before heating.*) Bake in a preheated 350° oven, 15 to 20 minutes for au gratin dish, about 10 minutes for scallop shells, or until bubbly and lightly browned.

VEAL BIRDS WITH BROWN SAUCE

8 slices veal, cut from leg, each about ½ inch thick	½ pound veal, ground twice
4 tablespoons brandy	2 tablespoons chopped parsley
1 teaspoon salt	1 teaspoon dried tarragon
½ teaspoon freshly cracked white pepper	1 beaten egg
¾ cup finely chopped onion	¼ pound smoked cooked tongue, all in 1 piece
1 finely chopped clove garlic	Black truffle
5 tablespoons butter	1 recipe basic brown sauce (see p. 281)

Place veal slices between 2 sheets of waxed paper and pound thin. Brush them with 2 tablespoons brandy and sprinkle with ½ teaspoon salt and ¼ teaspoon pepper. Cook onion and garlic over high heat in 2 tablespoons butter, stirring with a wooden spatula, until onion is transparent—do not let it brown. In a bowl, mix together ground veal, onion, garlic, chopped parsley, tarragon, beaten egg, and remaining salt and pepper. Spread ground veal mixture over veal slices. Cut tongue into fingers and lay 1 finger down the center of each piece of veal. Put a wedge of black truffle in the center. Roll up the veal around the tongue and tie ends loosely with string. Heat remaining 3 tablespoons butter in a heavy skillet and sauté veal birds in butter, over high heat, turning them to brown on all sides. Flame with remaining 2 tablespoons brandy and remove from pan. Add basic brown sauce to pan and bring it to a boil over high heat, scraping up the brown bits. Return veal birds to pan. (*Recipe may be done ahead to this point and refrigerated, or frozen for up to 1 month.*) Cook veal, covered, over low heat, for about 20 minutes. Arrange on serving platter, remove strings, and pour on sauce.

FRENCH-FRIED ZUCCHINI

8 small zucchini	1 teaspoon salt
½ cup flour	½ teaspoon freshly cracked
2 cups vegetable shortening	white pepper

Peel the zucchini with a vegetable peeler and cut into matchsticks. Dredge the sticks with flour, put them in a coarse sieve, and bang it to shake off excess flour. In a heavy saucepan, electric skillet, or deep-fat fryer, heat vegetable shortening to 375°. Fry zucchini sticks, a handful at a time, until light brown, about 3 minutes. Remove them with a slotted spoon and drain on brown paper or paper towels. Keep warm in a low oven while you fry remaining sticks. (*Or prepare ahead to this point. To reheat, spread sticks on brown paper set over cake racks on a baking sheet, and warm in a 350° oven for several minutes.*) Salt and pepper the zucchini and heap in a serving dish.

BERRIES WITH COLD ZABAGLIONE

Follow the directions for Zabaglione on page 203, but reduce ingredients to 1 egg, 2 egg yolks, 3 tablespoons sugar, and 3 tablespoons Marsala. When zabaglione is thick and creamy, remove from heat, set the pot or bowl in a bowl of ice, and continue beating over ice until mixture is cold. Whip 1 cup heavy cream to the same consistency as zabaglione and fold in. Cover and store in refrigerator until serving time. Spoon over raspberries or strawberries in dessert bowls.

An Informal Alsatian Dinner
for 6

Lentil salad
Choucroute garni
Steamed potatoes with caraway
and melted butter
Tart Tatin

LENTIL SALAD

½ pound lentils
3 slices bacon
1 finely minced onion
  Juice of ½ lemon
1 teaspoon salt
½ teaspoon freshly cracked
  white pepper
2 teaspoons mustard

2 tablespoons red wine vinegar,
  or tarragon vinegar
4 tablespoons olive oil
1 chopped clove garlic
1 2-ounce can flat anchovy
  fillets
6 black olives
2 tablespoons chopped parsley

Put lentils in a saucepan, cover with cold water, and bring to a boil. Turn heat to simmer, cook lentils for about 35 minutes, and test for doneness: if a lentil gives between your fingers when you pinch it, it is done. Drain and set aside. Cut bacon into large dice and partly fry it, over high heat—it should remain limp. Stir in onion and wilt it; this takes about 2 minutes. Add lentils, mix, and heat through. Pour into a large bowl and sprinkle with lemon juice. Make a dressing by beating or shaking together salt, pepper, mustard, vinegar, olive oil, and garlic; pour over warm lentils and toss to mix. (*Recipe can be made a day ahead to this point.*) Serve at room temperature, garnished with anchovies, black olives, and chopped parsley.

CHOUCROUTE GARNI

A marvelous traditional dish with a gala presentation.

½ pound salt pork, about
2 pounds sauerkraut
2 apples, peeled, cored, and sliced
2 medium-size onions, cut in eighths
4 juniper berries
1 bay leaf
¼ teaspoon ground coriander seed
2 whole cloves
2 mashed cloves garlic
½ teaspoon freshly cracked white pepper
1 pound bacon, uncut

6 smoked pork chops
3 pounds pork tenderloin, optional
1 2-pound smoked pork butt, cut in ¾-inch slices, optional
1 rack spareribs, optional
1 garlic sausage
6 knackwurst, optional
1 cup Riesling dry white wine
1 cup chicken stock (see p. 278)
1 potato
1 split champagne, optional

Cut a few strips of salt pork and lay them in the bottom of a large flameproof casserole. Rinse and drain the sauerkraut and put it in the casserole along with apple slices, onions, juniper berries, bay leaf, coriander, cloves, garlic, and pepper. Dice the bacon and spread it over sauerkraut. Add meats, except sausage and knackwurst, and pour in wine and chicken stock. (*Recipe can be prepared ahead to this point.*) Cover, bring to a boil over high heat, and place casserole in a preheated 350° oven to cook for 1½ to 2 hours, or longer if you wish—sauerkraut must be thoroughly cooked. About 45 minutes before serving time, add sausage and knackwurst and grate the raw potato into the casserole to absorb any sour taste and excess salt. (*May be made ahead and reheated in oven or on top of stove.*)

To serve, arrange smoked meats at ends of platter. Remove bay leaf, toss the sauerkraut, salt pork, and bacon dice together, and spoon into the center of the platter. Bring platter to the table, uncork the champagne, and pour it over the sauerkraut. Put the platter over a spirit lamp and flame the champagne. Cover with another platter and let it simmer for 15 minutes to absorb the champagne.

STEAMED POTATOES WITH CARAWAY AND MELTED BUTTER

24 peeled small new potatoes
2 cups water
1 chopped celery rib
½ chopped onion
1 tablespoon salt

½ teaspoon freshly cracked black pepper
2 tablespoons caraway seeds
6 tablespoons hot melted butter

"Turn" or shape the potatoes with a paring knife so that they are all the same size, or cut larger ones into smaller pieces and trim. Put them in a steamer basket over water flavored with celery, onion, salt, and pepper. Cover and steam until potatoes are tender—test with the point of a knife after 10 minutes. Just before serving, sprinkle with caraway seeds and pour on butter; roll potatoes around in the pan to coat them well. *You can peel potatoes ahead; keep them covered with cold water to prevent darkening. Measure ingredients into steamer bottom ahead, too—but do not cook potatoes until ready to serve.*

TART TATIN

2 tablespoons softened butter
2 cups sugar
8 medium-size apples, greenings, if available
2 tablespoons Calvados, apple brandy, or brandy
½ teaspoon freshly grated nutmeg
½ cup butter

1 recipe pâte brisée (see p. 288)
2 tablespoons confectioners' sugar
Whipped cream or vanilla ice cream, optional
3 tablespoons confectioners' sugar, optional
3 tablespoons Calvados or apple brandy, optional

Spread butter over bottom and sides of a 9-inch ovenproof glass pie pan. Add 1 cup sugar and shake the pan to distribute sugar evenly. Peel, core, and slice apples ⅛ inch thick; heap them in the pan, making a dome in the center—the pan will look overflowing, but the apples cook down. Sprinkle apples with Calvados, nutmeg, and remaining 1 cup sugar. Dot all over with ½ cup butter. Roll a pastry circle ¼ inch thick and place over apples, turning back the edge of the pastry all around so that it does not touch the rim of the pan—leave about ¼ inch gap. Place pan on the bottom shelf of a preheated 375° oven and bake for 30 minutes. Turn oven to 325° and bake 2 hours longer (time is correct). Do not put foil around the dish to catch drippings and do not set pan on a baking sheet. (These directions are necessary to caramelize the tart; it helps to have a self-cleaning oven.) If crust begins to get too brown, lay aluminum foil loosely over the top.

Remove from oven and cool 5 minutes. Run a knife around the edge of the tart, lifting up as you go, and invert onto an oven-proof serving plate. If you find, when you turn it out, that the bottom of the tart isn't caramelized, run it under the broiler for a minute or two. (*May be baked ahead and served at room temperature or reheated in a 350° oven for 15 minutes.*) Sift confectioners' sugar around edge of tart just before serving (stir it through a small sieve with a teaspoon). If desired, whip 1½ cups heavy cream; leave unsweetened, or flavor it with 3 tablespoons confectioners' sugar and 3 tablespoons Calvados or apple brandy. Or serve tart with ice cream.

A Game Dinner
for 6

Trout amandine
Venison Bourguignonne
Red cabbage
Kartoffelklösse
Chestnut tart

TROUT AMANDINE

6 trout, about 1 pound each	½ teaspoon freshly cracked
1 tablespoon lemon juice	white pepper
1 quart water	½ cup vegetable oil
1 cup milk	½ cup butter
1 cup flour	¾ cup sliced blanched almonds
1 teaspoon salt	

Scale, clean, and split (but do not halve) trout—or ask your fish seller to do it—leaving heads and tails intact. Wash trout in a mixture of water and lemon juice and dry them. Dip in milk, roll in flour, pat off excess flour, and season with salt and pepper. Heat oil in large skillet and sauté trout for 6 minutes over medium-high heat, without moving them. Turn them over carefully with 2 spatulas and cook 6 minutes on the other side. Remove to serving platter and keep warm. Pour oil out of pan and add butter; when it's hot, add almonds. Sauté almonds for 3 to 4 minutes over medium-high heat, shaking the pan, and pour almonds and butter over fish.

VENISON BOURGUIGNONNE

3 pounds venison, rump or loin, cut into 1½-inch cubes
4 tablespoons butter
½ cup brandy
24 small white onions, peeled
½ pound mushrooms
2 teaspoons tomato paste
1 teaspoon meat glaze (see p. 280)
3 teaspoons potato flour
½ cup dry red wine
½ cup dry sherry

2 cups chicken stock (see p. 278)
1 teaspoon freshly cracked black pepper
1 teaspoon red currant jelly
1 bouquet garni (see p. 283) but substitute 1 tablespoon fresh tarragon or 1 teaspoon dry tarragon for the thyme
½ pound finely diced salt pork
2 tablespoons finely chopped parsley

In a heavy casserole, over high heat, brown the venison cubes in 3 tablespoons hot butter, a few pieces at a time—do not let them touch. When all cubes are brown, put them all back in the pan and flame with ¼ cup brandy. Remove meat and set aside. Add remaining 1 tablespoon butter to pan and stir in the peeled onions; cook, stirring, for about 3 minutes. Stir in mushrooms—cut any large mushrooms in half—to coat well with butter. Remove from heat, stir in tomato paste, meat glaze, and potato flour; mix until smooth. Add red wine, sherry, and chicken stock and mix until smooth. Return to medium-high heat and bring to a boil. Add black pepper, currant jelly, and the bouquet garni. Return venison to casserole. (*Can be made ahead to this point or fully cooked the day before and reheated.*) Cover with foil and a heavy lid and place in a preheated 350° oven to cook for 1½ to 2 hours or until tender. Baste it 4 times during cooking, adding a tablespoonful of brandy each time. Remove the bouquet garni after 45 minutes.

When venison is nearly done, blanch, drain, and sauté the diced salt pork until crisp, and add to casserole. When ready, sprinkle with parsley and serve from the casserole.

RED CABBAGE

Follow recipe on p. 96, but while cabbage is cooking, prepare 4 green apples: peel, core, and slice the apples and sauté in 3 tablespoons butter. Add 2 tablespoons lemon juice and 1 tablespoon cinnamon and cook until tender. Add apples to cabbage in serving dish, pour on the cornstarch-thickened liquid, and mix lightly together.

KARTOFFELKLÖSSE

6 medium-size all-purpose potatoes
2 beaten eggs
½ cup flour
½ cup grated onion
1 tablespoon finely chopped parsley

¼ teaspoon freshly grated nutmeg
1 teaspoon salt
½ teaspoon freshly cracked black pepper
2 quarts chicken stock (see p. 278)

Peel potatoes, cover with cold water, and boil until tender. Put them through a potato ricer or food mill. Add eggs, flour, onion, parsley, nutmeg, salt, and pepper. Beat with a fork until fluffy. Roll the mixture into balls the size of walnuts. (*Can be done ahead to this point.*) When ready to cook, bring chicken stock to a boil; drop potato balls into stock and cook them at a low boil, covered, for 15 minutes. If you have a large pot, cook the potato balls all at once—they can be crowded together. Or cook them in relays, keeping those already cooked warm in a low oven (first removing the venison casserole, which can be held on top of the stove over a low flame, or in a hot water bath).

CHESTNUT TART

1 15-ounce can sweetened
    chestnut puree
1 cup unsalted butter
    Confectioners' sugar,
    optional
2 tablespoons kirsch
½ cup chopped toasted almonds

1 wholly baked 9-inch pâte
    brisée shell (see p. 288)
1 cup heavy cream, whipped
2 tablespoons confectioners'
    sugar
12 whole marrons

Beat chestnut puree and butter together with an electric mixer or wooden spatula until smooth and creamy. Taste for sweetness and add confectioners' sugar to taste. Stir in kirsch and toasted almonds. Spread mixture into baked pastry shell, smooth the top, and garnish with rosettes of whipped cream sweetened with 2 tablespoons confectioners' sugar and piped from a large pastry bag fitted with a star tube. Place whole marrons around edge of tart. Serve cold. *Tart may be fully assembled 3 to 4 hours before serving.*

A Chinese Dinner
for 6 to 8

Puffed shrimp
Paper-wrapped chicken
Barbecued spareribs
Stir-fried beef
Fried rice
Glacéed apples and bananas

If you don't like to cook in front of your guests, don't attempt Chinese food. All of these dishes should be cooked at the last minute to retain flavor, texture, and crispness. You can do the chopping, measuring, and preparing ahead of time, but then it's cook-and-serve—fast! I recommend that you serve the shrimp, chicken, and spareribs together. Then let your guests take a break —they won't mind!—while you prepare a second course of beef and rice. The apple and banana dessert, a real treat, makes up the third course.

PUFFED SHRIMP

30 to 35 medium-size shrimp
  Vegetable shortening for
    deep frying
  Flour for coating shrimp

1 recipe beer batter (see p. 285)
Soy Dipping Sauce (recipe follows)

Clean the shrimp but leave the tails on. Heat 2 inches of vegetable shortening in a wok, electric skillet, deep-fat fryer, or heavy saucepan to 375°. Flour shrimp, patting off excess flour, dip in beer batter, and drop them, 2 or 3 at a time, into hot fat. Cook until nicely browned—do not overcook. Drain on paper towels. (*May be prepared ahead and reheated. To reheat: set cake racks on a baking sheet, cover with brown paper, lay shrimp on paper, and heat for a few minutes in a 350° oven.*) Serve hot with Soy Dipping Sauce.

SOY DIPPING SAUCE

Mix together ¾ cup soy sauce, ¾ cup red wine vinegar, ¼ cup vegetable oil, and 2 very finely chopped cloves of garlic.

PAPER-WRAPPED CHICKEN

3 whole chicken breasts
1 teaspoon salt
2 tablespoons plus 1 pint
    peanut oil
2 tablespoons chopped
    scallions
¼ cup soy sauce

1 teaspoon ground ginger
3 tablespoons sherry
30 pieces of baking parchment, waxed paper or aluminum foil, about 5 inches square

Skin and bone chicken breasts and cut meat into pieces about 1 inch square. Put them into a bowl, cover with salt, 2 tablespoons peanut oil, chopped scallions, soy sauce, ground ginger, and sherry. Stir to mix well and marinate for 2 hours. Lay 1 or 2 chicken pieces on each paper or foil square. Fold 1 corner over chicken, fold in both side corners (like an envelope); then fold this squared end once more and tuck remaining free corner into resulting pocket to make a tight, secure package. (*May be made ahead to this point.*) Heat 1 pint peanut oil in wok or skillet to the point of smoking. Add chicken parcels, 3 or 4 at a time, and fry 5 minutes only. Hold cooked chicken parcels in a 350° oven to keep warm. Serve chicken pieces directly from their paper packages. Use chopsticks or forks to open packages and eat chicken.

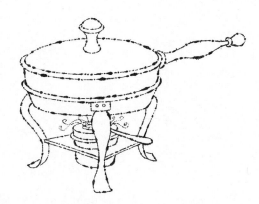

BARBECUED SPARERIBS

Chinese 5-spice powder is a strong and pungent mixture of star anise, peppercorns, fennel, cloves, and cinnamon and is readily available in Chinese and gourmet shops. Very little is used, as too much will overpower any dish.

3 pounds spareribs	1 tablespoon sugar
5 tablespoons soy sauce	2 teaspoons ground ginger
2 tablespoons sherry	1 tablespoon finely chopped
½ teaspoon Chinese 5-spice	garlic
powder	¼ cup honey

Trim excess fat and gristle from ribs and cut between every 2 ribs, but do not separate completely. Mix together soy sauce, sherry, 5-spice powder, sugar, ginger, and garlic, and marinate ribs for 2 hours, turning frequently. Place ribs on a rack in a roasting pan, pour 1 inch hot water into bottom of pan (to help keep ribs moist), and bake in a preheated 350° oven for 1 hour, turning ribs frequently. After 30 minutes, glaze ribs with honey and continue baking. *Ribs can be baked ahead and reheated in a 350° oven for 15 minutes.*

Note: Another way to bake the ribs is to hang them in the oven over the pan of hot water. Bend wire or strong paper clips into S-hooks, hook one end into meat, and hang the other end over rung of oven rack.

STIR-FRIED BEEF

2½ pounds beef, sliced ¼ inch
    thick
4 tablespoons soy sauce
2 tablespoons sherry
½ teaspoon salt
½ teaspoon sugar
1 teaspoon Chinese 5-spice
    powder
1 pound vegetables (choose
    any 5 or 6 from the fol-
    lowing: celery, mush-
    rooms, scallions, red
    onion, green pepper,
    snow peas, fresh or

frozen, Chinese cabbage,
    bean sprouts, canned
    water chestnuts, drained,
    or canned bamboo
    shoots, drained)
4 tablespoons peanut oil
1 chopped clove garlic
2 chopped slices fresh ginger
    root
2 teaspoons cornstarch
1½ cups chicken stock (see
    p. 278)
¼ cup walnuts or almonds,
    optional

Cut slices of meat into 1-inch squares. Mix together soy sauce, sherry, salt, sugar, and 5-spice powder, stir into meat, and let marinate for 1 hour. Slice all vegetables except bean sprouts and snow peas into 1-inch pieces; cut celery, Chinese cabbage, and scallions on the diagonal. Set aside. Heat 2 tablespoons oil in the wok, or large skillet. Add chopped garlic and gingerroot and stir-fry over high heat for 1 minute. Add beef and stir-fry for 2 minutes. Remove beef and set aside. Add remaining 2 tablespoons oil, stir in vegetables (except snow peas), and return meat to wok. Stir cornstarch into chicken stock and add. Cook, stirring, until sauce thickens, about 5 minutes. Put lid on wok and cook over high heat until all vegetables are tender-crisp, about 5 minutes. Add snow peas the last minute of cooking, and the nuts last, just to heat through.

Note: Ingredients may be collected, measured, and chopped ahead of time, but stir-fry cooking is always done at the last minute.

FRIED RICE

5 cups cooked cold rice (about
    1¾ cups uncooked)
5 eggs
3 tablespoons water
¼ cup peanut oil

1 teaspoon salt
½ teaspoon freshly cracked
    black pepper
¼ cup chopped scallions or
    Chinese parsley

Dampen hands and separate rice grains so fried rice won't be lumpy. Beat eggs with water and set aside. Heat peanut oil in wok or large skillet almost to smoking. Add rice and stir-fry over high heat until rice is heated through. Season with salt and pepper. Pour in beaten eggs and quickly fold eggs and rice together with a spatula or large spoon. Sprinkle with chopped scallions or Chinese parsley and serve hot. Stir-frying time is no more than 5 minutes—can be done while beef (previous recipe) simmers.

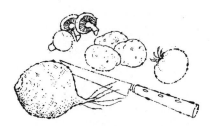

GLACÉED APPLES AND BANANAS

This dessert creates a spectacular effect when served using chopsticks; each guest dips pieces of glazed fruit into a bowl of ice-cold water. As the fruit comes in contact with the water, the glaze hardens instantly, surrounding the soft fruit with a crackly, crunchy syrup shell.

6 to 8 apples (1 per person)	¼ teaspoon cream of tartar
3 or 4 bananas (½ per person)	¾ cup flour
4½ cups (2 pounds) sugar	4 beaten eggs
1 cup water	Peanut oil
2 tablespoons light corn syrup	6 to 8 bowls of iced water

Peel and core apples and cut in eighths. Peel bananas and cut in chunks about ½ inch thick. Mix sugar, water, corn syrup, and cream of tartar together in a saucepan and bring to a boil over high heat, stirring until sugar dissolves. Turn heat to medium and cook syrup to the hard-crack stage (300° to 320° on a candy thermometer). Remove pan from heat and immediately put it in a pan of warm water to stop the cooking. Roll fruit pieces in flour and shake off excess. Dip in beaten egg. Heat 2 inches of peanut oil in wok or skillet. Deep-fry fruit a few pieces at a time in hot fat until golden, about 1 minute. Remove and drain on paper towels. While still hot, dip fruit into sugar syrup (use tongs or chopsticks—syrup is hot) and place dipped fruit on a buttered platter. Serve hot with bowls of iced water into which the glazed fruit is dipped.

A Thanksgiving Dinner
for 8

Jerusalem artichoke soup
Roast capon or turkey with tarragon butter
Wild rice ring
Bibb lettuce salad (see p. 111)
Chestnut tart (see p. 141)

JERUSALEM ARTICHOKE SOUP

The Jerusalem artichoke does not look anything like the globe artichoke and resembles it only slightly in flavor. It doesn't come from Palestine either. Actually, it's a species of North American sunflower, cultivated by Indians at the time of the Pilgrims and introduced to France at the beginning of the seventeenth century. The tuber is the edible part. You'll find Jerusalem artichokes on the market in winter; they're knobby-looking but should be very firm, with no wrinkles.

2 pounds Jerusalem artichokes	2 teaspoons salt
4 cups chicken stock (see p. 278)	1 teaspoon freshly cracked white pepper
3 cups milk	¼ teaspoon freshly grated nutmeg
4 tablespoons butter	
1 cup chopped onion	4 egg yolks, optional
2 cups chopped celery	1 cup heavy cream
2 tablespoons chopped shallots	2 tablespoons chopped parsley

Scrub and slice (but do not peel) Jerusalem artichokes. Put them in a large soup kettle and cover with chicken stock and milk. Melt butter in a skillet, add onion, celery, and shallots, and toss over high heat for about 5 minutes. Add to soup kettle along with salt, pepper, and nutmeg. Bring to a boil, cover, and simmer until vegetables are tender, 20 to 30 minutes. Puree the soup through a food mill, using the medium disk. Taste for seasoning. (*Recipe can be made ahead to this point.*) Beat egg yolks into heavy cream and whisk into soup. Bring to the boiling point, but do not boil. Serve from a tureen, sprinkled with chopped parsley.

ROAST CAPON OR TURKEY
WITH TARRAGON BUTTER

1 6- to 7-pound capon or small turkey

¾ cup butter

1 tablespoon fresh or 1 teaspoon dried tarragon

1 tablespoon chopped parsley

½ roughly chopped black truffle

Salt and pepper

1 finely chopped carrot

1 finely chopped celery rib

1 finely chopped onion

1 cup dry red wine

1 bunch watercress

1 lemon

1 truffle

2 Sautéed Fluted Mushroom Caps (see p. 284)

Loosen the skin on the breast of the bird—and, if possible, the legs, too—by working your hands under the skin, next to the flesh. Try not to tear it. Cream butter with tarragon, parsley, chopped truffle, ½ teaspoon salt, and a few grinds of pepper. With a wooden spatula, place tarragon butter, a dollop at a time, under the skin; press down on skin with your hand while you withdraw spatula, leaving butter under skin. Then pat and press the bird to spread the butter around. Truss bird. (*May be prepared ahead to this point, wrapped in foil, and refrigerated.*)

Place bird on its side on rack in roasting pan. Spread a *mirepoix*—chopped carrot, celery, and onion—together with giblets, the neck from the bird, and ½ cup red wine in the bottom of the roasting pan. Salt and pepper the bird and put it into a preheated 475° oven for 15 minutes. Baste and turn bird to its other side for another 15 minutes. Baste again. Turn bird breast up, reduce oven heat to 425°, and roast until done, basting every 15 minutes. Each time you baste, add 2 tablespoons red wine to pan juices, draw juices up with bulb baster, and squirt over bird. To calculate roasting time, count 20 minutes per pound, including the first half hour at high heat. Remove bird from oven and let rest for 15 minutes before bringing to the table.

To make a sauce strain pan juices and cook to reduce by half, skimming off fat. Prepare a garnish for bird: make zigzag cuts around center of lemon with a small knife and pull lemon halves apart. Thread lemon halves on an *attelet*—skewer-shaped utensil with an ornamental top—along with 1 whole black truffle and 2 fluted mushroom caps, and spear into breast of bird. Stuff cavity entrance with a bunch of watercress. To carve a small bird: cut off legs and cut thigh from drumstick through the joint. Cut down center of breast and take off each side of breast meat in 1 piece.

Cut each breast piece in two across the middle. Pass sauce separately in a sauceboat.

WILD RICE RING

1 cup wild rice
3 teaspoons salt
½ cup pine nuts
4 tablespoons butter
1 cup finely chopped onion

½ teaspoon freshly cracked
   black pepper
½ cup melted butter
1 bunch watercress

Soak rice overnight in cold water. Next day, drain it, put it in a saucepan, add water to cover, stir in 2 teaspoons of the salt, and bring to a boil. Reduce heat to simmer, cover pan, and cook 45 minutes or until barely tender. Drain. Spread pine nuts on a baking sheet and brown in a 350° oven for 10 to 15 minutes. Melt butter in a small skillet and stir in chopped onion; cook over high heat until limp, about 5 minutes. Combine cooked rice, browned pine nuts, and onions, and season with remaining 1 teaspoon salt and the pepper. Add melted butter and mix well. Taste for seasoning. Oil heavily a 4-cup ring mold and pack rice *firmly* into mold. (*Can be made ahead to this point. Cooked rice also freezes well. Bring to room temperature before reheating.*) Set mold in a pan of hot water and place in a preheated 350° oven for 30 minutes. Remove from oven and let stand for 5 minutes. Unmold rice onto a serving plate and fill center of ring with a bunch of watercress.

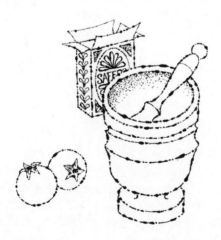

A Hearty Christmas Dinner
for 8

Smoked salmon with caviar
Mushroom broth garnished with
mushroom rounds (see p. 51)
Roast goose with giblet sauce
Braised turnips
Relish dish: radishes, black and green olives,
celery, scallions, cherry tomatoes
Mincemeat roll with hard sauce

Roast goose is rich, but for many families, it's not Christmas without it. The relish dish—raw vegetables and olives, unadorned—offers the necessary something crisp and crunchy. Incidentally, don't plan to serve the apple stuffing—you'll find it much too greasy. The apples give flavor to the goose.

SMOKED SALMON WITH CAVIAR

On individual plates arrange very thinly sliced smoked salmon—top quality—2 slices on each plate. In the center of each, put a small demitasse spoonful of black caviar, also the best. Serve with a lemon wedge and garnish each plate with watercress. Pass the black pepper mill.

ROAST GOOSE WITH GIBLET SAUCE

1 goose, 10 to 12 pounds	1 cup boiling water
8 apples	1 bunch watercress
1 tablespoon salt	Giblet Sauce (recipe
1 tablespoon butter	follows)

Wash and dry goose. Peel, core, and quarter apples, stuff them into cavity, and truss legs with string. Secure neck skin onto the back with a skewer, and twist wings behind back. Rub the bird with salt and prick all over with a fork. Spread butter over breast and place the bird on a rack in a roasting pan. Add boiling water to pan and put the goose in a preheated 375° oven. Count 20 minutes per pound. Turn the goose so that it browns lightly on all sides, and baste frequently during roasting with the simmering giblet stock. When goose is done, remove trussing strings and skewers, place on a serving platter, and keep warm while you complete the giblet sauce. Decorate platter with a bunch of watercress and place paper frills on drumsticks.

GIBLET SAUCE

While goose is roasting, simmer neck, heart, and gizzard in chicken stock to cover, adding 1 onion, salt to taste, a pinch of thyme, ½ carrot, and ½ celery rib. After 2 hours, strain the stock and set aside. Chop the heart and gizzard. Sauté the liver in butter and chop it. When goose is done, pour off all but ¼ cup fat from the roasting pan and stir into it 2 teaspoons potato starch. Cook, stirring, over high heat for about 5 minutes. Gradually add 1½ cups of strained giblet stock to the pan and cook, stirring, for another 5 minutes. Add the chopped giblets and serve sauce separately.

BRAISED TURNIPS

32 small white turnips	2 teaspoons salt
½ cup butter	1 teaspoon freshly cracked
2 teaspoons sugar	white pepper

Peel turnips, cutting off root and stem ends, parboil 5 minutes, and drain. Put into a heavy pan with butter and seasonings and place in preheated 350° oven or over high heat and bake or cook until tender—about 30 to 35 minutes. Shake the pan frequently to avoid scorching turnips. *Can be cooked ahead and reheated.*

MINCEMEAT ROLL WITH HARD SAUCE

1 recipe Sandy's piecrust (see p. 287)	1 egg yolk
1 1-pound jar mincemeat	1 tablespoon water
4 tablespoons brandy	Hard Sauce (see p. 79)

Roll out piecrust pastry on a lightly floured board to a rectangle 17 by 10 inches and ⅛ inch thick. Trim edges. Spread with mincemeat ½ inch thick, sprinkle with brandy, and roll up, like a jelly roll, from the long side. Tuck in edges and place on baking sheet, seam side down. Beat egg yolk with 1 tablespoon water to make egg wash and brush on pastry. Cut 4 gashes to let out steam. (*Can be prepared ahead to this point. Baked roll will freeze, for up to 1 month. Thaw overnight in refrigerator before baking.*) Bake in a preheated 350° oven for 35 to 40 minutes, or until crust is brown and crisp. Slice and serve warm with Hard Sauce, flavored with brandy.

An Unusual Easter Dinner for 8

Eggs Andalouse
Roast fresh ham
Tyropita
Mustard ring
Paskha

This Easter dinner menu upholds tradition by beginning with eggs, which are stuffed and re-formed to look like whole eggs, then coated with sauce. The mustard ring with fresh roast ham is bity but smooth. Tyropita will introduce you to Greek feta cheese and filo pastry, and for dessert you'll learn how to make paskha, an Easter tradition in Russia. If you happen to have a paskha mold, you can shape it, as they do, into a four-sided pyramid. But it will taste as good formed in a sieve, as the recipe directs. Allow 4 hours to roast the ham; everything else is prepared ahead.

EGGS ANDALOUSE

10 hard-cooked eggs
 1 cup unsalted butter
1½ tablespoons tomato paste
 2 teaspoons salt
 ½ teaspoon freshly cracked
     white pepper

SAUCE:

1 cup mayonnaise (see p. 283)
½ cup sour cream
3 tablespoons tomato paste

Parsley, for garnish
Tomato roses, for garnish
(see p. 284)

Cut eggs in half; remove yolks and press them through a sieve. Beat butter with an electric mixer or by hand with wooden spatula until creamy; beat in sieved yolks, tomato paste, salt, and pepper. Fill egg whites with mixture and press 2 halves together to re-form whole eggs. Cover with plastic wrap and refrigerate. Prepare mayonnaise, seasoning it well; add sour cream and tomato paste; store in a jar in the refrigerator. (*Recipe can be made ahead to this point.*) When ready to serve, arrange eggs on platter, spoon sauce over each egg, and garnish with chopped parsley. Place 2 tomato roses on parsley bed in center of platter.

ROAST FRESH HAM

Do not remove skin from meat; it becomes beautifully crisp when roasted.

1 8-pound fresh ham (pork
   leg roast)
2 teaspoons coarse salt
1 teaspoon freshly cracked
   black pepper

1½ cups Madeira, about
 1 bunch watercress, for
     garnish
Spiced crab apples, for
   garnish

Score pork skin in diamond shapes and rub all over with salt and pepper. Lay fat side up in a roasting pan and roast in a preheated 325° oven for 30 minutes per pound, or about 4 hours, raising temperature to 350° for last half hour, while baking Tyropita. (Temperature on meat thermometer should read 170°, and never mind the listing on the thermometer for pork. This new lower temperature has general approval; pork will be thoroughly cooked but not dry and overdone.) Baste every 30 minutes while roasting with 2 tablespoons Madeira. When done, remove pork to a carving board and keep warm. Add ½ cup Madeira to pan juices and boil, scraping up brown bits. Reduce by half. Skim off fat, rectify seasoning, and pass in sauceboat. Garnish meat platter with a bunch of watercress and spiced crab apples.

TYROPITA

The best feta cheese—or Greek goat cheese—is packed in brine. Rinse off brine and taste the cheese; if it is overpoweringly salty, soak it in milk for 1 hour. Filo dough, a pastry thin as an onion skin, comes in sheets and is available in Greek or Armenian grocery stores. Because it is fragile and dries out rapidly, work with only 1 filo sheet at a time, keeping the remaining sheets covered with a damp, not wet, towel.

1 pound feta cheese	1 cup grated Parmesan cheese
3 tablespoons butter	4 beaten eggs
4 tablespoons flour	8 sheets filo dough, each
2 cups milk	about 11 inches by 15
½ teaspoon freshly cracked	inches
white pepper	½ cup melted butter
¼ teaspoon freshly grated	
nutmeg	

Drain cheese, mash it, and set it aside. Melt butter in a saucepan and stir in flour. Cook, stirring constantly, over high heat for 2 minutes; do not let it brown. Remove from heat, change to a whisk, and add milk, whisking vigorously. Return to high heat and cook, stirring with whisk, until sauce comes to a boil and thickens. Add pepper, nutmeg, and Parmesan cheese; whisk until cheese melts. Stir some of the hot sauce into the eggs, to warm them; then stir the warmed eggs into the sauce. Mix sauce with cheese and set aside. Brush an oven-to-table baking dish (about 7 by 11 or 8 by 10 inches) with melted butter. Line dish with 4 filo sheets, brushing each sheet with melted butter as you lay it in. Let edges hang over dish. Pour in cheese mixture. Cover with remaining 4 filo sheets, again brushing each sheet with melted butter. Fold the overhang back over the top and brush with butter. (*Recipe can be made ahead to this point, and refrigerated or frozen.*) Bake in a preheated 350° oven for 30 minutes or until brown; the crust will puff up nicely. Serve immediately.

Note: If making recipe ahead, brush top well with melted butter and cover with plastic wrap. Refrigerate it if holding for more than 1 hour; let it come back to room temperature, still covered with wrap, before you bake it. It can be frozen, ready to bake, too. Defrost in refrigerator and then bring to room temperature. If you bake this and reheat it, it will not puff.

MUSTARD RING

2 tablespoons oil, to oil ring mold
1 tablespoon (1 envelope) unflavored gelatine
¼ cup lemon juice
4 beaten eggs
¾ cup sugar

2 tablespoons Dijon mustard
½ teaspoon salt
½ cup cider vinegar
½ cup water
1 cup heavy cream
2 tablespoons chopped parsley

Oil 4-cup ring mold and set aside. Soften gelatine in lemon juice and place over hot water, stirring to dissolve. In a non-aluminum saucepan combine eggs, sugar, mustard, salt, vinegar, and water, and beat well. Add gelatine mixture and place over low heat; stir with a whisk and cook until mixture thickens to custard consistency. Cool in refrigerator until mixture is on the point of setting. Whip heavy cream and fold into mixture along with parsley; pour into prepared mold and chill in the refrigerator until firm, at least 2 hours, or overnight.

PASKHA

1 cup unsalted butter
2 pounds cream cheese
3 egg yolks
2 cups confectioners' sugar
1 pint large-curd cottage cheese, optional
2 teaspoons vanilla extract
¾ cup toasted slivered almonds

8 ounces candied fruits *or* 8 ounces citron *or* 8 ounces mixed dark and light raisins
Fresh strawberries, for garnish
Angelica, for garnish

Bring butter, cheese, and egg yolks to room temperature. Put butter in large mixer bowl and beat, using the flat whip if you have a heavy-duty mixer, or beat by hand with wooden spatula. Beat in cream cheese and egg yolks, and add sugar a little at a time, lowering mixer speed as you do so. Drain cottage cheese (if adding it), press it through a sieve, and beat into mixture on low speed. Add vanilla, almonds, and candied fruits or raisins. Line a large sieve (or other container with drainage) with a double thickness of cheesecloth wrung out in cold water. Spoon in cheese mixture, smooth the top, and fold the cheesecloth over. Rest the sieve on the rim of a large bowl, so it can drain, and place in refrigerator overnight. When ready to serve, unmold dessert on a serving plate and decorate with 4 strawberry halves at center top and whole berries around base. Cut angelica into leaf shapes and add to berry decoration.

A Dinner for 6
Special Friends

Mussels en brochette, Béarnaise
Veal Orloff
Grilled tomatoes
Watercress salad
Macédoine of fruit
Sand tarts

Veal Orloff is a marvelous main course on two counts: it's rich and satisfying, so accompaniments can be simple and light. And it can be *completely* prepared a day ahead, ready for reheating. The mussels on skewers are deep-fried but exceedingly light. To serve 6, you'll want to halve the recipes for grilled tomatoes (p. 33) and macédoine of fruit (p. 61); and add an extra bunch of watercress to stretch the salad (p. 122). Any leftover sand tarts (see p. 62) can be frozen for later use.

MUSSELS EN BROCHETTE, BÉARNAISE

36 mussels
¼ cup dry white wine
Flour
1 recipe beer batter (see p. 285)

Fat for deep frying
1 recipe Béarnaise Sauce (see p. 282)

Scrub mussels well, remove beards, and wash in several changes of cold water. Put them in a pan with wine, cover, and shake over high heat until mussels open. Remove mussels from shells (the broth in the pan belongs to the cook), dip in flour, and thread on skewers—6 mussels to a skewer. (*Can be prepared ahead to this point.*) Dip the whole skewer in beer batter and deep-fry, 1 skewer at a time, in 3 inches of hot vegetable shortening (370° on frying thermometer), until brown and crisp, about 3 to 5 minutes. Drain on paper towels and keep warm in a low oven while you fry remaining mussels. Serve with Béarnaise Sauce.

Note: Mussels can be fully prepared ahead and reheated. To reheat: set cake racks on a baking sheet, cover with brown paper, lay skewers on the paper, and place in a 350° oven for several minutes.

VEAL ORLOFF

You can use almost any cut of veal—rump, shoulder, sirloin, or loin; loin is the most expensive. Have it boned and tied every inch to make a cylinder about 4 inches in diameter.

1 3-pound roast of veal, boned and tied (reserve bones)	Bouquet garni (see p. 283)
3 tablespoons butter	½ cup (more if needed) chicken stock (see p. 278) or dry white wine
1 tablespoon coarse salt	Soubise filling (recipe follows)
1 teaspoon freshly cracked black pepper	Mornay sauce (recipe follows)
1 tablespoon vegetable oil	
1 cup sliced onions	¼ cup bread crumbs
1 cup sliced carrots	1 tablespoon softened butter
1½ cups sliced celery	

Rub veal with 2 tablespoons butter, coarse salt, and pepper. Heat 1 tablespoon butter and the oil in a heavy casserole and brown the meat on all sides over high heat. Remove from casserole and brown the bones (this helps flavor the juices, which you'll use later to make the sauce). Stir in onions, carrots, and celery and cook over high heat until wilted. Return veal to casserole and add a bouquet garni and chicken stock or dry white wine. Cover pan with aluminum foil and casserole lid, and place in a preheated 325° oven to braise for about 1 hour. Veal is done when juices run clear when you prick it, or when meat thermometer reaches 170°. While the veal braises, prepare soubise filling.

When veal is done, remove it from the casserole and strain

the drippings into a 2-cup measure. Deglaze the casserole by pouring in a little chicken stock or white wine, letting it boil for 1 minute, and scraping up the brown bits. Add this liquid to drippings, along with enough chicken stock to make 1½ cups; prepare Mornay sauce, using this liquid. Carve the veal into slices about ¼ inch thick. Spoon about ½ cup of the Mornay sauce into a buttered ovenproof serving platter or au gratin dish. Spread each slice of veal with soubise filling and arrange the slices, overlapping, in the serving dish. Spread any remaining soubise over top of meat. Cover with Mornay sauce, sprinkle with bread crumbs, and dot with softened butter. (*Recipe can be made the day before to this point, covered with plastic wrap, and refrigerated; or it can be frozen for up to 1 month—thaw in refrigerator before reheating.*) Reheat before serving in a 400° oven until sauce bubbles; or run it under broiler to glaze.

SOUBISE FILLING

4 tablespoons butter	¼ cup heavy cream
4 cups chopped onions	2 egg yolks
6 tablespoons raw rice	1 tablespoon lemon juice
⅔ cup (more if needed) chicken stock (see p. 278)	1 teaspoon salt
	½ teaspoon pepper

Melt butter in a heavy ovenproof saucepan. Stir in onions and rice and cook for a minute, stirring, over high heat, to coat well with butter. Add chicken stock and bring to a boil. Cover tightly and set in preheated 325° oven. Look at it in 20 minutes; if dry, add a little more hot chicken stock. Continue cooking until onions and rice are tender, about 40 minutes total time. Puree through a food mill and stir in heavy cream, egg yolks, and lemon juice. Add more cream if necessary—the sauce should fall lazily from a spoon. Season with salt and pepper.

MORNAY SAUCE

3 tablespoons butter	½ cup heavy cream
4 tablespoons flour	¼ cup grated Swiss cheese
1½ cups liquid (drippings from veal plus chicken stock)	Salt
	Freshly cracked white pepper

Melt butter in a saucepan and stir in flour with a wooden spatula. Cook, stirring constantly, over high heat for at least 2 minutes. Do not let the flour brown. Take the pan off heat and add liquid all at once, beating vigorously with a whisk. Return pan to high heat and cook, stirring, until mixture thickens and comes to a boil. Stir in heavy cream and grated cheese; cook until cheese melts. Season to taste.

Dinner for 8,
with an American Flavor

Cherry tomatoes stuffed with guacamole
Sautéed crab meat on Virginia ham
Cornish hens with tangerines
Whipped sweet potatoes
Pecan pie

American foodstuffs and specialties highlight this unusual and satisfying menu. Serve the stuffed cherry tomatoes with drinks; they make a colorful, one-bite appetizer. Tangerines and juniper berries give the sauce for the Cornish hens a light, bright flavor, not at all sweet, and buttered and seasoned sweet potatoes are perfect with the birds. You'll find the recipe for Sautéed Crab Meat on Virginia Ham on page 34—but cut it back to serve 8. Use 8 slices of ham and 2 pounds of crab meat. The all-American ending is pecan pie.

CHERRY TOMATOES STUFFED
WITH GUACAMOLE

These are excellent served with drinks. Guacamole also makes a good dip. Keep the avocado pit buried in the mixture until serving time, to help keep it from discoloring, and serve with deep-fried pappadoms.

32 cherry tomatoes
 1 large ripe avocado
 1 tablespoon lime juice
 2 tablespoons grated onion
 1 tablespoon canned green
      chili sauce

 1 teaspoon salt
 2 teaspoons olive oil
 ¼ teaspoon ground coriander
      seed

Hollow out cherry tomatoes with a grapefruit knife. Peel and mash the avocado, add lime juice, grated onion, green chili sauce, salt, olive oil, and coriander seed, and whip with a whisk until smooth. Fill cherry tomatoes with mixture. *May be prepared ahead and refrigerated.*

CORNISH HENS WITH TANGERINES

 4 tangerines
 8 12- to 14-ounce Cornish hens
 6 tablespoons butter
 2 tablespoons vegetable oil
 ¼ cup brandy
 ¼ cup chopped shallots
 ½ pound sliced mushrooms
 1 tablespoon lemon juice
 1 teaspoon salt
 ½ teaspoon freshly cracked
      white pepper

 1 cup dry Marsala
 1 teaspoon potato starch or
      cornstarch
 1 tablespoon cold water
20 crushed juniper berries or
      2 tablespoons gin
 ½ teaspoon meat glaze,
      optional (see p. 280)
 1 bunch watercress

Peel the tangerines and separate them into segments; stuff into hens and truss. Heat 4 tablespoons butter and the oil in a heavy skillet and, over high heat, brown the hens all over. Place them in a large heavy casserole. Pour off fat from skillet and deglaze the pan with brandy; pour brandy over hens. Heat remaining 2 tablespoons butter in the skillet, add shallots, and cook for a minute or two, then add mushrooms, lemon juice, salt, and pepper. Toss over high heat for 3 minutes. Add Marsala and heat to boiling. Remove from heat; stir in potato starch dissolved in cold water. Return to heat and cook over high heat until sauce thickens. Pour mushroom sauce over hens in casserole. Sprinkle crushed juniper berries over (or substitute 2 tablespoons gin). Cover casserole with foil and heavy lid. (*May be prepared ahead to this point.*) Place casserole in a preheated 400° oven for about 30 minutes, or until birds test done (juices run clear when you prick the thick part of leg with a fork). Remove trussing strings, arrange birds on a serving platter, and keep warm. Taste the sauce, adding salt if necessary. If sauce is too thin, cook it down over high heat to reduce. Add ½ teaspoon meat glaze, if desired, to intensify flavor. Spoon sauce with mushrooms over each bird and decorate platter with watercress garnish. *If you wish to make dish completely ahead, undercook the birds by 15 minutes; cool to room temperature and refrigerate. Bring to room temperature before reheating; cook until birds test done, about 15 minutes.*

WHIPPED SWEET POTATOES

10 medium-size sweet potatoes
¾ cup butter
2 teaspoons salt
1 teaspoon freshly cracked white pepper
½ cup heavy cream

Scrub potatoes and put in a saucepan; cover with cold water. Bring to a boil, cover pan, reduce heat to maintain a low boil, and cook until potatoes are tender. Drain and peel while warm. Put through a potato ricer or food mill (medium disk). Put riced potatoes in mixer bowl and beat in ½ cup butter, salt, pepper, and heavy cream. Beat until fluffy. (*Recipe can be made ahead to this point. Reheat in pan over simmering water. Before serving, beat again with wooden spatula.*) Pile in serving dish and bury remaining ¼ cup butter in the middle.

PECAN PIE

½ recipe Sandy's piecrust (see p. 287)
1 cup dark corn syrup
1 cup sugar
4 beaten eggs
2 teaspoons vanilla extract
½ teaspoon salt
1 cup pecan halves

Roll out piecrust and fit into 9-inch pie pan. Mix together dark corn syrup and sugar. Stir in beaten eggs, vanilla, salt, and pecan halves. Pour into shell and bake in a preheated 350° oven for 50 to 60 minutes, or until knife inserted in center of pie comes out clean. *The pie can be completely baked ahead, and also frozen. Thaw it, in wrappings, at room temperature. Just before serving, reheat it for 5 minutes in a 350° oven.*

Early Dinner for 8
Before a Gala

Chicken with almonds
Gnocchi à la Parisienne
Watercress salad with cherry tomatoes
and chives
Poached pears in cassis

CHICKEN WITH ALMONDS

5 to 6 pounds chicken pieces,
mixed breasts, thighs,
and legs
2 teaspoons salt
1 teaspoon freshly cracked
white pepper
8 tablespoons butter
1½ cups finely chopped onion
3 finely chopped cloves garlic

1½ cups (more if needed)
chicken stock (see p. 278)
½ cup dry Madeira
1 cup blanched almonds,
finely ground
12 drops Tabasco sauce
2 tablespoons chopped
parsley

Wash and dry the chicken pieces and sprinkle with salt and pepper. Melt 6 tablespoons butter in a heavy casserole and brown chicken pieces. Remove from pan and keep warm. Add remaining 2 tablespoons butter to casserole, stir in onion and garlic, and cook, stirring, until onion is transparent—do not let it brown. Pour on chicken stock and Madeira and bring to a boil. Return chicken to casserole, turn heat to simmer, and cook, covered, for about 30 minutes, or until chicken is tender. Remove chicken from casserole and keep warm. Add ground almonds and Tabasco to casserole (12 drops is correct—this dish should have a hot taste), mix together, and puree in a blender. Return sauce—if it's too thick, thin it with a little chicken stock—and chicken to casserole. (*Recipe can be made ahead to this point.*) Before serving, heat through and sprinkle with chopped parsley.

GNOCCHI À LA PARISIENNE

1¾ cups water
4 tablespoons butter
1¾ cups lightly spooned flour
3 eggs
1 teaspoon Dijon mustard

2 teaspoons salt
1 teaspoon freshly cracked
   white pepper
¾ cup grated Parmesan cheese
4 tablespoons melted butter

Put water and 4 tablespoons butter, cut in pieces, into a saucepan and bring to a boil. As soon as butter melts, dump in the flour all at once and mix vigorously with a wooden spatula until mixture forms a smooth ball. Add eggs, 1 at a time, beating well. Beat in mustard, salt, pepper, and ½ cup grated Parmesan cheese. Pack mixture into a pastry bag fitted with a dime-size plain round tube and pipe it into a large pan three-quarters full of simmering water. Rest the bag on the side of the pan and press out the dough steadily, cutting it off in 1-inch pieces with a small knife. Simmer 15 minutes. With a slotted spoon, remove gnocchi to a buttered serving dish. (*May be made ahead to this point and reheated.*) Dress with 4 tablespoons melted butter and sprinkle with remaining ¼ cup grated cheese.

WATERCRESS SALAD WITH CHERRY TOMATOES AND CHIVES

Wash 4 bunches of watercress, remove stems, roll in towels, and chill. When ready to serve, toss with 16 cherry tomatoes, 2 tablespoons finely chopped fresh chives, and French vinaigrette dressing (see p. 282).

POACHED PEARS IN CASSIS

8 firm but ripe pears
2 cups sugar
3 cups water
2 inches of vanilla bean,
   or 1 teaspoon vanilla
   extract

SAUCE:
½ cup butter
1 cup sugar
¾ cup cassis syrup or crème
   de cassis
¼ cup kirsch

Peel but do not core pears and leave stems on. Cut a thin slice from bottoms so pears will stand upright. Heat sugar and water in saucepan, stirring until sugar dissolves. Cut vanilla bean lengthwise and scrape seeds into sugar water. Add the pod, too. Stand pears in syrup, cover pan with lid or aluminum foil, and simmer until pears are tender, basting occasionally. This may take from 5 to 25 minutes—it depends on ripeness of pears. Do not overcook; pears should not be mushy. (*Recipe may be prepared ahead to this point. Hold pears in poaching liquid.*)

To make sauce, melt butter and sugar in skillet, stirring constantly. When mixture is thick and white, like taffy—this takes about 5 minutes—add cassis and cook until sugar is completely dissolved. Remove pears from poaching liquid, put in sauce in skillet, and baste with sauce to warm them through. Warm kirsch in a small long-handled pan, ignite, and pour over pears. Serve pears with sauce.

A Dinner for 6
Frogs' Legs Lovers

Mushroom, onion, and sausage flan
Frogs' legs Provençale
Watercress and Belgian endive salad
Pears poached in white wine

Frogs' legs may be fried ahead of time, but don't try to keep them warm. Put them in a heatproof serving dish and let stand; when it's time to serve them, cover them with Provençale sauce and reheat on top of the stove. The flan may be made ahead and reheated. To adjust the Watercress and Belgian Endive Salad recipe (p. 42) for 6, use 4 instead of 6 heads of endive.

MUSHROOM, ONION, AND SAUSAGE FLAN

1 partly baked pâte brisée shell (see p. 288); use an 8-inch pan, 2 inches deep
1 recipe onion pie filling (see p. 85)
½ pound bulk sausage
½ pound sliced mushrooms
2 tablespoons butter
1 tablespoon lemon juice
½ teaspoon salt
¼ teaspoon freshly cracked black pepper

Prepare pâte brisée shell and onion pie filling. Cook sausage in a dry skillet over high heat, crumbling and stirring it until done. Drain on paper towels and cool. Sauté sliced mushrooms in butter, sprinkling with lemon juice, salt, and pepper, over high heat for 2 or 3 minutes; let cool. Stir drained sausage and mushrooms into onion pie filling and pour into the partly baked pastry shell. Bake in a preheated 350° oven for 20 to 25 minutes, or until custard tests done (when knife inserted in center comes out clean). *Flan may be reheated and it can be frozen.*

FROGS' LEGS PROVENÇALE

30 small frogs' legs	Fat for deep frying
¾ cup flour	Provençale Sauce (recipe
2 beaten eggs	follows)
¾ cup bread crumbs	

Dip frogs' legs in flour and then in beaten egg and roll in crumbs. Chill for about 15 minutes. Deep-fry a few at a time in 3 inches of hot vegetable shortening (365° to 370°) until brown and crisp, about 7 minutes. Drain on paper towels and place in heatproof serving dish. (*May be prepared ahead to this point.*) When ready to serve, pour Provençale Sauce over frogs' legs and simmer 10 minutes.

PROVENÇALE SAUCE

½ cup butter	½ pound sliced mushrooms
2 teaspoons finely chopped garlic	1 cup chopped green pepper
	2 tablespoons chopped parsley
2 tablespoons chopped shallots	2 cups chopped fresh or canned tomatoes
½ cup chopped onion	

Heat butter in saucepan. Cook garlic, shallots, and onion over high heat until onion is transparent, about 5 minutes—do not let them burn. Add mushrooms and green pepper and cook 5 minutes longer. Stir in chopped parsley and tomatoes and simmer for 15 to 20 minutes. *Sauce may be prepared ahead.*

PEARS POACHED IN WHITE WINE

8 firm but ripe pears
2 cups sugar

3 cups white wine, preferably
 dry
2 inches of vanilla bean

Peel pears, cut in half, and remove cores. Boil sugar and wine together, stirring until sugar dissolves. Cut vanilla bean length-

dinner with style.
wise, scraping seeds into syrup; drop the pod in, too. Add pears and cook over medium heat, basting them with the syrup, until they're tender but not mushy, about 10 to 15 minutes. Remove pears to a serving dish and boil syrup rapidly to reduce by one half. Pour syrup over pears. Serve warm or chilled.

A Chic Spring Dinner for 8

Poached shad roe, Hollandaise
Squabs or Cornish hens, à l'orange
Brown rice pilaf
White asparagus vinaigrette (see p. 115)
Almond torte

Ask me how to celebrate spring, and the first food I think of is shad roe. Rather than sautéing it, my mother always poached it; this is a twist you may like, too. Shad roe introduces a poultry

POACHED SHAD ROE, HOLLANDAISE

4 pairs shad roe
4 cups dry white wine
2 tablespoons chopped
 parsley

Hollandaise Sauce (see
 p. 281), substituting cooled
 cooking wine for lemon
 juice

Put roe in a shallow pan and cover with white wine. Bring to a boil, reduce heat, and simmer for 5 minutes. Carefully remove roe to a platter and keep warm. Sprinkle with chopped parsley, and serve with Hollandaise Sauce on the side.

SQUABS OR CORNISH HENS, À L'ORANGE

8 squabs, 1¼ to 1½ pounds, or
  8 Cornish hens, 12 to
  15 ounces
2 tablespoons coarse salt
2 teaspoons freshly cracked
  black pepper
4 oranges
½ cup sugar
½ cup red wine vinegar or
  cider vinegar
4 cups basic brown sauce
  (see p. 281)

¾ cup dry red wine
¼ cup Grand Marnier
1¼ cups bitter orange
  (Seville) marmalade
2 teaspoons potato starch or
  cornstarch, optional
3 tablespoons dry red wine,
  optional
1 bunch watercress, for
  garnish

Wash and dry birds thoroughly. Remove giblets, necks, and wing tips. Truss birds and rub them all over with salt and pepper. Place on racks in a roasting pan, add giblets and trimmings, and roast in a preheated 350° oven—1 hour and 15 minutes for squabs, 1 hour for Cornish hens, or until juices run clear when you prick leg.

While birds roast, prepare blanched orange peel for sauce: with a potato peeler, thinly peel 2 of the oranges. Cut peelings into slivers, that is, julienne them, with a chef's knife. Put the slivers into a saucepan, cover with cold water, bring to a rolling boil, drain, and rinse in cold water to set the color. Set aside. Reserve peeled oranges for garnish. Prepare a caramel for sauce: in a heavy pan dissolve sugar in vinegar, stirring, over low heat. When sugar is dissolved, tip the pan back and forth (without stirring) over medium-high heat until it turns to caramel, about 15 minutes. (Caramel will look like thin molasses and be very sticky.) Slowly add brown sauce to caramel, then ½ cup dry red wine and the Grand Marnier. Add the blanched orange peel, along with ¼ cup bitter orange marmalade. Taste for seasoning. Thicken sauce if you wish with potato starch, dissolved in 3 tablespoons dry red wine, or boil to reduce and thicken. You should have about 1½ cups sauce. (*Sauce may be made ahead to this point.*)

Fifteen minutes before birds are done, remove them from the oven and, with a pastry brush, spread over them the remaining 1 cup bitter orange marmalade. Return to oven to glaze. When birds are done, remove them to serving platter and keep warm. Pour off fat from roasting pan and deglaze pan with the remaining ¼ cup wine. Boil wine to loosen the brown bits, scraping at them if necessary, and strain into sauce. Decorate the serving platter with a bunch of watercress, orange sections from peeled and reserved oranges or serrated orange slices: with a lemon stripper, cut longitudinal grooves into the skin of the 2 remaining oranges, slice, then cut slices in half. Spoon a little sauce over each bird and pass the remainder.

BROWN RICE PILAF

Follow recipe for Brown Rice Pilaf with Pine Nuts (see p. 105), but omit pine nuts.

ALMOND TORTE

The flavor of torte layers is enhanced if they are baked 2 or 3 days in advance. Store at room temperature, covered with plastic wrap.

¾ pound blanched almonds, about—to make 3 cups ground	1 teaspoon almond extract
	2 tablespoons flour
	2 teaspoons baking powder
Oil for baking pans	⅛ teaspoon salt
6 eggs, separated	2 cups heavy cream
1½ cups plus 1 tablespoon sugar	4 tablespoons confectioners' sugar, plus more for sifting
2 teaspoons vanilla extract	

The day before baking torte layers, grind almonds in a blender and spread on a baking sheet to dry overnight. (Do not buy ground almonds—they're too fine.) Oil 2 8-inch round cake pans with vegetable oil, line with waxed paper, and oil paper; or line with baking parchment. Set aside. Beat egg yolks in an electric mixer bowl; add 1½ cups sugar gradually and continue beating until very thick and mixture forms ribbons. Beat in 1 teaspoon vanilla and ½ teaspoon almond extract. Mix flour and baking powder with nuts and fold into egg yolk mixture—batter will be stiff. Beat egg whites, adding 1 tablespoon sugar and the salt after they foam, and beat to stiff but not dry peaks. Fold into egg yolk–nut mixture. Spread in pans and bake in a preheated 375° oven for 25 to 30 minutes. Test with toothpick—if it comes out clean, torte is done. Cool on racks before removing torte from pans.

To serve, whip heavy cream, flavoring it with 4 tablespoons confectioners' sugar, 1 teaspoon vanilla, and ½ teaspoon almond extract. Spread half of whipped cream on bottom layer; top with second layer. Lay 2 strips of waxed paper across cake to make a cross and sift confectioners' sugar over exposed part of cake. Remove waxed paper. Pack remaining whipped cream into a pastry bag fitted with a star tube and pipe a rosette onto each quarter of cake. Pipe 8 ribbons of whipped cream up the sides of cake.

Cooking Lesson Show-off
Dinner for 8

Quenelles de brochet
Orange leg of lamb en croûte
Hearts of palm salad
Cold chocolate almond soufflé

When checking out a new restaurant, a knowledgeable gourmet frequently will order quenelles—an exacting test of a chef's skill. Undoubtedly this is why students in cooking school always want to learn how to make them; prepared correctly, nothing is more "show-off." The Orange Leg of Lamb en Croûte is an original recipe and a specialty of my school. Serve the salad with the lamb in this menu (although hearts of palm are usually served as a separate course).

QUENELLES DE BROCHET

1 pound boneless pike or
    haddock
4 tablespoons butter
1 cup water
1 cup lightly spooned flour
2 eggs
2 egg whites
¾ cup butter, at room
    temperature

⅓ cup heavy cream
3 teaspoons salt
½ teaspoon freshly grated
    nutmeg
Sauce (recipe follows)
¼ cup freshly grated
    Parmesan cheese
Butter to dot top of serving
    dish

Using the fine blade of a meat grinder, grind fish twice and set aside. To make a *panade,* or thickener, add 4 tablespoons butter, cut in chips, to water in saucepan and heat slowly until butter melts and water begins to boil. Dump in flour all at once and beat until the mixture clears the sides of the pan. Remove from heat and beat in eggs, one at a time. Add egg whites little by little and beat them in. Put *panade* in a bowl and, if you have a heavy-duty mixer, use the flat whip to beat in the ground fish 1 teaspoonful at a time. Otherwise, beat by hand, using a wooden spoon—mixture will clog a regular electric mixer attachment.

In another bowl, again using the flat whip, beat ¾ cup butter until light. Gradually beat in the fish mixture, 1 tablespoon at a time. Then beat in heavy cream, salt, and nutmeg. Cover and chill in refrigerator at least 30 minutes or overnight. While mixture chills, prepare sauce.

On a lightly floured board, shape quenelles into sausagelike pieces about 3 inches long. (*Quenelles can be prepared ahead to this point.*) Poach quenelles in simmering water for about 20 minutes. Drain well and arrange in a shallow ovenproof serving dish. Spoon hot sauce over them, sprinkle with grated Parmesan, and dot with butter. Run the dish under the broiler to brown lightly—about 5 minutes, but watch closely. *May also be fully prepared, including browning under broiler, and reheated in oven with the lamb (following recipe).*

SAUCE FOR QUENELLES DE BROCHET

FISH STOCK:
Skin, head, and bones of pike
  or a small piece of fish
1 cup dry white wine
3 cups water
½ cup chopped celery
½ cup chopped carrot
½ cup chopped onion
3 sprigs parsley
2 teaspoons salt

SAUCE:
6 tablespoons butter
4 tablespoons flour
1½ cups strained fish stock
½ cup light cream
¼ cup freshly grated
  Parmesan cheese
2 egg yolks
2 tablespoons dry sherry

Put skin, head, and bones of pike into a saucepan, or cut up small piece of fish. Add dry white wine and water and bring to a boil. Skim. Add celery, carrot, onion, parsley, and salt. Simmer about 1 hour, strain, and reserve.

To make sauce, melt butter in saucepan, stir in flour, and cook over high heat, stirring with wooden spatula, for 2 minutes— do not let it brown. Remove from heat, change to a whisk, and add strained fish stock, whisking vigorously. Return to medium-high heat and cook, stirring, until sauce comes to a boil and thickens. Stir in ⅓ cup of the light cream and the grated Parmesan cheese. Beat egg yolks lightly with a fork. Beat in sherry and remaining light cream. Stir in some of the hot sauce to warm egg yolks, then stir egg yolk mixture into the sauce. Return to heat and cook until sauce thickens—do not let it boil. Taste for seasoning. *Sauce may be prepared ahead and reheated.*

ORANGE LEG OF LAMB EN CROÛTE

1 6- to 7-pound leg of lamb, partly boned
Peel of 1 orange
½ cup butter
2 teaspoons rosemary
1 chopped clove garlic
2 tablespoons vegetable oil
2 teaspoons coarse salt
½ teaspoon freshly cracked black pepper
Pastry (recipe follows)
1 egg yolk
1 bunch watercress, for garnish
1 orange, for garnish

Remove center (thigh) bone from lamb, leaving the end bone. Cut a thin peel about 5 inches long from the orange and cut into slivers. Poke slivers into the meat by inserting the point of a small knife in the fatty side and using the knife blade as a slide to push slivers down into the meat. Grate the remaining orange peel; you should have 1 tablespoonful. Cream butter with grated orange peel, 1 teaspoon rosemary, and the chopped garlic. Pack this butter into the cavity where thigh bone was removed. Brush lamb all over with oil and rub with salt, pepper, and remaining 1 teaspoon rosemary. Place lamb on a baking tray and roast in a preheated 500° oven for 15 minutes to sear meat. Remove from oven and cool to room temperature.

On a floured board roll out pastry ¼ inch thick, in a rectangular shape to cover lamb. Trim off irregular edges (save trimmings for decoration), roll pastry over pin, and unroll over lamb, pressing around meat but not covering meat on bottom side. Paint crust with egg yolk mixed with 1 tablespoon cold water. Cut trimmings into petal and leaf shapes, apply to crust, and paint with egg wash. Prick crust all over with tip of knife. (*Can be done ahead to this point and refrigerated or frozen. If frozen, defrost in refrigerator and bring to room temperature before baking.*) Place the wrapped lamb on a baking tray and bake in a preheated 375° oven 12 minutes per pound for very rare lamb, 15 minutes for medium, and 18 for well done. Garnish platter with a bunch of watercress and an orange cut in half with a zigzag, serrated cut.

PASTRY

2 teaspoons salt
3 cups lightly spooned flour
1¾ *sticks* butter (¾ cup plus 2 tablespoons)

4 tablespoons solid vegetable shortening
½ cup iced water

Stir salt into flour and cut in butter and shortening until mixture looks like coarse meal. Add just enough ice water (no more than ½ cup) so you can gather the mixture into a ball. Wrap the ball in waxed paper or plastic wrap and refrigerate at least ½ hour or overnight.

HEARTS OF PALM SALAD

3 1-pound cans hearts of palm
8 lettuce leaves

1 recipe French vinaigrette dressing (see p. 282)
3 tablespoons chopped parsley

Rinse and dry hearts of palm. Cut in rounds or leave in strips; count 2 strips per person. Arrange on lettuce leaves on individual salad plates. Spoon 2 tablespoons vinaigrette over each salad and sprinkle with chopped parsley.

COLD CHOCOLATE ALMOND SOUFFLÉ

2 tablespoons (2 envelopes) unflavored gelatine
½ cup rum
8 ounces dark sweet chocolate
2 cups light cream
1 cup confectioners' sugar

½ teaspoon salt
5 cups heavy cream
½ cup slivered toasted salted almonds
¾ cup shaved chocolate

Make a waxed paper collar for a 2-quart soufflé dish by folding paper in half, lengthwise, brushing inside edge with vegetable oil, and tying it around the top of the dish so that it extends 4 to 5 inches above it. Set aside. Sprinkle gelatine into rum in a cup, let stand a few minutes, then set the cup in a pan of boiling water and stir to dissolve gelatine. In a saucepan, over medium-high heat, melt chocolate in light cream and beat with a whisk until smooth. Beat in dissolved gelatine, confectioners' sugar, and salt. Remove from heat and let cool until the mixture is almost at the point of setting. Whip 4 cups of the heavy cream and gradually beat in the chocolate mixture a little at a time, whisking until smooth after each addition. Fold in almonds. Pour into prepared dish and refrigerate for at least 3 to 4 hours. (*Recipe can be done to this point the day before.*) Whip remaining 1 cup heavy cream. Remove paper collar and decorate soufflé with rosettes of whipped cream. Sprinkle with shaved chocolate.

A Dinner for 6
Sweetbread Lovers

Ris de veau, velouté sauce
Broccoli timbales
Cherry tomatoes vinaigrette
Oranges Grand Marnier (see p. 84)

RIS DE VEAU, VELOUTÉ SAUCE

6 pairs calves' sweetbreads
½ cup flour
1½ cups heavy cream
6 tablespoons butter
4 tablespoons Calvados
1 finely chopped truffle
1 teaspoon finely chopped garlic

1 teaspoon tomato paste
2 cups chicken stock (see p. 278)
1 teaspoon salt
½ teaspoon freshly cracked white pepper
2 tablespoons chopped parsley

Put sweetbreads in a pan and cover them with cold water. Slowly bring them to a boil, reduce heat, and simmer, uncovered, for 5 to 7 minutes. Turn over once during cooking. Drain and plunge immediately into ice water. Carefully remove the skin, sinews, and tubes. Cut them in half lengthwise and lay them on a plate. Cover with another plate and weight; place in the refrigerator for at least 1 hour.

When ready to cook, dry sweetbreads with paper towels and dust lightly with ¼ cup flour. Barely whip the heavy cream—just past the foaming stage—and set aside. Heat 4 tablespoons butter in a large skillet, over high heat. When butter is foaming, add sweetbreads—do not let them touch each other—and cover them with a flat lid and weight, to keep them flat. Brown 1 minute on each side. Flame them with Calvados; when flames die, remove sweetbreads and set aside. Scrape up brown bits. Stir in truffle and garlic and cook 1 minute. Add tomato paste and remaining 2 tablespoons butter. Stir in remaining ¼ cup flour with a wooden spatula and cook, stirring, for 2 minutes—do not let it brown. Remove from heat, change to a whisk, and add chicken stock, whisking vigorously. Return to high heat and cook sauce until it thickens and comes to a boil, stirring. Beat heavy cream into the sauce. Season with salt and pepper. Return sweetbreads to skillet, basting them with the sauce. (*Recipe can be made ahead to this point, covered, and refrigerated.*) Cover skillet with aluminum foil and a heavy lid and simmer over low heat for 15 minutes. Arrange on a serving platter and spoon sauce over; sprinkle with chopped parsley.

BROCCOLI TIMBALES

Follow recipe for Spinach Timbales, on page 121, but substitute frozen chopped broccoli for the spinach, omit the nutmeg, and add 1 tablespoon lemon juice.

CHERRY TOMATOES VINAIGRETTE

Count 8 cherry tomatoes per person; put them in a salad bowl with French vinaigrette dressing (see p. 282) and 2 tablespoons chopped parsley. Mix well and marinate for 2 hours at room temperature, turning occasionally, before serving.

An Old-Fashioned
Shore Dinner for 8

Clams on the half shell (see p. 266)
Baked stuffed fish
Corn on the cob
Beefsteak tomatoes and chives
marinated in sour cream dressing
Strawberries over homemade
vanilla ice cream

BAKED STUFFED FISH

1 whole striped bass, 4 to 6
    pounds, or other whole
    fish such as bluefish or
    mackerel
1 tablespoon salt
1 teaspoon freshly cracked
    black pepper
    Juice of ½ lemon
3 tablespoons butter
3 tablespoons chopped
    shallots
1½ to 2 cups chopped mush-
    rooms

    Salt and pepper
2 tablespoons chopped parsley
½ cup bread crumbs
½ cup plus 2 tablespoons dry
    white wine
4 tablespoons melted butter
    Mushroom Sauce (recipe
    follows)
1 thinly sliced lemon, for
    garnish
2 tablespoons chopped parsley,
    for garnish

Scale and clean the fish—or ask fish seller to do it—with the head and tail left intact. Wash the fish well in cold water and trim the tail neatly. To make more room for the stuffing, cut 2 pockets in the fish, one each side of the backbone, by slitting from the belly, with the knife blade parallel—and close—to the backbone. Be careful not to cut through the back of the fish. Salt and pepper the 2 cavities you've made and sprinkle with lemon juice. To make stuffing, melt butter in a skillet and add the shallots. Cook for a minute or two over high heat, then add the chopped mushrooms and toss over high heat. Add salt and pepper to taste, parsley, and bread crumbs. Moisten with 2 tablespoons dry white wine. Pack the stuffing into the fish along the bone and skewer the opening crosswise. Butter an ovenproof serving dish and curl the fish into it, belly down—the skewers will form a platform to hold the fish in position. Cover fish's head and tail with aluminum foil. Sprinkle fish with salt and pepper and brush with one third each of the melted butter and ½ cup dry white wine. Place in a preheated 400° oven and bake for about 30 minutes (figure about 8 minutes per pound), but test for doneness after 25 minutes— touch fish with a toothpick to see if it flakes. Baste fish with butter and wine 2 times while baking. When done, use a bulb baster to take up the juice in the serving dish and add it to the Mushroom Sauce. Decorate the back of the fish with lemon slices dipped in parsley and serve fish at once from cooking dish. Pass sauce separately.

MUSHROOM SAUCE

4 tablespoons butter
4 tablespoons flour
2 cups fish stock, if available
   (see p. 279) or clam juice
1 cup sliced mushrooms
¼ cup dry white wine
1 teaspoon salt

½ teaspoon freshly cracked
   black pepper
1 tablespoon chopped parsley
3 egg yolks, optional
3 tablespoons heavy cream,
   optional

Melt butter in a saucepan and stir in flour with a wooden spatula. Cook over high heat, stirring constantly, for 2 minutes to cook flour, but do not let it brown. Remove from heat, change to a whisk, and add the fish stock all at once, whisking vigorously. Return to heat and bring to a boil, whisking. In another pan, cook mushrooms in white wine over high heat until all liquid is absorbed. Do not let the mushrooms burn—shake the pan as they cook. Pour the sauce into the mushrooms, add salt, pepper, and parsley. (*May be prepared ahead to this point.*) When ready to proceed, add juices from pan in which fish has cooked, and enrich the sauce if you wish: beat together egg yolks and heavy cream, stir a little hot sauce into the egg yolk—cream mixture to warm it, and stir this mixture back into the sauce. Heat sauce through, but do not let it boil.

CORN ON THE COB

Count 1 or 2 ears per person. Buy it on the same day you plan to serve it, store in refrigerator, and husk just before cooking. Drop ears into a big kettle of unsalted boiling water. (Add 1 teaspoon sugar if you think your corn is a bit mature.) Boil from 3 to 6 minutes after water returns to boil—do not overcook. Serve hot with plenty of melted butter, salt, and pepper in a mill.

BEEFSTEAK TOMATOES AND CHIVES MARINATED IN SOUR CREAM DRESSING

5 or 6 beefsteak tomatoes
¼ cup chopped chives
¾ cup dairy sour cream
2 tablespoons tarragon vinegar

1 teaspoon salt
½ teaspoon freshly cracked pepper

Peel tomatoes if you wish and slice ½ inch thick. Allow 3 slices per person. Overlap in a flat serving dish and sprinkle with chopped chives. Mix sour cream with vinegar, salt, and pepper and pour over tomatoes. Let marinate for 1 hour in refrigerator before serving.

STRAWBERRIES OVER HOMEMADE VANILLA ICE CREAM

3 cups light cream
4 eggs, separated
1½ cups sugar
2 tablespoons cornstarch

1 tablespoon vanilla extract
½ teaspoon salt
2 cups heavy cream
3 pints strawberries

In a nonaluminum pan, scald the light cream. Beat egg yolks and beat in 1 cup sugar and the cornstarch. Slowly pour scalded cream onto egg yolk mixture, stirring, and place over low heat. Cook until custard coats the back of a spoon, about 10 minutes, stirring constantly. Let cool. When cool, stir in vanilla. Beat egg whites with salt until stiff and fold them into custard. Pour into freezer trays and chill until the mixture is a heavy mush. Put it into a bowl and beat it until fluffy. Whip the heavy cream—not too stiff—and fold it into the mixture. Return to freezer trays.

Make ice cream a few hours ahead to be sure it chills thoroughly and becomes really firm.

If you have an ice-cream freezer, do not whip the heavy cream. Instead, add it, unwhipped, to the egg yolk custard along with the beaten egg whites. Pour the mixture into freezer can and freeze following directions for your freezer.

Prepare strawberries about 1 hour before serving. Hull the berries, dip them quickly in and out of water, and leave them whole or slice them in half. Sprinkle with ½ cup sugar and let stand. Mash them slightly before serving if you wish.

An Adult Birthday Dinner
for 4 to 6

Beef Burgundy
Barley pilaf
Carrot salad
Gâteau Saint-Honoré

St. Honoré is the patron saint of pastrycooks and bakers and the "cake" that is named in his honor is a *tour de force* of the pastry chef's artistry. It's not an American-style layer cake. The base is rolled-out pastry baked with a ring of cream puff paste. The center that results from this construction is filled with pastry cream, and the cake is further embellished with tiny cream puffs around the rim and a lacy network of caramel threads over the top. It is chilled before serving, so you can do it all ahead.

BEEF BURGUNDY

3 pounds beef round, sirloin, or chuck, cut in 2-inch cubes
6 tablespoons butter
1 teaspoon salt
½ teaspoon freshly cracked black pepper
½ cup brandy, about
2 teaspoons chopped garlic
3 tablespoons chopped shallots
2 teaspoons dried or 2 tablespoons fresh tarragon
1 teaspoon tomato paste
4 teaspoons potato starch or cornstarch
2½ cups chicken stock (see p. 278)
1 cup dry red wine
1 bouquet garni (see p. 283)
12 small white onions
12 mushroom caps
2 tablespoons finely chopped parsley

Dry beef cubes with paper towels. Heat 4 tablespoons butter in a heavy casserole and brown the beef cubes on all sides over high heat—do not let pieces touch. Sprinkle with salt and pepper and flame with 3 tablespoons of the brandy. (*Warm brandy in a small pan, ignite, and pour it, flaming, over beef.*) Remove beef from pan, add the remaining 2 tablespoons butter, and stir to loosen brown bits. Stir in garlic and shallots and cook for a minute. Then stir in tarragon, tomato paste, and potato starch and let cook 2 minutes more. Add chicken stock, wine, and bouquet garni. Return beef to casserole. (*May be prepared ahead to this point.*) Bring sauce to a boil, cover the casserole with aluminum foil and a heavy lid, and place in a preheated 350° oven to simmer for about 1½ hours or until beef is tender. Baste 3 times during cooking with 2 tablespoons brandy each time. While beef simmers, peel onions and parboil for 15 minutes, and clean and trim mushroom caps. Add them to casserole the last 30 minutes of cooking. When ready to serve, sprinkle with chopped parsley. *May be completely made ahead and reheated. If you plan to do this, undercook the dish slightly and wait until the reheating to add onions and mushrooms.*

BARLEY PILAF

4 tablespoons butter
1½ cups chopped onions
1¾ cups pearl barley
3½ to 4 cups chicken stock (see p. 278)
1 teaspoon salt
½ teaspoon freshly cracked black pepper

Melt butter in a heavy casserole, stir in onions and cook, stirring, over high heat until onions are transparent. Add barley and continue cooking and stirring until golden brown. Pour on 1¾ cups of the chicken stock, add salt and pepper, and bring to a boil. Cover and place in a preheated 350° oven. Bake for 30 minutes; add 1¾ cups more chicken stock and continue baking for 30 minutes longer. If barley looks dry, add another ½ cup chicken stock. Bake 20 minutes longer or until barley is tender but not mushy.

CARROT SALAD

1 pound carrots
½ cup French vinaigrette
  dressing (see p. 282)
¼ cup grated orange peel

2 tablespoons mayonnaise
  Salt and pepper, optional

Marinate the grated orange peel in vinaigrette dressing for 1 hour. Shred the carrots—you should have about 2½ to 3 cups. Mix dressing with mayonnaise and toss with carrots. Taste for seasoning and add salt and pepper if desired.

GÂTEAU SAINT-HONORÉ

½ recipe for pâte brisée pastry
  (see p. 288)
1 recipe pâte à choux (cream
  puff paste, see p. 286)
1 egg yolk

1 tablespoon water
  Pastry cream (recipe fol-
  lows)
  Caramel (recipe follows)

Prepare pâte brisée pastry, wrap it in waxed paper, and put it in the refrigerator to chill. Prepare pâte à choux paste and pack it into a large pastry bag fitted with a round tube. Roll out the pâte brisée pastry ⅛ inch thick and trim it to make an 8-inch circle. Place the pastry circle on a baking tray lined with baking parchment (if you do not have baking parchment, grease the baking tray) and prick it all over with a fork. Beat egg yolk with water and brush it around the edge of the pastry circle. Pipe a ring of pâte à choux paste around the edge of the pastry circle, ¼ inch inside. Pipe a second ring on top of the first. Pipe out remaining paste onto the baking parchment to make 8 to 10 individual small puffs. With the back of a spoon, flatten any points on the puffs and brush the *tops only* of ring and puffs with egg yolk mixture; don't let it dribble down the sides, or the puffs won't rise. Place in a preheated 425° oven and bake for 15 minutes. Quickly poke the tip of a knife into the sides of both the puffs and the rings in 4 places; return to oven and bake for 20 minutes more at 375°. While pastry circle is baking, prepare pastry cream.

When both pastry ring and pastry cream filling are cool, fill the shell with the pastry cream. Also, split the individual puffs and fill them with pastry cream. Prepare the caramel, dip the bottoms of the filled puffs in the hot caramel, and stick them to the top of the ring. When caramel spins a thread, dip a fork into it and wave it over the cake, round and round; continue until the cake is laced with caramel threads. *May be fully prepared ahead; serve chilled.*

PASTRY CREAM

1 egg	1 cup scalded milk
1 egg yolk	1 teaspoon vanilla extract
3 tablespoons sugar	1 cup heavy cream
3 tablespoons flour	2 tablespoons confectioners'
2 teaspoons unflavored gelatine	sugar

Combine egg, egg yolk, sugar, and flour in a bowl and beat well with a whisk. Stir in gelatine. Slowly pour scalded milk into egg mixture, whisking constantly. Return mixture to saucepan (nonaluminum) and stir it over low heat until it thickens. Mixture scorches easily, so move the whisk all around the pan; let it bubble just once and remove from heat. Add vanilla. Set the pan in a bowl of ice to chill, and stir constantly for about 5 minutes; or chill it in the refrigerator, stirring frequently, for about 20 minutes. When cool, whip the heavy cream, sweetening it with confectioners' sugar, and fold whipped cream into pastry cream.

CARAMEL

Put ⅔ cup sugar, ½ cup water, and ¼ teaspoon cream of tartar into a small skillet and cook over medium heat, stirring until sugar dissolves. Then tip the pan over heat, swirling the mixture, until it turns quite brown. This takes about 15 minutes. Remove from heat immediately.

Buffets

Buffets are the dinners (or lunches or breakfasts) you plan when your guest list grows beyond the capacity of your dining table, or when you expect to manage things yourself without help. Your guests serve themselves—and save you a good deal of work.

Not only the ease of buffets but the help-yourself fun of them have made them increasingly popular. Many of the dinners in the preceding chapter can be served as buffets, although you may want to make a change or two in the menus. Successful buffet food must be a little more durable than food served directly from the kitchen to already seated guests. Electric hot trays and carts are invaluable for maintaining food at the proper temperature without further cooking. Chafing dishes, sectioned serving dishes set over hot water, even a spirit lamp or Sterno are other alternatives. There's no reason to rule out a three-course menu. You can serve a first course with drinks and later offer desserts at a separate buffet table, which you might set up in another room, with coffee.

If possible, I like to seat my guests at tables even when I serve buffet-style, particularly if they will need to use both a fork *and* knife. If this means setting up card tables, or even individual tables, fine—any surface is better than your lap. When guests don't have to carry their own silver and napkins, I count it a plus.

When you're in the planning stages for your party, bring out your serving dishes and decide early on what goes in what. Compose a logical and interesting arrangement, playing off round, square, oblong, and oval shapes for contrast. An effective buffet also has an up-and-down dimension, and a tiered server can help you out in this. Remind yourself of food colors as you read recipes. Guests should get hungry just approaching your table.

A Lap Buffet
for 12

Salami cornucopias on pumpernickel (see p. 63)
Coulibiac of beef with mustard Hollandaise
Baked tomatoes with Soubise
Endive, mushroom, and cucumber salad
Pistachio Bavarian cream

COULIBIAC OF BEEF
WITH MUSTARD HOLLANDAISE

1 recipe brioche (see p. 11)
PANADE:
2 cups water
1 teaspoon salt
6 tablespoons farina
2 eggs
3 tablespoons butter
¼ cup freshly grated Parmesan
   cheese
1 teaspoon dry mustard
1 teaspoon Dijon mustard

FILLING:
2 thinly sliced mushrooms
2 teaspoons butter
   Few drops of lemon juice
¼ teaspoon salt
⅛ teaspoon freshly ground
   black pepper

2 tablespoons fresh chopped
   dill
1 teaspoon finely chopped
   garlic
1 tablespoon finely chopped
   shallots
1 cup sour cream
1½ pounds fillet of beef, cut in
   finger-size pieces
3 finely chopped hard-cooked
   eggs

¼ cup melted butter
1 egg yolk
1 tablespoon water
2 teaspoons Dijon mustard
1 recipe Hollandaise Sauce
   (see p. 281)

Make brioche dough the day before and refrigerate it overnight. Prepare the *panade,* or thickener: heat water in a saucepan
to boiling, add salt, and slowly pour in farina, stirring constantly.
Cook, stirring, over high heat, until thick. Remove from heat and
beat in eggs—do this quickly, so eggs won't scramble. Beat in
butter, grated cheese, and mustards and place in refrigerator to
chill, at least ½ hour. Sauté the mushrooms for the filling in butter

for 2 minutes, sprinkling them with lemon juice, salt, and pepper; set aside. Stir dill, garlic, and shallots into sour cream and set aside. (*May be prepared ahead to this point.*)

To assemble coulibiac: brush a 6 x 10 x 3-inch loaf pan with oil. Turn the refrigerated brioche dough out onto a lightly floured board; dough will be sticky. Cut off about one quarter of the dough and put it back in the refrigerator. Roll out remaining dough to make a rectangle about 12 x 16 inches, and line the pan with it, tucking dough into corners and pinching it over the edge of the pan. Brush dough with ¼ cup melted butter. Spread about a third of the farina *panade* into the mold and then add, in layers, half of each of the sour cream, beef, mushrooms, and hard-cooked eggs. Repeat layers, ending with a final layer of farina. Roll out reserved brioche dough to make a lid. Beat the egg yolk with the 1 tablespoon water (to make egg wash) and brush top edges of brioche in pan with it; press lid in place, pinching edges together. Cover with a towel and let stand about 20 minutes. Cut slits in lid and brush dough all over with more egg wash. (*Recipe can be made ahead to this point and refrigerated.*) Place pan on a baking sheet and bake in a preheated 425° oven for 40 minutes. If crust browns too fast, cover it loosely with aluminum foil.

To unmold coulibiac, loosen it around the edges with a knife and ease it out with a wide spatula. Or serve it in the pan, dressed up in a pleated paper ruffle around outside of pan. If you bake coulibiac in a throwaway aluminum pan, you can cut the pan away to unmold it. Serve with Mustard Hollandaise, made by adding—after sauce is made—2 teaspoons Dijon mustard to 1 recipe Hollandaise Sauce.

BAKED TOMATOES WITH SOUBISE

6 to 8 tomatoes
1 teaspoon salt
½ teaspoon freshly cracked
　black pepper

1 recipe soubise filling (see
　p. 157)
¼ cup freshly grated Parmesan
　cheese

Slice tomatoes ½ inch thick; allow 2 slices per person. Sprinkle with salt and pepper and lay on a baking tray. Put 1 tablespoonful of soubise filling on each tomato piece and top with 1 teaspoon Parmesan cheese. (*May be prepared ahead to this point.*) Bake in a preheated 350° oven until tops are bubbly, about 15 to 20 minutes, or at 425° for about 10 minutes.

ENDIVE, MUSHROOM, AND CUCUMBER SALAD

6 heads Belgian endive
1 pound white mushrooms
2 cucumbers
2 tablespoons finely chopped
   parsley

2 tablespoons finely chopped
   shallots
French vinaigrette dressing
   (see p. 282)

Trim root ends of endive, removing any discolored leaves, and wash and drain. With a chef's knife, cut into julienne pieces. Clean mushrooms in acidulated water (1 tablespoon lemon juice to 1 quart water), trim stems, and slice thinly. Peel cucumbers with potato peeler and slice thinly. Put in a chilled bowl and sprinkle with chopped parsley. Add chopped shallots to vinaigrette and, just before serving, pour over vegetables and toss to mix.

PISTACHIO BAVARIAN CREAM

5 eggs, separated
5 rounded tablespoons sugar
2 tablespoons (2 envelopes)
   unflavored gelatine
1½ cups scalded milk
2 to 3 tablespoons dark rum
3 or 4 drops green food
   coloring

1½ cups heavy cream
½ cup plus 2 tablespoons
   chopped natural pistachio
   nuts
1 tablespoon confectioners'
   sugar

Oil a 9 x 1½-inch pan with loose bottom and set aside. With a whisk, beat egg yolks, sugar, and gelatine until thick and sticky. Scald milk (do not use aluminum pan) and slowly pour into egg yolk mixture in a thin stream, whisking. Return mixture to pan and cook over low heat, stirring constantly, until it coats the back of a spoon. Remove from heat and cool—stir it over ice, or place in refrigerator, stirring a few times, until cooked base is syrupy, on the point of setting. Flavor with rum and tint with food coloring. Beat egg whites to soft peaks and fold into base. Whip ¾ cup of heavy cream—not too stiff—and fold it into base, along with ½ cup chopped pistachios. Pour into prepared pan and place in refrigerator to set for at least 2 hours, preferably overnight. (*Recipe can be made ahead to this point; it will freeze.*) Unmold on serving plate and decorate with rosettes of remaining ¾ cup heavy cream, sweetened with 1 tablespoon confectioners' sugar. Sprinkle with remaining 2 tablespoons chopped pistachios.

A Sit-down Buffet
for 12

Mussels marinière
Beef à la mode
Garniture bourgeoise
Russian gnocchi
Beet salad
Mont Blanc

MUSSELS MARINIÈRE

10 quarts mussels
1½ cups chopped celery
1½ cups chopped onions
3 tablespoons chopped shallots
2 tablespoons chopped parsley, plus ½ cup for garnish

6 thin slices lemon
1 teaspoon freshly cracked black pepper
1 teaspoon salt
½ teaspoon thyme
3 cups dry vermouth

Scrub mussels, using several changes of cold water, and remove beards with a stiff brush or knife. This is a difficult job and will take time; discard any mussels that are open. Put the scrubbed mussels into a *very* large pot with remaining ingredients (except parsley for garnish), cover, bring to a boil, turn down to simmer, and cook, shaking the pot often, for about 12 minutes, or until all mussels open. Discard any mussels that do not open during cooking. When ready to serve, remove mussels with a slotted spoon to soup plates. Divide the broth among the plates and sprinkle with chopped parsley.

BEEF À LA MODE

1 8-pound beef roast, eye of
   the round or boned rump,
   cut in a long narrow
   shape
1 cup chopped onions
1 cup chopped carrots
1 cup chopped celery, including leaves
1 chopped clove garlic
1 bay leaf
½ teaspoon thyme
5 or 6 sprigs of parsley

2½ cups dry red wine
1 teaspoon salt
½ teaspoon freshly cracked
   black pepper
⅓ cup plus 2 tablespoons
   brandy
2 tablespoons butter
2 tablespoons oil
1 veal knuckle or calf's foot
1 teaspoon potato starch or
   cornstarch, optional
1 bunch watercress

Tie, or have the butcher tie, the meat every 2 inches so that it will retain its round shape. In a nonaluminum casserole large enough to hold beef, mix together the onions, carrots, celery, garlic, bay leaf, thyme, parsley, wine, salt, pepper, and ⅓ cup brandy, and marinate meat, in the refrigerator, for at least 12 hours or overnight, turning it over with wooden spatulas every 2 hours or so. Remove meat—reserving marinade—and pat dry with paper towels. Heat the butter and oil in a heavy skillet and brown the meat thoroughly, over high heat—take at least 20 minutes for this. Pour off excess fat from pan, warm 2 table-spoons brandy in a small long-handled pan, ignite it, and pour it over meat. When flames die, return meat to casserole. Scrape up brown bits in skillet and add them to the marinade in the cas-serole. Add the veal knuckle or calf's foot. Cover casserole with aluminum foil and a heavy lid and braise in a preheated 350° oven for 2½ to 3 hours. Turn the meat at least twice during cook-ing. Beef is done when a fork can be easily inserted into meat. (*Recipe can be made ahead to this point the day before and re-heated gently on the top of the stove—in flameproof casserole—or in 350° oven.*)

Remove beef to carving board and keep warm. Skim fat from liquid in casserole. If meat has rendered a lot of juice, cook it over high heat to reduce and concentrate the sauce to 3 cups. Taste for seasoning. Serve it as is, or puree it through a food mill, using fine disk, or in the blender. Thicken it, if you wish, with potato starch dissolved in a little cold water or wine. Let beef rest 15 minutes before carving into thin slices. Arrange slices, overlapping, on a serving platter, spoon sauce over beef, and decorate platter with a bunch of watercress.

GARNITURE BOURGEOISE

24 small white onions	½ teaspoon freshly cracked
5 or 6 carrots	black pepper
Suet	2 tablespoons melted butter
½ teaspoon salt	1 teaspoon sugar

Peel onions and parboil about 15 minutes. Cut carrots diagonally into 24 pieces and parboil 15 minutes. Fry suet over high heat to render beef fat—you need about ¼ cup. Arrange vegetables 1 layer deep in an ovenproof serving dish, sprinkle with salt and pepper, and spoon melted butter and beef fat over them, being sure to coat each piece. Sprinkle with sugar to give them a glaze. Place on bottom shelf of a preheated 350° oven and bake until brown and crisp, about 1 hour, basting occasionally. Serve in separate dish to accompany Beef à la Mode. *May be made ahead and reheated.*

RUSSIAN GNOCCHI

Very delicate, Russian gnocchi are also an excellent accompaniment to Beef Stroganoff or any kind of beef stew.

1 pound cottage cheese	½ teaspoon freshly cracked
½ pound cream cheese	white pepper
2 beaten eggs	¾ cup freshly grated
¼ to ½ cup lightly spooned flour	Parmesan cheese
1 teaspoon plus 1 tablespoon salt	10 tablespoons melted unsalted butter

Push the cottage cheese and cream cheese through a fine sieve into a mixing bowl. Add the beaten eggs and beat well with a wooden spatula. Stir in flour, 2 tablespoons at a time, adding just enough to bind the mixture. Season with 1 teaspoon salt and the pepper, cover, and refrigerate for at least 30 minutes. Bring about 3 inches of water to boil in a large pan or deep skillet. Add 1 tablespoon salt to water. Reduce heat to simmer and drop cheese mixture by the teaspoonful into simmering water. (It helps to dip the spoon in cold water and to use a second spoon as a pusher.) Simmer gnocchi—do not let boil—for about 20 minutes. When cooked, they'll rise to the surface and be firm to your touch. (*Recipe may be made ahead to this point, cooled in water, and gently reheated at serving time.*) Drain gnocchi and sprinkle with Parmesan cheese and melted butter.

BEET SALAD

8 medium-size beets
6 hard-cooked eggs
1 red onion
1 teaspoon salt
½ teaspoon freshly cracked
    black pepper
½ cup tarragon vinegar
¾ cup oil
    Romaine lettuce leaves to
    line salad bowl
2 tablespoons chopped parsley

Scrub fresh beets with a brush. Cut stems 2 inches above beet crowns but do not trim roots. Cover with salted water and cook, covered, over high heat, until tender, 30 minutes to 1 hour, longer for older beets. Drain and rub off skins under cold water. Cut off stems and roots, and slice beets into a bowl. Chop the hard-cooked eggs—setting aside about ¼ of them—and onion and combine with beet slices. Mix salt, pepper, vinegar, and oil and pour over beets. Mix thoroughly. Line salad bowl with romaine. When ready to serve, spoon beet mixture into bowl, and sprinkle with reserved chopped egg and parsley.

MONT BLANC

Make this rich, sweet dessert fantasy by filling a ring of egg-shaped meringues with chestnut butter cream and decorating it with meringue mushrooms and whipped cream.

MERINGUE:
9 egg whites
½ teaspoon cream of tartar
1¾ cups sugar
1 ounce finely grated dark
    sweet chocolate

CHESTNUT BUTTERCREAM:
1½ cups sugar
¾ cup water
½ teaspoon cream of tartar

4 egg yolks
1½ cups unsalted butter,
    chilled
1 15-ounce can unsweetened
    chestnut puree
2 tablespoons kirsch

GARNISH:
1 cup heavy cream
1 tablespoon kirsch

To make meringues, beat egg whites and cream of tartar with an electric mixer until soft peaks form. Gradually beat in sugar, a tablespoonful at a time, and continue beating until mixture is thick and glossy, like marshmallow, and feels smooth when you pinch it. Put three quarters of mixture into a pastry bag fitted with a plain round tube. Line a baking tray with baking parchment or brown paper and pipe out 12 large egg shapes, 12 rounded domes in several sizes to resemble mushroom caps, and an equal number of pointed cones to make mushroom stems. Put remaining meringue mixture into another pastry bag fitted with a star tube and pipe a ring of stars or dots around a large, round ovenproof serving plate, inside the rim. Place meringues (including ring of stars) in a preheated 250° oven and bake for about 45 minutes or until they are hard to the touch and creamy white, not brown. When "eggs" are baked, glue them together in a ring inside the ring of stars on the serving plate using a bit of meringue saved for this purpose. Dip the bottoms of the mushroom caps into grated chocolate and push the pointed ends of stems into caps.

To make chestnut buttercream, boil together sugar, water, and cream of tartar, stirring until sugar dissolves. Boil until mixture spins a thread (230° on candy thermometer). Beat egg yolks with an electric mixer until light and fluffy. Pour sugar syrup onto beaten egg yolks in a thin stream, beating constantly until mixture cools. Beat in butter, 1 tablespoonful at a time, then chestnut puree. Flavor with kirsch. When ready to pipe cream—meringue should be cooled—put mixture into a pastry bag fitted with very small plain round tube and pipe it, like vermicelli, crisscrossing in a long, thin, continuous stream, into the center of the meringue ring. Decorate the chestnut "mountain" with meringue mushrooms. Garnish with rosettes made from whipped cream flavored with kirsch and piped out from a pastry bag fitted with a star tube. Serve cold. *The meringues and chestnut buttercream can be made a day ahead and the Mont Blanc assembled a few hours before serving.*

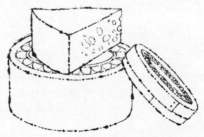

A Make-Your-Own Salad Buffet
for 24

Hot or cold watercress soup
Salad assortment, with French, Roquefort,
and Russian dressings
Assorted breads and breadsticks with butter
Assorted cheeses, with crackers and fruits

This is a simple and pleasing way to entertain a number of people for luncheon or perhaps an early supper—and fun for your guests as well. They literally put together their own meals. As hostess, you can, of course, prepare this buffet for as few or as many people as you choose by varying the kinds and quantities of ingredients you offer.

WATERCRESS SOUP

8 large, roughly chopped
    potatoes
8 roughly chopped onions
2 roughly chopped carrots
4 roughly chopped ribs celery,
    including leaves
4 cups chicken stock (see
    p. 278), more if needed
2 peeled cloves garlic

2 tablespoons salt
2 teaspoons freshly cracked
    white pepper
1 cup butter
4 large bunches watercress
2 cups light cream, more if
    needed
2 cups heavy cream
2 tablespoons chopped parsley

Put the potatoes, onions, carrots, and celery in a large kettle and cover with chicken stock. Add garlic and 1 inch water. Add salt and pepper and lay the butter on top. Bring to a boil, reduce heat to simmer, cover, and cook until vegetables are mushy. Trim heavy stems from watercress if you plan to puree the soup in a food mill (leave them on if you're going to puree it in a blender) and add cress to soup; cook, stirring, for not more than 5 minutes. Puree soup, using electric blender or medium disk of food mill. (*May be prepared ahead to this point.*)

If serving soup hot, return puree to kettle, stir in light and heavy cream, bring just to the boiling point, and taste for seasoning. If pureed in a blender, it may need to be thinned with up to 2 cups more of light cream, milk, or chicken stock. If serving cold, chill the puree. At serving time, stir in chilled light cream and heavy cream and taste for seasoning. Chilled foods usually need more salt. Ladle from a tureen, garnishing with chopped parsley, into mugs for easy handling.

SALAD ASSORTMENT

Romaine	Carrot curls
Bibb lettuce	Sliced radishes
Watercress	Cucumber rings
Chinese cabbage	Black olives
Chicory	Tomato wedges
Avocado slices	Scallions or chives
Red onion rings	Green pepper rings

SALAD DRESSINGS

FRENCH

Beat together 2 teaspoons coarse salt, 1 teaspoon freshly cracked black pepper, ¼ cup tarragon vinegar, and 1 cup French olive oil.

ROQUEFORT

Mash ½ pound Roquefort cheese and add it and 1 teaspoon Worcestershire sauce to basic French dressing.

RUSSIAN

Beat ¼ cup chili sauce into 2 cups mayonnaise (see p. 283).

ASSORTED CHEESES

For a crowd of 24, plan on between ¼ and ½ pound of cheese apiece, depending on anticipated appetites. A good selection would include different flavors—strong to mild—and textures—soft, semisoft, and hard. You might care to feature an international medley: for example, the French Pont l'Evêque, Brie or Camembert, Port du Salut, Chevret (made from goats' milk), and Muenster (an Alsatian specialty), the Swiss Gruyère, Italian Bel Paese, Dutch Gouda, and English or American Cheddar. Serve at room temperature with unsalted water biscuits and a selection of apples and pears.

Note: Make a cheese crock from any cheese left over. Add to it one half its weight in butter and 1 to 2 shots of brandy, mix well, pack into a crock, and refrigerate. It will keep for months.

A New Year's Eve Sit-down Buffet for 16

Gigot Provençale
Onion crêpes
Tossed green salad
Meringue torte with chocolate buttercream

GIGOT PROVENÇALE

Prepare 2 legs of lamb for 16 guests. Have your husband or a male guest carve the legs of lamb in front of the guests. If this does not seem practical to you, carve them in the kitchen but arrange the slices on the platter as prettily as possible, with the bone ends of the lamb at one end of the platter for a better effect.

2 2-ounce cans flat anchovy fillets	½ cup olive oil
10 slices bacon	1½ cups white wine
2 legs of lamb, 6 to 7 pounds each	1 cup water
2 tablespoons coarse salt	½ cup brandy
2 teaspoons freshly cracked black pepper	40 cloves garlic
	2 bunches watercress, for garnish

Cut up the anchovies and dice 4 strips of the bacon. With the point of a small knife, cut slits over the entire surface of the lamb and poke bits of anchovy and bacon into the slits, using the tip of the knife as a slide. Rub the lamb all over with coarse salt and pepper. Heat olive oil in a heavy skillet and brown the legs thoroughly over high heat. Put legs of lamb on 2 racks, fatty side up, in a roasting pan. Pour excess fat from skillet, deglaze it with 4 tablespoons white wine, and pour juices into roasting pan, together with another cup white wine, the water, and 4 tablespoons of the brandy. Cut remaining 6 slices bacon into squares and add to pan. (*May be prepared ahead to this point.*) Cover lamb closely with heavy aluminum foil, pinching it around pan edges to seal tightly. Place in a preheated 325° oven and roast 18 minutes per pound or about 1¾ hours for each 6-pound leg of lamb. Lamb will be rare.

While lamb roasts, peel garlic cloves, place in a saucepan, cover with water, and boil over high heat until garlic is very soft, about 15 minutes. Drain and push through a sieve or food mill, using the fine disk, or puree in a blender. Set aside.

When legs of lamb are done, remove them to a carving board and keep warm. Remove bacon pieces from roasting pan. Add remaining 4 tablespoons white wine and 4 tablespoons brandy and set pan over high heat. Add pureed garlic; cook and stir 5 minutes over high heat until well blended and reduced slightly. Taste sauce for seasoning—it may need pepper.

When brought to the table, a leg of lamb should wear a frill over the bone end—it looks better and keeps the carver's hands clean. To make frill, cut white paper to a 10 x 15-inch rectangle. Fold it in half lengthwise, without creasing, and make cuts about 3 inches deep at ½-inch intervals along the folded edge. Unfold it and refold it, inside out, again without creasing, to make frill puffier. Coil it to a diameter of 1½ inches to fit over bone, and fasten it with staples or cellophane tape. Garnish platter with watercress and serve sauce separately in a warmed bowl.

ONION CRÊPES

3 tablespoons butter	1 recipe soubise filling (see
1½ cups very finely chopped	p. 157)
onions	1 cup melted butter
2 recipes basic crêpes (see	1 cup freshly grated Parmesan
p. 285)	cheese

Heat 3 tablespoons butter in a skillet, stir in onions, and cook, stirring, until they are limp but not brown, about 15 minutes.

Drain and cool and add to crêpes batter. Fry crêpes—7-inch size. Fill each crêpe with 1 tablespoon soubise filling and roll up. Brush an au gratin dish with 2 tablespoons of the melted butter and arrange crêpes. Sprinkle them with remaining melted butter and Parmesan cheese. (*Recipe can be made ahead to this point.*) Place in a preheated 350° oven for about 15 to 20 minutes, or a 325° oven for 20 to 25 minutes, or until heated through.

TOSSED GREEN SALAD

3 or 4 heads of tender lettuce
2 cucumbers
4 heads of Belgian endive
½ pound mushrooms

2 tablespoons chopped parsley
French vinaigrette dressing
(see p. 282)

Separate and wash lettuce leaves, roll up in towels, and re-frigerate to crisp. Peel cucumbers and shave them into strips, the length of the cucumber, with a potato peeler. Wash Belgian endive heads, discarding discolored outer leaves, and cut into julienne pieces. Wipe mushrooms clean with acidulated water (1 table-spoon lemon juice to 1 quart of water), trim stems, and slice very thinly. When ready to serve, put all greens and vegetables into a chilled salad bowl, sprinkle with chopped parsley, and toss with vinaigrette dressing.

MERINGUE TORTE
WITH CHOCOLATE BUTTERCREAM

10 egg whites
½ teaspoon cream of tartar
2½ cups sugar
½ cup toasted flaked almonds

1 recipe chocolate buttercream (recipe follows)
1 cup heavy cream
Confectioners' sugar

In electric mixer bowl, beat egg whites until foamy. Add cream of tartar and continue beating while adding sugar, 1 table-spoon at a time. Beat until mixture looks like marshmallow and no longer feels grainy when you pinch it. Pack the meringue into a big pastry bag fitted with a star tube. Line 2 trays with baking parchment and draw a 9-inch circle on each (trace around a 9-inch cake pan). Following the outline, pipe out a ring of meringue and spiral into the center to make an entire layer of meringue. Decorate one of the layers (the top layer when you assemble torte) with some scallops. Also pipe out separately some shell shapes by humping the extrusion just a bit. (Lift or push up the pastry bag a little so that a rounded shell shape emerges.) Sprinkle layers and shells with toasted almonds and bake in a preheated 250° oven for about 1 hour or until firm. This will be a somewhat chewy meringue—not a dry, crisp one. Let cool.

Make buttercream and pack it into a pastry bag fitted with a star tube. Pipe over bottom layer of meringue in loose curlicues. Place top layer over filling and pipe remaining buttercream in a floral design on top. (*May be made to this point the day before.*) Whip the heavy cream, pack it in a pastry bag fitted with star tube, and decorate sides of torte. Push the meringue shell shapes into the whipped cream at intervals around edge of torte. Dust the entire torte with confectioners' sugar stirred through a sieve. Cut into wedges for guests to help themselves. *May be decorated a few hours ahead—whip heavy cream over ice with a piano-wire whisk so it will hold up.*

Note: Instead of a single torte, you can make individual meringue shells; fill each with buttercream and decorate with a rosette of whipped cream.

CHOCOLATE BUTTERCREAM

6 ounces dark sweet
   chocolate
2 tablespoons water
2 tablespoons rum
1 cup sugar
⅔ cup water

¼ teaspoon cream of tartar
1 tablespoon lemon juice
3 egg yolks
1½ cups chilled unsalted butter
1 tablespoon vegetable
   shortening, if needed

Melt chocolate with 2 tablespoons water and the rum. In another pan combine sugar, ⅔ cup water, the cream of tartar, and the lemon juice. Stir over high heat until sugar dissolves; then cook until syrup spins a thread (230° on a candy thermometer). Meanwhile, beat egg yolks in an electric mixer bowl until thick and lemony. When syrup is ready, pour it in a *thin* stream into egg yolks, beating constantly at high speed. Continue beating until bowl feels cool to touch. When mixture is cool, beat in the unsalted butter, a bit at a time. Have vegetable shortening measured and ready in case the mixture curdles. If it does, beat in shortening—this will bring it back. Beat in cooled chocolate mixture.

A "Cook-in" Buffet
for 6 to 8

Sautéed blowfish
Rack of lamb with green peppercorns
Carrot soufflé
Leeks Mornay
Baked Alaska

A "cook-in" buffet is one of my favorite methods of entertaining. I invite a small group of people—no more than can move around my kitchen easily—and have *them* do the cooking, under my supervision. When the food is ready, we set it up on a table, admire it, then eat. We usually eat the first course standing up around the kitchen, then present the main course at the buffet table. Dessert is served separately.

SAUTÉED BLOWFISH

24 blowfish (sea squabs)
Flour for dredging
¾ cup butter
1 teaspoon salt
½ teaspoon freshly cracked
white pepper

2 teaspoons finely chopped
garlic
2 tablespoons finely chopped
parsley
Juice of ½ lemon

The edible part of blowfish—a saltwater fish usually available in eastern markets—is the white meat on both sides of the backbone—a delicacy. When it is trimmed out of the blowfish and sold commercially, it is called sea squab, and it looks something like a frog's leg. To prepare the fish, cut off the head about 1 inch behind the eyes, strip off the skin and cut away the entrails. Leave backbone in. Wash and dry meat and dredge with flour, patting off excess. Heat ½ cup butter in a heavy skillet; when it's foaming, sauté the blowfish over high heat for about 3 minutes on each side—do not overcook. Sauté a few at a time—just one layer in pan. Season with salt and pepper, remove to a serving plate, and keep warm. Wash the skillet and heat the remaining ¼ cup butter. Add garlic, parsley, and lemon juice; swirl the pan for 1 minute only over high heat and pour over the fish.

RACK OF LAMB
WITH GREEN PEPPERCORNS

Green peppercorns, grown mainly in Madagascar, are picked before they are ripe, and strong in taste.

2 racks of lamb	1 cup basic brown sauce (see
2 tablespoons coarse salt	p. 281)
2 teaspoons freshly cracked	2 tablespoons drained green
black pepper	peppercorns
2 slivered cloves garlic	1 tablespoon butter

Have the butcher remove the chine bones, to make carving easier, and trim the racks so that 1½ to 2 inches of bone are exposed on each chop. Rub the lamb all over with salt and pepper. With the point of a small knife, cut slits in the fatty side of the meat and push garlic slivers into the slits, using the tip of the knife as a slide. Place lamb, fatty side up, on a rack in a baking pan and roast in a preheated 425° oven for 45 minutes. Lamb will be pink. Let rest 15 minutes before carving. For sauce, combine basic brown sauce and drained green peppercorns and bring to a boil. Add butter and swirl over heat just until butter melts.

CARROT SOUFFLÉ

4 or 5 carrots	5 beaten egg yolks
1 tablespoon grated orange	1 teaspoon salt
peel	½ teaspoon freshly cracked
4 tablespoons butter	white pepper
4 tablespoons flour	2 tablespoons chopped parsley
¾ cup milk	7 egg whites
¼ cup orange juice	½ teaspoon cream of tartar

Use a 6-cup soufflé dish, or prepare a 4-cup soufflé dish with a paper collar: fold a strip of waxed paper lengthwise and tie it around the top of the soufflé dish so that it extends 4 to 5 inches above the dish. Oil the inside of the collar and set dish aside. Peel and slice carrots crosswise into 1-inch pieces; boil them in water to cover over high heat until tender and puree them in a blender or a food mill, using the fine disk—you should have 1 cup puree. Stir in grated orange peel and set aside. Melt the butter in a saucepan and stir in flour with a wooden spatula. Cook, stirring, over high heat for 2 minutes—do not let it brown. Remove from heat, change to a whisk, and add milk and orange juice, whisking vigorously. Return to heat and cook, stirring, until mixture thickens. Remove from heat and add beaten egg yolks—beat them in quickly so they won't scramble. Add salt, pepper, carrot puree, and chopped parsley and blend thoroughly. (*May be prepared ahead to this point.*) When ready to proceed, beat egg whites until foamy, add cream of tartar, and beat until stiff but not dry. Fold egg whites into soufflé base and pour into soufflé dish. Bake in a preheated 425° oven for 25 minutes.

LEEKS MORNAY

12 leeks	⅛ teaspoon freshly grated
2 cups water	nutmeg
1 tablespoon salt	6 tablespoons grated Gruyère
2 tablespoons butter	cheese
2 tablespoons flour	2 tablespoons cream
1½ cups milk	1 egg yolk
½ teaspoon salt	2 tablespoons freshly grated
¼ teaspoon freshly cracked	Parmesan cheese
white pepper	

Clean leeks: cut off the roots; cut off tops, leaving about 4 inches of green, and split leeks lengthwise. Hold under running water, separating the layers, to wash thoroughly. Put them in a saucepan, cover with salted water, bring to a boil, and simmer, uncovered, until barely tender, about 15 minutes. Drain and set aside. In another pan, over high heat, melt butter and stir in flour. Cook, stirring with a wooden spatula, for 2 minutes—do not let flour brown. Remove from heat, change to a whisk, and add milk, whisking vigorously. Return to heat and cook, stirring, until sauce thickens. Season with salt, pepper, and nutmeg. Stir in Gruyère cheese. Beat the cream into the egg yolk, warm it with 2 tablespoons of the sauce, and then stir it into the sauce. Heat through over medium-high heat but do not boil. Arrange leeks in an ovenproof baking dish. Spoon sauce over leeks and sprinkle with Parmesan cheese. (*May be prepared ahead to this point.*) Bake in a preheated 350° oven for about 15 minutes or until bubbly. Glaze under the broiler before serving.

BAKED ALASKA

1 9-inch layer gold cake (recipe follows)	¼ teaspoon salt
	½ teaspoon cream of tartar
3 tablespoons white crème de cacao	1¾ cups finely granulated sugar
	1 quart chocolate ice cream, softened
6 egg whites	

Cover a heavy wood board (such as a cutting board for bread or the back of a carving board) with baking parchment and place cake layer on paper in the center of the board. Sprinkle cake with crème de cacao, poking holes in top of cake with a fork so liqueur will soak in. Beat egg whites with an electric mixer until foamy. Add salt and cream of tartar. Continue beaing until soft peaks form. Add 1 cup sugar gradually, 1 tablespoon at a time, beating constantly. Continue beating until mixture looks glossy, like marshmallow, and no longer feels grainy when you pinch it. Quickly fold in ½ cup sugar and put meringue into a large pastry bag fitted with a star tube. Spread softened ice cream on the cake, leaving a 1-inch margin around the edge. Pipe the meringue all over the cake and ice cream, covering both completely. Dust the top with the remaining ¼ cup sugar and place the cake, on the board, into the freezer for 15 minutes to set. (*Can be made ahead to this point and stored in freezer.*) Preheat oven to 450°; move the cake, still on the board, from freezer directly to oven and bake for about 5 minutes, or until meringue is delicately brown. Serve immediately.

GOLD CAKE

1 tablespoon solid vegetable shortening	½ cup butter
4 eggs, separated	1½ cups lightly spooned cake flour
1½ cups sugar	½ cup cornstarch
½ cup cold water	½ teaspoon salt
2 teaspoons vanilla extract	4 teaspoons baking powder

Grease 2 9-inch layer pans with solid shortening. Line with waxed paper. Beat egg whites until foamy; beat in ½ cup sugar, adding it 1 tablespoon at a time, until mixture looks like marshmallow. With an electric mixer this takes about 5 minutes; by hand, about 15 minutes. In a separate bowl, whisk together egg yolks with cold water for 3 to 4 minutes, or until foamy. Add vanilla. In a third bowl, cream butter with the remaining cup of sugar. Add egg yolk mixture to butter mixture and combine well. Don't worry if mixture looks curdled. Sift together flour (if using all-purpose flour use 3 tablespoons less), cornstarch, salt, and baking powder. Add to butter mixture. Beat well for 2 minutes and fold in egg white mixture. Bake in 375° oven for 35 minutes. *This cake freezes well for 1 month.*

Italian Buffet
for 8

Stuffed zucchini
Fettuccini with pesto sauce
Braised fennel (see p. 102)
Grissini
Zabaglione
Pignolia cookies (see p. 249)
Espresso coffee

STUFFED ZUCCHINI

8 small zucchini	½ teaspoon oregano
1 pound ground beef	2 slices of bread
1 egg	¼ cup olive oil
2 finely chopped cloves garlic	2 tablespoons chopped parsley
2 teaspoons salt	

Wash zucchini. Cut off ends and seed with an apple corer. In a bowl, mix ground beef, egg, garlic, salt, oregano, and bread—soak the bread in water first, and squeeze it dry. Put meat mixture into a pastry bag fitted with a plain tube and pipe it into the zucchini from both ends. Sauté zucchini in olive oil over high heat until lightly browned. Arrange in a baking pan and pour on oil remaining in skillet. Bake about 20 minutes in a preheated 350° oven, or until tender. (*Can be made the day before and reheated for 10 minutes in a 350° oven, or served at room temperature.*) To serve, sprinkle with chopped parsley.

FETTUCCINI WITH PESTO SAUCE

1 recipe homemade pasta
  (see p. 286)
8 quarts boiling water

1 tablespoon salt
  Pesto alla Genovese (recipe
    follows)

Prepare and roll pasta; cut into noodles (use the wide noodle setting if you have a pasta machine, or cut noodles ¼ to ⅜ inch wide with a sharp knife). Let them dry at least 2 hours before cooking. (*They can be made ahead, packaged in plastic bags, and stored in the refrigerator for a day or two; or frozen for up to 1 month.*)

To cook noodles, bring water to a rolling boil, add salt, and add noodles gradually. Cook, stirring and lifting noodles with a wooden fork, until done, about 7 minutes. Test them by biting them—they should be *al dente*, slightly resistant. Drain in a colander and pour into warmed serving bowl. Toss with Pesto sauce and serve at once.

PESTO ALLA GENOVESE

You can keep this for weeks in the refrigerator—pack it into a small jar and float a little olive oil over the top to preserve it.

1½ cups fresh basil leaves
¾ cup olive oil
4 tablespoons soft butter
¼ cup pine nuts
¾ cup grated Parmesan cheese

2 tablespoons chopped parsley
2 teaspoons chopped garlic
1 teaspoon salt
½ teaspoon freshly cracked
    black pepper

Put all ingredients except salt and pepper in a blender. Blend on low, then higher speed until mixture looks like pea puree. (If you have no blender, puree with a pestle and mortar, but this takes some time.) Season with salt and pepper. To serve with pasta, thin pesto with 6 tablespoons water drained from cooking noodles. Spoon over noodles and toss.

ZABAGLIONE

You can beat zabaglione the cautious way, over hot water. But you should learn to work with eggs on a direct flame or burner—and making zabaglione is a great way to learn. There's even a special pot for it of heavy copper, with a dome-shaped bottom so that your whisk can reach everywhere to whip the zabaglione to thick, sweet creaminess. But if you don't have a zabaglione pot, you could use a copper or stainless-steel mixing bowl.

3 eggs	⅔ cup sugar
6 egg yolks	¼ cup sweet Marsala

Put eggs, egg yolks, sugar, and Marsala into zabaglione pot or metal bowl and beat with a whisk until blended. Hold pot over high heat and beat continuously, raising and lowering the pot so that it never gets too hot. *Or* put ingredients into a large glass bowl, stand the bowl in a pan of hot water over high heat, and beat with whisk or electric beater. When zabaglione is thick and creamy—it takes about 10 minutes over direct heat, 5 to 10 minutes longer over hot water—serve immediately.

Just Desserts Buffet for 25

Carlsbad Oblaten cake
Grape tart
Cold chocolate soufflé
La Tourinoise
Crème caramel
Savarin
Chestnut mousse
Trifle
Orange almond torte
Macédoine of fruits (see p. 61)

Everybody has friends who are "dessert freaks." These are people who read the list of desserts on a menu first, then build their dinner around their dessert choice. Why not invite them to a dessert orgy—perhaps after a community meeting or tryouts for an amateur play or just for the fun of it. If there are leftovers, either your guests can take extras home with them or you can freeze the leftovers. The Oblaten cake, soufflé, Tourinoise, savarin, mousse, and torte all freeze well. I always supply lots of coffee and sometimes champagne or a sweet dessert wine.

CARLSBAD OBLATEN CAKE

Oblaten, usually available in German or gourmet stores, are plain, gaufrette-type wafers.

9 ounces dark sweet chocolate	1 tablespoon solid vegetable
2 tablespoons rum or brandy	shortening, if needed
2 tablespoons water	2 cups heavy cream
1 cup sugar	4 tablespoons confectioners'
⅔ cup water	sugar
⅛ teaspoon cream of tartar	1 package round Oblaten
3 egg yolks	(8-inch-diameter wafers)
1½ cups chilled butter	1 8-ounce jar apricot jam

Melt 6 ounces of the chocolate in a small pan with the rum and 2 tablespoons water. Stir it over low heat and watch that it doesn't burn. Set aside to cool. Separately, melt remaining 3 ounces of chocolate over low heat. With a teaspoon, spread rounds of this chocolate, like coins, on waxed paper set on a pan or on cardboard, and refrigerate. Make sugar syrup by cooking sugar, ⅔ cup water, and cream of tartar together in a small saucepan, over high heat, until syrup spins a thread (230° to 234° on a candy thermometer). Beat egg yolks in mixer bowl until light and fluffy. When syrup is ready, pour it in a thin stream into the egg yolks, beating all the while. Continue beating until mixture is cool. Beat in the butter a bit at a time. (Don't worry if mixture gets thin; it will get thick again. If it curdles, beat in a tablespoon of vegetable shortening to bring it back.) Finally, beat in the cooled chocolate-rum mixture and place the bowl of chocolate pastry cream in the refrigerator to chill for a few minutes.

Line a serving plate with triangles of waxed paper. (When you've finished putting the cake together, you can pull out the waxed paper, leaving a clean plate.) Whip the heavy cream until stiff, sweetening it with confectioners' sugar. Put the whipped cream into a pastry bag fitted with a star tube. Spread one of the wafers with jam to within 1 inch of the edge. Lay it on the serving plate and pipe whipped cream rosettes around the edge—4 rosettes on each layer. Spread jam on a second wafer, stack it on the first, pipe with whipped cream rosettes. Continue until all wafers are used, but do not put jam on the top wafer. Pipe bands of whipped cream vertically, up the sides of the stacked cake, leaving about 1½ inches between each band. Bring cream up just over the top edge. Fill another pastry bag, also fitted with a star tube, with the chocolate pastry cream. Pipe bands of pastry cream between the bands of whipped cream on sides of cake. Cover top of cake with pastry cream rosettes and decorate with the chocolate coins. Chill cake overnight in the refrigerator before serving. Cut slices carefully with a sharp knife.

GRAPE TART

2 tablespoons bread crumbs	2 tablespoons rum
1 wholly baked 9-inch pâte brisée shell (see p. 288)	1 bunch black grapes
	1 bunch seedless white grapes
1½ cups heavy cream	1 cup apricot jam
3 tablespoons confectioners' sugar, plus more for sifting	¼ cup light rum

Sprinkle bread crumbs into pâte brisée shell. Whip the heavy cream, adding 3 tablespoons confectioners' sugar and the rum, until stiff. Spread into tart shell. Remove stems from grapes. Carefully seed black grapes, pressing halves back together so they look whole. Cover the tart with grapes arranged in alternating rings of black and white. Make glaze: mix apricot jam with rum and stir over high heat until it dissolves. Rub through a strainer and brush grapes with apricot glaze. (*May be made ahead and refrigerated.*) Just before serving, sift confectioners' sugar around edge of tart.

COLD CHOCOLATE SOUFFLÉ

Follow recipe for Cold Chocolate Almond Soufflé (see p. 171) but omit toasted almonds.

LA TOURINOISE

1 cup butter	1 teaspoon vanilla extract
1 15-ounce can unsweetened chestnut puree	2 tablespoons brandy or rum
1 cup sugar	½ cup toasted slivered al-monds, optional
½ pound unsweetened choco-late, melted and cooled	Confectioners' sugar
	1 cup heavy cream

Oil a 6-cup loaf mold. Put the butter into an electric mixer bowl and beat it until light and creamy. Add chestnut puree 1 tablespoonful at a time and continue beating; mixture should be very creamy. Gradually beat in sugar, then cooled chocolate. Add vanilla, brandy, and almonds. Pack into the oiled mold and bang the mold on the counter to settle the mixture. Refrigerate overnight. To serve, turn out onto a serving dish and sift with confectioners' sugar. Cut in very thin slices and serve with unsweetened whipped cream.

CRÈME CARAMEL

1½ cups plus 6 tablespoons sugar	2 teaspoons vanilla extract
4 eggs	⅛ teaspoon salt
3 egg yolks	1 quart milk

Make the caramel first, to coat the inside of an 8-cup soufflé dish. Put 1½ cups sugar in a heavy pan—an iron skillet is ideal. Place over high heat and stir until sugar dissolves. Use a wooden spatula and be sure you get into the corners of the pan. The sugar will lump at first; then it will dissolve and come to a boil. Watch carefully when it turns a butterscotch color; remove from heat when you see it give off small puffs of smoke. After a minute or two, pour the caramel into the soufflé dish and rotate the dish to spread caramel all over bottom and sides. Be careful; melted sugar is very hot. Set aside.

To make custard, whisk eggs and egg yolks in a large bowl just until blended. Whisk in remaining 6 tablespoons sugar and stir in the vanilla, salt, and milk. Strain this mixture through a fine sieve 10 times. Then pour into the caramel-coated soufflé dish and set it in a baking pan filled with 1 inch of hot water. Place in a preheated 350° oven and bake for 45 to 50 minutes. Custard is done when a knife, inserted near the edge of the dish, comes out clean. Remove from oven, take out of water bath, and let cool to room temperature. Then place custard in the refrigerator to chill. (*May be made to this point the day before.*) When ready to serve, unmold the custard on a rimmed serving dish. Baking dissolves the caramel, and you'll find a delicious pool of caramel sauce around the custard.

SAVARIN

Follow recipe for Rum Babas (see p. 247) but instead of putting dough in *baba au rhum* molds, form it into a roll and fit it into a 4-cup savarin or ring mold. Bake for 25 minutes in a preheated 375° oven. Make a syrup by stirring ½ cup light rum, 1¼ cups sugar, and ¼ cup water over high heat until sugar dissolves. Simmer 10 minutes and then soak the hot savarin in rum syrup. Mix 1 cup apricot jam with ¼ cup light rum and stir over high heat until jam dissolves. Rub apricot glaze through strainer and brush savarin with it. Decorate with candied cherry halves and leaves cut from angelica. (*May be made the day before to this point.*) When ready to serve, fill the center of the ring with 1 cup heavy cream, whipped and sweetened with 2 tablespoons confectioners' sugar.

CHESTNUT MOUSSE

2 tablespoons (2 envelopes) unflavored gelatine
1½ cups light cream
½ cup sugar
4 eggs, separated
1 15-ounce can unsweetened chestnut puree

4 tablespoons dark rum
2 tablespoons confectioners' sugar
3 cups heavy cream
1 8-ounce can whole marrons glacés

Oil a 6-cup soufflé dish and set aside. Sprinkle gelatine over light cream in a saucepan; stir in sugar. Place over low heat and stir until gelatine and sugar dissolve—do not boil. Beat egg yolks very well. Stir a little of the hot cream into egg yolks, to warm them, then stir into cream and cook, stirring constantly, until mixture thickens enough to coat the back of a spoon, about 10 minutes. Cool in refrigerator. Put the chestnut puree in an electric mixer bowl and add the rum. Beat it until very fluffy. When gelatine mixture has cooled just to the point of setting, beat it into the chestnut puree, a little at a time, until well blended. Beat egg whites until foamy; add confectioners' sugar and beat until stiff. Fold into chestnut mixture. Whip 2 cups of the heavy cream and fold into mixture. Pour into prepared soufflé dish and chill for several hours.

When ready to serve, whip the remaining 1 cup heavy cream and pack it into a pastry bag fitted with a star tube. Unmold the mousse onto a chilled platter and decorate all over with whipped cream rosettes. Press whole marrons glacés into rosettes.

TRIFLE

JELLY ROLL:
4 eggs
½ cup sugar
⅓ cup flour
⅓ cup potato flour
½ cup jelly or seedless jam
2 tablespoons sherry, or
    Madeira, Marsala,
    brandy, or rum

BAVARIAN CREAM:
3 eggs, separated
½ cup sugar
6 tablespoons sherry, or
    Madeira, Marsala,
    brandy, or rum

1 tablespoon (1 envelope)
    unflavored gelatine
1½ cups milk
1 cup heavy cream

¼ cup sherry, or Madeira,
    Marsala, brandy, or rum

¼ cup heavy cream
1 tablespoon confectioners'
    sugar

Candied violets, for
    garnish, optional

Oil the jelly-roll pan, line it with waxed paper, and oil the paper; set aside. Beat eggs with sugar until very light and fluffy; this will take several minutes using an electric mixer. Mix the two flours and fold gently into the egg mixture. Spread batter in the jelly-roll pan and bake 10 minutes in a preheated 375° oven. Remove cake from oven and loosen around edges. Lay 2 strips of waxed paper on the counter, overlapping lengthwise. Turn cake out on waxed paper, peel off lining paper. Let cool for a minute or two; then spread with jelly. Roll up and cut the roll in 1-inch slices. Line a glass serving bowl with about half of the jelly-roll slices, reserving the rest, and sprinkle them with 2 tablespoons sherry.

To make the Bavarian cream, whisk the 3 egg yolks in a bowl. Add ½ cup sugar and whisk until thick. Pour ¼ cup sherry into a measuring cup, sprinkle it with the gelatine, and let stand for about 5 minutes. Then set the cup in a pan of boiling water and stir until gelatine dissolves. Whisk the dissolved gelatine into the egg yolk mixture. Add milk all at once and transfer to a heavy nonaluminum saucepan. Set over high heat and cook, whisking constantly, until mixture coats the back of a spoon. It will not be thick. Set the pan over ice and continue whisking until mixture is cool. Flavor with 2 tablespoons sherry. Beat egg whites until stiff peaks form and whip 1 cup of the heavy cream. When the cooked mixture is cool, fold in egg whites and whipped cream; mixture will be thin.

Spoon about half of the Bavarian cream over the jelly roll in the glass bowl. Lay remaining jelly-roll slices on the cream, sprinkle with remaining ¼ cup sherry, and spoon on the rest of the Bavarian cream. Refrigerate. (*Can be made the day before.*) When ready to serve, whip remaining ½ cup heavy cream, sweetening it with the confectioners' sugar. Put it in a pastry bag fitted with a star tube and pipe rosettes of whipped cream around the edge of the dessert. Decorate with candied violets.

ORANGE ALMOND TORTE

Follow the directions for torte layers given in the recipe for Almond Torte (see p. 167), but omit vanilla and almond extracts and flavor the torte with 2 tablespoons freshly grated orange peel and 2 tablespoons Grand Marnier or other orange liqueur. To serve, whip 1½ cups heavy cream and flavor it with 3 tablespoons confectioners' sugar, 1 tablespoon freshly grated orange peel, and ¼ cup fresh orange juice. Spread over bottom layer of torte, reserving about ½ cup for decorating top of torte; top with second layer and decorate with whipped cream rosettes.

A Summertime Seafood
Buffet for 8

Scallops and prosciutto
Poached flounder paupiettes stuffed
with fish mousse, shrimp sauce
Lima beans with black butter
Hot violet soufflé, crème Anglaise

SCALLOPS AND PROSCIUTTO

1½ pounds sea scallops
1 tablespoon chopped garlic
Juice of 2 limes or 2 lemons
2 teaspoons salt
½ teaspoon freshly cracked
white pepper

½ teaspoon basil or oregano
or tarragon
½ pound thinly sliced
prosciutto ham
Melted butter, optional

Cut sea scallops in half. Marinate them in the refrigerator overnight in garlic and lime juice. When ready to serve, season them with salt, pepper, and basil. Wrap in ham and serve raw, on picks. Or brush with melted butter and bake in a preheated 450° oven for about 10 minutes or until they sizzle.

POACHED FLOUNDER PAUPIETTES
STUFFED WITH FISH MOUSSE

1½ pounds fresh salmon or
halibut
4 egg whites
2 tablespoons chopped fresh
dill
3 tablespoons finely chopped
shallots
¼ teaspoon very finely
chopped garlic
¾ cup light cream, about

2 teaspoons salt
½ teaspoon freshly cracked
white pepper
8 medium-size flounder fillets
1 cup dry white wine
½ cup water
1 bay leaf
6 peppercorns
Shrimp Sauce (recipe
follows)

Grind the salmon or halibut and put it into the bowl of an electric mixer. Beat it about 5 minutes. Add egg whites a little at a time, still beating, and add dill, shallots, and garlic. Beat in cream, 1 tablespoonful at a time, just enough so that mixture will drop easily from a spatula. Add salt and pepper. Set aside. Lay flounder fillets on waxed paper, skin side up. Sprinkle generously with white wine. Spread each fillet with fish mousse and roll up like a jelly roll; fasten with toothpick. Place paupiettes in a baking dish; they may touch. Pour on remaining wine and the water and add bay leaf and peppercorns. Cover fish with buttered waxed paper. (*May be made ahead to this point and refrigerated.*)

Bake in a preheated 350° oven for 15 to 20 minutes, or until fish flakes when you touch it with a toothpick. Remove from oven and arrange in serving dish; use the poaching liquid to make the shrimp sauce. Remove toothpicks from the paupiettes, spoon on shrimp sauce, and reheat briefly in the oven before serving, about 5 minutes. *May be completely prepared ahead, covered with plastic wrap, and refrigerated. To reheat, bring to room temperature, then place in a 350° oven for 15 minutes, or glaze under the broiler for 1 minute.*

SHRIMP SAUCE

2 tablespoons butter
1 tablespoon chopped shallots
2 tablespoons flour
1 tablespoon tomato paste
1 cup liquid, from poaching
    fish

½ cup light cream
1 tablespoon brandy, optional
½ pound chopped cooked
    shrimp

Melt butter in a saucepan, stir in shallots, and cook over high heat for 2 minutes—do not let them burn. Stir in flour and tomato paste and cook for 2 minutes more, stirring constantly. Remove from heat, change to a whisk, and add poaching liquid all at once, whisking vigorously. Return to high heat and bring to a boil, stirring constantly. Add cream, and brandy if desired, and bring to a boil again. Season to taste, add shrimp, and heat through. Spoon sauce over paupiettes.

LIMA BEANS WITH BLACK PEPPER

Fresh lima beans are available in the summer mostly. Although you can substitute frozen lima beans (4 cups—preparing them according to package directions), the fresh limas are far superior.

3 pounds lima beans (about 4 cups, shelled)
2 teaspoons salt
½ cup butter

2 tablespoons vinegar
½ teaspoon freshly cracked black pepper

Shell the lima beans and put them into a saucepan, add just enough cold water to cover, and 1 teaspoon salt. Bring to a boil, reduce heat, and simmer, uncovered, until barely tender, about 20 to 30 minutes. Heat butter very slowly in a small skillet until it turns dark brown, about 10 to 15 minutes. Set aside. Put vinegar, remaining 1 teaspoon salt, and the pepper in a very small pan and simmer until it reduces to 1 tablespoon. Stir vinegar reduction into cooled butter; reheat and pour over lima beans. Toss them well and add seasoning, if necessary.

HOT VIOLET SOUFFLÉ

3 tablespoons butter
3 tablespoons flour
1 cup milk
⅓ cup sugar
5 egg yolks
1 teaspoon vanilla extract
2 tablespoons crème de violette liqueur

1½ cups chopped crystallized violets
7 egg whites
¼ teaspoon cream of tartar
Crème Anglaise (recipe follows)

Melt butter in a nonaluminum pan. Stir in flour and cook over high heat, stirring constantly, for 2 minutes. Do not let it brown. Remove from heat, change to a whisk, and add milk, whisking vigorously. Return to high heat, add sugar, and cook, stirring constantly, until mixture comes to a boil and is thick and smooth. Set aside to cool slightly; then beat in egg yolks 1 at a time. Flavor with vanilla and violet liqueur. (*May be prepared ahead to this point and refrigerated. Warm the mixture slightly before folding in egg whites.*) When ready to bake, fold crystallized violets into base. Beat egg whites with cream of tartar until stiff, fold into base mixture, and pour into 6-cup soufflé dish (or use a 4-cup soufflé dish fitted with a paper collar). Bake on the bottom shelf of a preheated 375° oven for 30 minutes, or a 425° oven for 25 minutes. Serve immediately with Crème Anglaise.

CRÈME ANGLAISE

2 cups light cream
4 egg yolks

½ cup sugar
¼ cup crème de violette liqueur

Scald the cream. Beat egg yolks with sugar until very thick and lemony. Add the hot cream slowly, stirring constantly. Return to high heat and cook until the mixture coats the back of a spoon, stirring constantly. Flavor with crème de violette. Serve warm.

Suppers

I think of suppers as late night entertainment—light and un-elaborate meals offered around eleven or eleven-thirty. It's always fun, for instance, to say "Come home with us" after an art opening or an evening at the theater or ballet. When you're excited about a show, you want to talk about it with friends.

If my invitation is impromptu, we collect in the kitchen and I pull out my omelette pans. But if I've planned and cooked ahead, the menu may be more elegant and may well include champagne. Still, the first rule for late nights is keep it simple. The best foods are completely prepared ahead, ready to go into the oven or chafing dish for quick reheating. Curried Chicken Pancakes or Lobster Thermidor are excellent choices. You'll be ready with either before your guests have had a round of drinks!

Supper for 8 after
the Theater, Ballet, or Opera

Pea pod soup
Curried chicken pancakes
with chutney
Stuffed oranges

PEA POD SOUP

If the peas in your market are not fresh, don't make this soup. If fresh pods are available, they make a deliciously unusual soup, totally different from dried pea soup.

2 quarts washed pea pods
   (not snow peas)
6 cups strong chicken stock
   (see p. 278)
1 cup shredded lettuce, well
   packed
1 cup chopped onion
1 quart light cream
1 bay leaf
4 sprigs parsley

2 teaspoons salt
½ teaspoon freshly cracked
   white pepper
¼ teaspoon freshly grated
   nutmeg
2 egg yolks
4 teaspoons butter
4 teaspoons finely chopped
   parsley

In a large saucepan, combine pea pods, chicken stock, lettuce, and onion. Bring to a boil, reduce heat, cover, and simmer until pea pods are barely tender, about 20 to 30 minutes. Puree this mixture through a food mill, using the fine disk, or in a blender. Return to high heat and stir in light cream, bay leaf, and parsley. Bring to a boil. Season with salt, pepper, and nutmeg. (*Can be made ahead to this point.*) Beat egg yolks, warm them with a little of the hot soup, and stir them into soup. Heat just to boiling, but do not boil. Serve in individual soup bowls, garnished with butter and finely chopped parsley.

CURRIED CHICKEN PANCAKES
WITH CHUTNEY

1 4-pound chicken
4 cups chicken stock (see p. 278)
½ rib celery
4 whole peppercorns
1 small onion
2 whole cloves
¾ cup butter
2 cups chopped onions
½ cup chopped carrots
½ cup chopped celery

1 medium-size apple, unpeeled, but cored and chopped
3 to 4 tablespoons curry powder
3 tablespoons flour
1 cup light cream
1 cup canned unsweetened coconut milk
¼ cup finely chopped mango chutney
16 7-inch crêpes (see p. 285)
¼ cup melted butter

Poach the chicken in chicken stock, adding celery, peppercorns, and onion stuck with cloves. Cool in broth. Remove meat from bones and cut into cubes. Set aside. Strain stock and set aside. Melt butter in a heavy skillet and add chopped onions, carrots, celery, and apple and cook over high heat until onions are transparent. With wooden spatula, smooth curry powder and flour into the vegetable mixture, and cook, stirring, for 2 minutes. Stir in 2 cups of reserved chicken stock and cook about 15 minutes, or until vegetables are tender. Add cream and coconut milk and cook a few minutes longer. Puree the sauce through a food mill, using the medium disk, or in a blender. Taste for seasoning. Mix half the sauce with chicken, adding the chopped chutney. Lay out the crêpes, light side up, and put 2 heaping tablespoons of chicken mixture on each; roll up and lay, seam side down, in a buttered ovenproof serving dish. Spoon remaining sauce over rolled crêpes. Drizzle with melted butter. (*Dish may be prepared ahead, covered with plastic wrap, and refrigerated, or frozen for up to 1 month. Any leftover chicken mixture may be frozen.*) When ready to serve, heat through in a 350° oven until brown and bubbly, about 10 to 15 minutes.

STUFFED ORANGES

8 large navel oranges
2 tablespoons bitter orange
   marmalade
8 tablespoons orange liqueur
1 pint orange sherbet

3 egg whites
⅛ teaspoon cream of tartar
1 cup sugar
8 candied violets

Remove tops from oranges—in a slice about 1 inch thick—and scoop out the pulp with a grapefruit knife. Separate fruit from membranes and put fruit into a bowl. Add marmalade and stir to mix. Set aside. Spoon 1 tablespoon orange liqueur into each orange shell and fill shells with orange-marmalade mixture, dividing it equally among the 8 shells. Top each with a scoop of orange sherbet and set into the freezer for at least 15 minutes. (*Oranges may be filled in advance and stored in the freezer.*)

Make meringue: beat egg whites until foamy, add cream of tartar, and beat until soft peaks form. Gradually beat in sugar, 1 tablespoon at a time; continue beating until mixture looks like marshmallow and feels smooth, not grainy, when you pinch it. Put meringue into a large pastry bag fitted with a large star tube and pipe the meringue onto the oranges, covering sherbet and cut edge of orange shells completely. Place on a baking sheet and set in a preheated 450° oven for about 5 minutes, or until meringue is set. (*Baked orange shells may be frozen for 1 month; when frozen, wrap them in plastic wrap or foil for longer storage. To serve, defrost at room temperature for a few minutes, until meringue softens.*) The oranges look particularly pretty served on glass plates each lined with a big green leaf; garnish each orange with a candied violet.

A Late Night Champagne Supper for 6

Lobster thermidor
Watercress salad (see p. 122)
Raspberry ice with cassis (see p. 56)

Lobster and champagne are about as elegant an offering as a hostess can make—delicious and unexpected after a play, opera, dance, or art show. I like to serve champagne before and during supper. Invite only those friends who would appreciate it.

LOBSTER THERMIDOR

3 live lobsters, about 1½ pounds each
8 tablespoons butter
2 tablespoons oil
2 tablespoons brandy
2 cups minced onion
1½ teaspoons salt
½ teaspoon freshly cracked white pepper

1 cup dry white wine
3 tablespoons flour
1 tablespoon plus 1 teaspoon Dijon mustard
4 or 5 drops Tabasco sauce
2 cups heavy cream
4 tablespoons freshly grated Parmesan cheese
1 tablespoon melted butter

To kill lobsters: place lobster on cutting board with claws to your left and shell side up. Insert a knife point into center of cross on head (this is clearly marked); split lengthwise. Remove sac behind eyes and the spinal cord (the little membrane running the length of the lobster). Cut off large claws with knife or scissors. Cut off little claws and remove any tomalley and red coral (the roe). Heat 2 tablespoons butter and the oil in a large skillet until hot, add all lobster pieces (including tomalley and red coral), cover, and cook over medium-high heat for 3 minutes. Remove cover. Heat brandy in a small pan just until warm; ignite it and pour it over the lobster. Shake pan until flames die. Cover pan again and cook lobster briskly over medium-high heat for 5 minutes. As soon as lobster is cool enough to handle, remove meat from shells, being careful to keep shells intact, and from large claws. Meat comes out of shells easily—just pull it out with your fingers. To get meat from large claws, crack them with nutcracker and pull meat out. Cut into good-size pieces, and set aside, with any tomalley and red coral. Reserve shells, little claws, and pan juices.

In a saucepan, melt 3 tablespoons butter and stir in minced onion, 1 teaspoon salt, and the pepper. Cook over high heat, stirring, until onion is transparent; do not let it brown. Add white wine to onion and cook over high heat until wine completely evaporates. Leave the pan uncovered and stir occasionally; do not let onion burn. Set aside. In another pan, melt remaining 3 tablespoons butter, stir in the flour with a wooden spatula, and cook, stirring constantly, over high heat for 2 minutes to eliminate the raw flour taste; do not let it brown. Add ½ teaspoon salt, the mustard, Tabasco, and pan juices from flaming lobster. Remove pan from heat, change to a whisk, and add the heavy cream all at once, whisking vigorously. Return pan to high heat and cook, whisking, until sauce thickens. Add onion mixture to sauce and simmer for 3 to 5 minutes. Stir in 2 rounded tablespoons grated Parmesan cheese. Add lobster meat and any tomalley or coral to sauce and spoon it into reserved shells. Sprinkle lobster halves with remaining Parmesan cheese and drizzle with melted butter. (*Recipe may be made ahead in morning to this point, covered with plastic wrap, and refrigerated. Reheat in 350° oven for 10 to 15 minutes before glazing.*) Run under the broiler to glaze. Garnish the top of each serving with the tiny claws.

A Robust Supper
for 12 Poker Players

Potage Saint-Germain
Steak tartare
Black radish salad
French and pumpernickel breads
Assorted pickles and olives
Crock of Stilton cheese
Coffeehouse mousse

This is a perfect menu for a group of men. Hearty pea soup can be served in mugs while the poker game is still on. Later, spread the tartare on thinly or thickly sliced bread and serve it with a crisp radish salad—biting in flavor and texture—and pickles and olives. After Stilton and crackers, the mousse adds a final filip.

POTAGE SAINT-GERMAIN

1½ pounds dried peas
6 cups chicken stock, more if necessary (see p. 278)
4 whole cloves
2 peeled onions
½ cup thinly sliced carrots
1 ham bone, with ham clinging to it
3 leeks
1 tablespoon salt, about
½ teaspoon freshly cracked white pepper

¼ teaspoon sugar
½ cup butter
½ cup fresh peas, cooked
½ pound ham, cut into shreds
½ cup light cream, heated, about
1 cup small croutons sautéed in butter
Fresh mint, optional

Soak the peas overnight in water to cover. Drain and wash them well and put them into a large heavy saucepan. Add chicken stock to cover. Bring to a boil and skim. Stick 2 cloves into each onion and add to soup, along with carrots and ham bone. Split leeks lengthwise and hold them under running water, separating layers, to wash away grit. Slice the leeks—use the white part plus 1 inch of the green—and add to soup. Bring back to a boil, turn heat to simmer, and cook slowly, partially covered, for about 1½ hours.

Remove the ham bone and puree the mixture through a food mill, using the medium disk, or in blender. Thin the soup, if you wish, with a little more hot chicken stock, but this soup should be thick. Season to taste with salt and pepper—add the salt 1 teaspoon at a time. Add sugar and beat in the butter, a teaspoonful at a time, using a whisk or wooden spatula. Add freshly cooked peas and shredded ham (cut from ham bone, or from another piece of ham), along with enough heated cream to thin soup to the consistency you want. (*Recipe can be made the day before and reheated.*) Reheat before serving. Garnish each serving with croutons and a sprig of fresh mint if you have it.

STEAK TARTARE

Use the very best prime-quality beef—sirloin or fillet—and grind the meat just before serving it, and never more than 1 hour ahead of time. If you have a respectable-looking meat grinder, it's fun to grind and prepare the meat in front of your guests.

3 pounds prime beef, very
freshly ground

3 egg yolks

1 cup chopped onion

½ cup capers, drained

3 tablespoons coarse salt

2 teaspoons freshly cracked
black pepper

6 finely chopped anchovy
fillets

¾ cup finely chopped parsley
or chives

Mix thoroughly all ingredients, except parsley or chives, with your hands or a wooden spatula. Taste for salt and pepper; it should be well seasoned. Form into a sausage shape and roll in finely chopped parsley or chives. Serve on a wooden plank or chopping board.

BLACK RADISH SALAD

4 large black radishes, about
3 inches diameter (see
p. 76)

2 egg yolks

1 teaspoon dry mustard

4 tablespoons vinegar *or* 2
tablespoons vinegar and 2
tablespoons lemon juice

1 teaspoon salt

½ teaspoon freshly cracked
white pepper

2 cups vegetable oil

2 tablespoons light cream

1 tablespoon Dijon mustard

2 tablespoons chopped parsley

Wash and peel the black radishes like potatoes, slice them about ⅛ inch thick, and cut slices into very fine julienne sticks. To make mayonnaise dressing, put egg yolks and dry mustard in a bowl and whisk. Add 2 tablespoons of vinegar and the salt and pepper and whisk. Continue whisking and begin to add oil, very slowly, 1 teaspoon at a time, until it starts to thicken. Pour in remaining oil in a thin stream, whisking constantly about 5 minutes, until mixture is thick and smooth. Beat in cream and flavor with remaining vinegar (or lemon juice) and Dijon mustard. Fold mayonnaise into julienne radish sticks, mound in a serving dish, and decorate with chopped parsley. *Can be made in the morning and refrigerated.*

COFFEEHOUSE MOUSSE

18 ladyfingers, split (see
   p. 265)
½ pound cream cheese
3 eggs, separated
6 ounces dark sweet chocolate
1 tablespoon (1 envelope)
   unflavored gelatine
2 tablespoons cold strong
   coffee
⅛ teaspoon salt

1 cup dark brown sugar
2 teaspoons vanilla extract
2½ cups heavy cream
3 tablespoons coffee liqueur
1 tablespoon coffee essence
1 tablespoon confectioners'
   sugar
   Chocolate candy coffee
   beans, optional, for
   garnish

Oil an 8-inch springform pan and line the sides with split ladyfingers. Let cream cheese and separated eggs come to room temperature. Melt chocolate and set aside. Soften gelatine in cold coffee. In electric mixer bowl, beat egg whites and salt until soft peaks form. Beat in ½ cup brown sugar, a spoonful at a time; add vanilla and continue beating until thick, smooth, and glossy. In a separate, chilled bowl, whip 1½ cups heavy cream until stiff. In a third bowl, beat cream cheese until fluffy; beat in remaining ½ cup brown sugar, a tablespoonful at a time. Flavor with 2 table-spoons coffee liqueur and the coffee essence. Beat in egg yolks, one at a time. Dissolve the softened gelatine by placing it over simmering water. Beat it into cream cheese mixture in a thin stream, along with melted chocolate. Fold in the beaten egg whites and whipped cream and pour into the prepared pan. Chill in the refrigerator for at least 2 hours or overnight. (*Recipe is better if made the day before.*) When ready to serve, whip remaining 1 cup heavy cream with confectioners' sugar and re-maining 1 tablespoon coffee liqueur until stiff. Put the cream into a pastry bag fitted with a star tube, unmold mousse, and decorate around top edge with rosettes of whipped cream. Garnish with chocolate coffee beans or with shreds of grated chocolate.

An Election Night Supper for 10

Stuffed artichokes
Fried oysters, shrimp, and mussels,
with tartar sauce
Broccoli with white wine
Romaine salad (see p. 58)
Cold caramel soufflé

A tasty meal for people staying up late for election results. If you wish to lighten the menu, serve either broccoli or salad, rather than both.

STUFFED ARTICHOKES

10 artichokes	1 teaspoon salt
2 tablespoons salt	½ teaspoon freshly cracked
5 cups chopped onions	black pepper
1¼ cups butter	Olive oil to film serving dish
⅓ cup bread crumbs	
1 cup freshly grated	
Parmesan cheese	

Break off stems and trim bases of artichokes so that they stand evenly. With scissors, cut the tips off the leaves, and with a knife, cut ½ inch off the very top of each. Put in a large kettle, cover with water, add 2 tablespoons salt, and bring to a boil. Do not cover. Boil about 25 to 35 minutes or until done. Drain upside down and cool until they can be handled. Spread leaves open and pull out the center cone. With a spoon, scrape out the hairy choke. Sauté chopped onions over high heat in 2 tablespoons of the butter, just until wilted. Mix with bread crumbs and Parmesan cheese; season with 1 teaspoon salt and the pepper. Melt remaining butter and use about ¼ cup of it to moisten the onion-cheese mixture. Stuff artichokes. (*Recipe can be made ahead to this point.*) Film an ovenproof serving dish with olive oil and arrange artichokes in dish. Drizzle with remaining butter and bake in a preheated 400° oven for 10 minutes.

FRIED OYSTERS, SHRIMP, AND MUSSELS, WITH TARTAR SAUCE

40 mussels
¼ cup dry white wine
40 raw shrimp
40 oysters
 1 cup flour

2 recipes beer batter (see
  p. 285)
Fat for deep frying
2 recipes Tartar Sauce (see
  p. 55)

Scrub mussels with a stiff brush and remove the beards with a knife. Rinse in several changes of cold water to remove sand. Discard any mussels that are open. Put mussels in a pan with white wine, cover, and shake over high heat just long enough to open mussels. Discard any that do not open. Remove mussels from shells (broth in pan belongs to the cook). Shell and devein the shrimp. Remove oysters from shells and drain (save juice for another use). Dry mussels, shrimp, and oysters on paper towels and roll in flour; pat off excess. Dip in beer batter. Heat 3 inches of fat in a heavy saucepan or deep-fat fryer to 375°. Fry seafood, a few pieces at a time, until puffed and brown, about 3 to 4 minutes. Place on brown paper on cake rack on baking sheet in 325° oven to keep warm as you fry them. (*Can be fried ahead of time and reheated in same way.*) Serve hot with Tartar Sauce.

BROCCOLI WITH WHITE WINE

 2 bunches broccoli
¼ cup olive oil
1½ cups dry white wine

1 teaspoon salt
½ teaspoon freshly cracked
  black pepper

Wash broccoli well and trim off stem ends. Put it in a saucepan with olive oil, wine, salt, and pepper. Bring to a boil, half-cover the saucepan, reduce heat, and simmer until broccoli is barely tender, about 15 to 20 minutes. Arrange broccoli on a serving dish and keep it warm. Boil liquid to reduce it to about 1 cup. Pour over broccoli.

Note: Broccoli cooked in wine is also good cold, as a salad. Reduce cooking liquid to 1 cup to use, chilled, as a dressing.

COLD CARAMEL SOUFFLÉ

2 cups sugar
⅔ cup boiling water
2 tablespoons (2 envelopes) unflavored gelatine
¼ cup rum

6 eggs, separated
2½ cups heavy cream
2 tablespoons melted currant jelly

Prepare a 6-cup soufflé dish with a paper collar. Cut a length of waxed paper long enough to go around the dish with some overlap. Fold it in half, lengthwise, and brush the inside edge with vegetable oil. Tie it around the soufflé dish so that it extends about 4 to 5 inches above it.

To make caramel, melt 1½ cups sugar in a heavy skillet over high heat. Stir the sugar with a wooden spatula until lumps disappear; then let it bubble until it turns a light caramel color. Remove from heat and let bubbles subside. Have boiling water ready and add it *carefully* to caramel—keep your hand behind the pan to avoid scalding steam. Stir the caramel-water mixture until well blended and let it cool for about 10 minutes. Soften gelatine in rum in a custard cup; then stand the cup in a pan of simmering water and stir to dissolve gelatine. With electric mixer, beat egg yolks until foamy; beat in remaining ½ cup sugar. Gradually add caramel mixture in a thin stream, beating constantly. Beat in gelatine mixture. Continue beating until mixture cools, about 10 minutes—set the bowl over ice to hasten cooling.

In another bowl, beat egg whites until soft peaks form. Fold them into the cooled caramel mixture, along with 2 cups heavy cream, softly whipped. Pour into prepared soufflé dish and chill for at least 3 hours, or overnight, in the refrigerator. To serve, remove collar. Whip remaining ½ cup heavy cream until stiff. Put it into a pastry bag fitted with a star tube and pipe rosettes of whipped cream around top of soufflé. Drizzle rosettes with melted currant jelly.

Cocktail Parties

There are two ways to look at a cocktail party. Undeniably, it's a useful way to pay off an unmanageable accumulation of social debts. But I take a more positive view: I love to give cocktail parties!

I like big, bashy affairs given to honor a friend or pay tribute to accomplishment. I invite as large a group as I can shoehorn into the house and set the party hours from four to six or five to seven. All the food is finger food, available on tables or, more usually, passed on trays constantly replenished in the kitchen. You need good help, including a good bartender, for a party of this kind.

If you want to feed your cocktail guests dinner in an informal way, invite them for a later hour and change your menu to more substantial food. At a cocktail buffet you might, for example, offer

227

your guests a Pâté en Croûte, Raw Vegetables with Olive Butter, Scallops and Prosciutto, Cold Baked Ham, Cold Fillet of Beef, and Tyropita—all recipes available in this book. Include a dessert, too, if you wish—a choice of crêpes makes a fantastic ending for a large party.

Now for party logistics. You'll be safe if you count six hors d'oeuvre per guest. There are twelve suggestions in the large cocktail party menu; you may want to fix fewer of these, doubling or tripling some of the recipes. Think hard about what you can manage, how much you can store in your refrigerator, even how many trays or plates you'll need.

Count four drinks per person. In addition to the usual hard liquors, be sure to offer your guests a choice of lighter drinks—white wine, or apéritifs such as sweet vermouth, white wine and cassis, or Lillet. My favorite advice for hassle-free bartending is to settle on one size glass for everything—perhaps a plain all-purpose wineglass (10-ounce size). Incidentally, for a large gathering, I find it simplest to rent all the glasses—they don't have to be washed, just rinsed and sent back.

Do everything you can ahead of time. Anything wrapped in bacon or deep-fried should be cooked well in advance, so that your house will be free of cooking odors when guests arrive. Prepare garnishes—giant fluted mushrooms, turnip and tomato roses—for your serving plates. Instruct your help to use fresh paper doilies when they refill trays. Lay in plenty of ice. Set out twice as many ashtrays as you think you'll need, and be sure someone's assigned to empty them and to pick up paper napkins and empty glasses.

Have fun!

A Large Cocktail Party
for 50

Pâté en croûte
Assorted canapés
Platter of raw vegetables with olive butter
Cherry tomatoes stuffed
with crab meat and guacamole
Onion pie, cut into wedges
Brandade of trout
Steak tartare
Shrimp maison
Roasted peppers and anchovies
Salami cornucopias on pumpernickel
Alpine logs
Fried oysters

Here is a generous selection of hors d'oeuvre from which you can pick and choose according to your tastes and the appetites of your guests. Several of these recipes appear elsewhere in the book: Onion Pie on p. 85, Steak Tartare on p. 221, and Salami Cornucopias on p. 63.

PÂTÉ EN CROÛTE

Pâté molds, imported from France, are made of tin and hinged so that you can take the pan away from the loaf after it's baked, without damaging the crust—like a springform pan. Molds may be oblong or oval; to make this recipe, you will need one with a capacity of 4 to 5 cups. First you line the mold with pastry, then line that with blanched bacon, and pack it with forcemeat and filling. You put on the top crust, decorate it, and bake the pâté. When cool, you finish it off with aspic, poured under the crust. This recipe can be prepared ahead in stages, and it can be frozen after baking, but *before* the aspic is added.

PASTRY:
- 2 cups lightly spooned flour
- 1 teaspoon salt
- 10 tablespoons butter
- 3 egg yolks
- 2 tablespoons olive oil
- ¼ cup ice water

- ½ pound sliced bacon, blanched

FORCEMEAT:
- ½ pound veal, ground twice
- ½ pound pork, ground twice
- 1 egg
- 1 egg white
- ½ cup finely chopped onion
- 1 finely chopped clove garlic
- 1 tablespoon chopped parsley
- 1 teaspoon freshly cracked black pepper

- 1 teaspoon salt
- 2 tablespoons brandy

FILLING:
- ¼ pound boiled ham or tongue, thinly sliced
- 1 truffle, sliced

EGG WASH:
- 2 egg yolks
- 1 tablespoon water

ASPIC:
- 2 cups chicken or veal stock (see p. 278 or p. 279)
- 2 teaspoons tomato paste
- 2 tablespoons (2 envelopes) unflavored gelatine
- 2 tablespoons dry Madeira
- 2 egg whites, beaten just to a froth

To make pastry, put flour in a bowl, stir in salt, and cut in butter with a pastry blender until mixture looks like coarse cornmeal. Make a well in the flour mixture and drop in egg yolks and olive oil. Work this up quickly with a pastry fork, adding just enough ice water so the mixture can be gathered together in a dough ball. Wrap the ball in plastic wrap and chill it for at least 1 hour.

To line pâté mold, roll pastry dough out on a floured board, ¼ inch thick. Rolled dough should be long enough to cover length plus ends of mold, and wide enough to cover bottom and both sides; reserve extra dough for top crust and decorations. Dust the surface of the rolled pastry with flour (so it won't stick to itself) and fold pastry in half, lengthwise. Pinch the ends together to make an envelope. Shape the envelope and fit it into the mold, pressing it against sides and into corners, but using care not to stretch the dough. Trim off excess pastry, leaving about ⅛ inch above rim of mold; this rim of dough will give you something to anchor the top crust to. Store pastry-lined mold in refrigerator until you're ready to fill it.

To fill mold, line the pastry-lined mold with overlapping strips of blanched bacon, letting the bacon hang over the sides of the mold. Put all ingredients for forcemeat in a bowl, flaming the brandy as you add it, and mix well. Pack about half the force-meat into the bacon-lined mold. Arrange the filling of ham slices and truffle down the center and cover with remaining forcemeat. Fold the bacon ends over to cover forcemeat completely.

Roll out remaining pastry, also ¼ inch thick, and trim it to fit top of mold. Beat egg yolks with water to make egg wash and brush the top edges of the pastry in the mold with this mixture. Lay top crust in place and pinch edges together with a pastry pincer or the back of a knife. The egg wash acts as a glue. Cut a little hole in the center of the top crust and insert a paper funnel. With a small leaf cutter, cut leaf shapes from pastry scraps; mark veins on leaves with a knife and place the leaves decoratively around the paper funnel, using the egg wash to hold them. Brush egg wash all over the top of the crust; this will make the crust brown and shiny when it's baked. (*If not baking immediately, cover the mold with aluminum foil and set in the refrigerator for up to 1 week or in the freezer for up to 1 month.*)

To bake pâté, bring mold from refrigerator or freezer and let it come to room temperature. Place it on a baking tray (protection in case the hinged mold oozes) and bake it in a preheated 375° oven for 1 hour; reduce heat to 300° and bake 30 minutes more. If pastry is not brown, bake another 15 minutes. Remove from oven, replace the paper funnel with a new one, and let cool. (*Refrigerate to chill thoroughly or freeze.*)

To make aspic, combine all ingredients in a saucepan, set over heat, and beat with a whisk until liquid comes to a rolling boil. Remove from heat; let stand 15 minutes. Line a fine sieve with a double thickness of cheesecloth wrung out in cold water and pour aspic through strainer into a bowl. Let the liquid drain through without stirring or forcing it in any way. Cool aspic over ice. When it's thick and syrupy, pour it down the funnel, to put a layer of aspic under the crust and on top of the meat. The meat shrinks away from the top crust when the loaf bakes, so there is space to fill. Remove funnel and refrigerate mold again until aspic sets, about ½ hour. Pour any extra aspic into a shallow pan and chill. To serve pâté, remove hinged mold and place pâté on a platter. Chop the chilled aspic and arrange it around the loaf of pâté. Slice pâté and serve on individual plates with fork.

CANAPÉS

To be at their best, canapés should be served as soon as possible after they're assembled and certainly within an hour. You'll need good kitchen help to manage this. Reserve a good-sized counter in the kitchen for the assembly line, and prepare all the makings in advance. To guide your help, make up samples ahead to be duplicated as needed.

I have included a number of specific suggestions for canapés, but use your imagination to create others. Decorate canapé platters with watercress, tomato roses (see p. 284), fluted mushrooms (see p. 284), and turnip roses. The following ingredients will make enough canapés for 50 people.

6 loaves white bread, firm-textured, sliced extra thin	2 large jars green stuffed olives
	6 tomatoes
	6 lemons
1½ cups egg salad	2 bunches parsley
1½ cups tuna salad	2 8-ounce packages cream cheese
3 dozen hard-cooked eggs	
2 pounds smoked salmon, thinly sliced	1 tablespoon light cream
	2 cups mayonnaise (see p. 283)
2 pounds boiled ham, thinly sliced	
	2 tablespoons Dijon mustard, about
8 ounces caviar, red and black	
2 7-ounce cans baby shrimp	1 pound butter, softened
4 4-ounce cans sardines	Horseradish
6 2-ounce cans flat anchovy fillets	Mustard
	Anchovy paste
3 bunches radishes	Lemon juice
3 cucumbers	

Cut bread in a variety of shapes—rounds, squares, rectangles, teardrops, fingers, diamonds, half-moons—using a knife or canapé cutters. For canapés that will be spread with soft fillings, lightly toast bread in a 350° oven and let it cool before spreading it. Since butter is not absorbed by cold toast, this will help prevent soggy canapés. Prepare egg and tuna salads using your favorite recipe; refrigerate until needed. Cool hard-cooked eggs rapidly and refrigerate. Cut some eggs in half and prepare balance for use as garnishing by sieving egg yolk and chopping egg white. Ready fish and meat for assembly and refrigerate. Prepare vegetables and garnishes: hollow out radishes. Slice cucumbers thinly on a vegetable cutter or mandoline; sprinkle with salt and refriger-ate. Slice stuffed olives. Peel and seed tomatoes and cut flesh into small pieces. Cut strips of lemon peel with a lemon stripper. Chop parsley (but reserve a few tufts unchopped). Cover and refrigerate all of these until needed. Soften cream cheese by bringing it to room temperature and thinning it with a bit of cream. Flavor mayonnaise with Dijon mustard, to taste (about 1 tablespoon mustard per cup of mayonnaise). Put cream cheese and mayonnaise into small pastry bags or paper cones fitted with cake decorating tubes, ready for piping out into rosettes or stripes. Blend softened butter with flavorings to taste—horseradish, mus-tard, anchovy paste, lemon juice—your choice. Pound solid food flavorers, such as shrimp or caviar, in a mortar; blend in butter and push it through a sieve.

INDIVIDUAL CANAPÉS

1. Fill hollowed-out radishes with caviar; decorate with a stripe of cream cheese.

2. Garnish hard-cooked egg halves with caviar and a tuft of parsley; pipe on a circlet of cream cheese.

3. Spread bread fingers with mustard mayonnaise. Lay 1 anchovy fillet on each. Dip 1 buttered end in chopped parsley and the other end in sieved egg yolk. Decorate with mayonnaise rosette.

4. Spread bread squares (including edges) with butter. Dip edges in chopped parsley. Pile on tuna salad; decorate with rosette of mayonnaise and a small piece of tomato.

5. Spread bread rectangles with butter, cover with egg salad, and decorate with olive slices.

6. Spread rounds with mustard mayonnaise. Cut thin boiled ham to fit bread, and decorate with cream cheese piped on a daisy design with a speck of caviar in the middle.

7. Spread half-moons (including edges) with butter. Dip in chopped parsley. Top with 2 slices of cucumber.

8. Spread bread fingers with mustard mayonnaise or lemon butter. Lay on 1 sardine, pipe on a wiggle of mayonnaise, and sprinkle with sieved egg yolk.

9. Spread bread teardrops with lemon butter and cover with baby shrimp. Pipe a U-shaped bit of cream cheese around shrimp and lay a strip of lemon peel across the U.

10. Butter squares (including edges) and dip edges in

chopped parsley. Lay on smoked salmon, decorate with an X shape of cream cheese, and sprinkle with sieved egg yolk.

11. Butter triangles with mustard mayonnaise. Heap with red caviar and chopped egg white.

PLATTER OF RAW VEGETABLES
WITH OLIVE BUTTER

Prepare as indicated and chill a selection of the following raw vegetables: celery sticks, carrot curls or sticks, baby turnip slices, zucchini slices or cubes, cauliflower flowerets, eggplant cubes, green or red pepper strips, white and red radishes, black radish slices, black olives, cherry tomatoes, fennel slices, and snow peas. Serve with olive butter, the recipe for which can be found on p. 68.

CHERRY TOMATOES STUFFED
WITH CRAB MEAT AND GUACAMOLE

Follow the recipe for Cherry Tomatoes Stuffed with Guacamole on p. 158, but double the quantity of tomatoes and stuff the rest with Crab-Meat Salad, the recipe for which is on p. 52.

BRANDADE OF TROUT

2 smoked trout
½ cup unsalted butter
½ cup heavy cream, about
   Juice of ½ lemon
½ teaspoon salt

¼ teaspoon freshly cracked
   black pepper
Chopped black olives, for
   garnish
1 loaf white bread, firm-
   textured, sliced extra thin

Skin and bone trout; you should have 1 pound of meat. Beat butter in electric mixer bowl, using the flat whip if you have a heavy-duty mixer. As butter gets creamy, add bits of the trout, about 1 teaspoonful at a time. Beat until mixture is smooth and very, very creamy; this will take about 15 to 20 minutes. Beat in just enough heavy cream to give mixture the consistency of whipped butter. Add lemon juice, salt, and pepper, and mix well. Pack it into a crock and chill thoroughly, at least 1 to 2 hours.

(*Can be made ahead and refrigerated up to 3 to 4 days.*) Serve pâté from the crock, its top decorated with chopped black olives. Serve with Melba toast, prepared by cutting bread into triangles and baking in a preheated 350° oven about 15 to 20 minutes or until brown, turning bread once.

SHRIMP MAISON

2 pounds small or medium-size raw shrimp
½ cup butter
6 finely chopped cloves garlic
Juice of 2 lemons
½ teaspoon salt
¼ teaspoon freshly cracked white pepper
¾ cup dry white wine
2 tablespoons chopped parsley

Shell and devein the shrimp. Melt butter in flameproof serving dish. When butter foams, add shrimp; sauté briefly over high heat, shaking the pan, but do not let them brown. Add chopped garlic (6 cloves is correct), lemon juice, salt, pepper, and wine. (*Can be made ahead to this point.*) Cook for about 7 minutes over high heat, uncovered, or until shrimp turn pink. Sprinkle with chopped parsley and keep warm on a hot tray or candle-warmer.

ROASTED PEPPERS AND ANCHOVIES

2 2-ounce cans flat anchovy fillets
2 tablespoons lemon juice
2 tablespoons olive oil
1 tablespoon finely chopped shallots
½ teaspoon finely chopped garlic
¼ teaspoon freshly cracked black pepper
4 tablespoons chopped parsley
1 tablespoon chopped fresh dill, optional
1 teaspoon chopped fresh chives, optional
1 12-ounce jar whole roasted peppers
Black olives, for garnish
Melba toast fingers (recipe follows)

Drain oil from anchovies into a bowl. Add lemon juice, olive oil, shallots, garlic, pepper, 2 tablespoons chopped parsley, the dill, and the chives and stir with a fork to make a paste. Put anchovy fillets into a sieve and rinse under cold water. Cut peppers in strips. Arrange anchovies and pepper strips on a serving platter (do not use a silver platter) and spoon paste over all. Sprinkle with remaining 2 tablespoons chopped parsley and garnish platter with black olives. Serve with Melba toast fingers.

MELBA TOAST FINGERS

Buy thin-sliced, firm-textured white bread of good quality and cut it into fingers. Paint fingers on both sides with melted butter, if you wish. Lay fingers on a baking sheet and bake in a preheated 350° oven until brown, about 15 to 20 minutes. Turn fingers over once while baking. *Can be baked ahead and stored in plastic bags.*

ALPINE LOGS

½ pound grated Swiss Appen- zeller cheese
½ pound finely chopped dried beef
2 slightly beaten eggs

2 tablespoons chopped parsley
2 tablespoons caraway seeds
2 to 3 sheets filo dough, each about 11 x 5 inches
¾ cup melted butter

Mix together the cheese, dried beef, eggs, parsley, and caraway seeds. Work with 1 sheet of filo dough at a time, keeping remaining sheets covered with a damp, not wet, towel. (Filo dough, an extrathin pastry, is available in Greek or Armenian grocery stores.) Lay a sheet of filo dough on a slightly damp towel and brush it all over with melted butter. Spoon the cheese mixture along one long edge of the sheet and roll it up like a jelly roll, brushing with more melted butter as you turn the roll. Repeat with remaining sheets and cheese mixture. Place on a baking sheet and brush all over with remaining melted butter. (*Can be made ahead to this point and covered closely with plastic wrap. Refrigerate if holding longer than 2 to 3 hours. May be frozen for up to 1 month; be sure it is fully thawed before baking.*) Bake in a preheated 350° oven for 15 to 20 minutes or until golden brown. Cut into 1-inch pieces. Serve hot or cold.

FRIED OYSTERS

60 oysters
1 cup flour
1½ recipes beer batter (see
    p. 285)

Fat for deep frying
1 recipe Soy Dipping Sauce
    (see p. 142)

Drain oysters and dry with paper towels. Roll in flour, patting off excess. Dip in beer batter and fry, a few at a time, in 3 inches of hot fat heated to 375°, until puffed and golden brown. Drain on paper towels. (*May be prepared ahead—to allow time for frying odor to dissipate—and reheated. Lay on sheets of brown paper on cake racks on baking tray and reheat in oven.*) Serve warm with Soy Dipping Sauce.

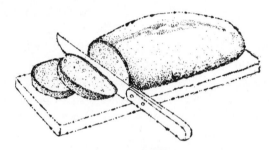

A Cocktail Party for 12

Crostini, Salsa di alici
Seafood in strudel
Duck pâté
Meat balls
Platter of raw vegetables
with olive butter (see p. 234)

This menu provides a good variety without an enormous number of dishes—cheese-flavored crostini, seafood, poultry, meat, and the crispness of the raw vegetables. It's easy, too, to make up your own menu using this as a guide. For example, you could substitute Cheese Puffs (see p. 246) for the Crostini, or Scallops and Prosciutto (see p. 210) for Seafood in Strudel. Other good recipes for a party menu are Cold Fillet of Beef (p. 258), Baked Ham (p. 259), and Tyropita (p. 153).

CROSTINI, SALSA DI ALICI

1 long loaf Italian bread, 1 day old
1 pound Swiss cheese
½ cup melted butter
½ teaspoon oregano

2 2-ounce cans flat anchovy fillets, drained and chopped
½ cup olive oil
2 finely chopped cloves garlic
2 tablespoons chopped parsley
¼ cup red wine vinegar

Cut ends off bread and cut into 2-inch squares, leaving crust on. Cut cheese into 1-inch cubes. Beginning and ending with bread, alternate bread and cheese cubes on 8-inch skewers; you'll fill 6 to 8 of them. Lay skewers in a buttered baking dish and brush generously with melted butter and oregano. (*Can be prepared the day before to this point.*) Bake in a preheated 350° oven until cheese begins to melt and bread browns a bit, about 10 to 15 minutes. Meanwhile, make sauce (*which also can be made ahead and reheated*). Mash the anchovies and combine with remaining ingredients. Heat to bubbling, stirring. To serve, bring Crostini to room on skewers; holding skewer in hand, with aid of fork, slip off contents onto platter. Pour sauce over and serve on plates with forks or toothpicks.

SEAFOOD IN STRUDEL

½ cup fine bread crumbs
½ cup freshly grated Parmesan cheese
2 teaspoons dry mustard
1 very finely chopped onion
1 tablespoon butter
1½ cups mixed seafood, cut in pieces (halved bay or sea scallops, cooked lobster meat, cooked shrimp, poached salmon, raw crab meat)

1 cup sour cream
½ teaspoon salt
¼ teaspoon freshly cracked white pepper
2 tablespoons chopped fresh chives
2 tablespoons chopped parsley
4 sheets filo dough, about 11 x 13 inches
1¼ cups melted butter
Juice of 1 lemon

Put bread crumbs, grated Parmesan, and dry mustard into a small bowl and mix well. Set aside. Cook onion in butter over high heat until transparent, but do not let it brown. Mix seafood with sour cream; add onion, salt, pepper, chives, and parsley. Work with filo sheets—extrathin Greek or Armenian pastry—one at a time, keeping the remaining sheets covered with a damp, not wet, towel. On a sheet of waxed paper, stack the filo sheets, brushing each sheet with some of the ¼ cup melted butter before adding the next one. Brush the top sheet with melted butter, too, and sprinkle with the cheese–bread crumb mixture. Spoon seafood mixture 1 inch from one long edge of filo sheets, leaving a 1-inch margin at each end. Start rolling up the seafood in the pastry, folding in the ends as you roll, so that the seafood is wrapped securely inside the pastry package. Brush the filo as you roll it with melted butter. Use the waxed paper to help you roll it. Place roll on a baking sheet and brush it all over with melted butter. (*Can be made ahead to this point, and refrigerated, or frozen up to 1 month. Bring to room temperature before baking.*) Place in a preheated 375° oven on the middle rack, and bake for 30 minutes or until crisp and light brown. Slice 1½ inches thick and serve hot with lemon butter, made by mixing remaining 1 cup melted butter with the lemon juice.

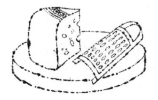

DUCK PÂTÉ

Follow directions for Pâté en Croûte (see p. 229), making the following changes: instead of ham, use uncooked duck meat for the filling. Remove skin from duck and cut breast and leg meat from carcass. Cut meat into long thin strips and marinate them in brandy (preferably Cognac) for 1 hour. Use the duck carcass to make stock and substitute this stock for the chicken stock when you make the aspic. To make stock, put the carcass in a saucepan, cover with cold water. Add 1 small peeled onion, stuck with 2 whole cloves, 1 small sliced carrot, and a bouquet garni (see p. 283). Bring to a boil, skim, turn heat to simmer, cover, and simmer for 1½ hours. Strain stock before using and season to taste with salt and pepper.

MEAT BALLS

1 pound veal, ground twice
1 pound pork, ground twice
4 eggs
1½ cups finely chopped
   onion
1 tablespoon finely chopped
   shallots
1 teaspoon finely chopped
   garlic
2 tablespoons chopped
   parsley
1 teaspoon salt
½ teaspoon freshly cracked
   black pepper
¼ teaspoon freshly grated
   nutmeg
¼ teaspoon ground cardamom
   Heavy cream, if necessary
4 tablespoons butter, more if
   necessary

SAUCE:
2 tablespoons brandy
2 tablespoons butter
2 teaspoons chopped garlic
2 tablespoons chopped shallots
2 finely chopped mushrooms
1 tablespoon tomato paste
1 teaspoon meat glaze
2 teaspoons potato starch,
   or cornstarch
½ cup dry Madeira, more if
   necessary
2 cups chicken stock, more if
   necessary (see p. 278)
1 tablespoon currant jelly
2 tablespoons orange
   marmalade
   Juice of ½ lemon
2 tablespoons chopped celery
6 chopped anchovy fillets

In a large bowl, mix together meat, eggs, onion, shallots, garlic, parsley, and seasonings. Mixture should be loose; if too stiff, thin it with heavy cream. Wet your hands and form meat balls. Do not compact the mixture; handle it lightly, moving the ball from palm to palm. Recipe makes about 70 small balls, 35 medium-size. (*Meat balls can be made ahead and frozen or refrigerated. Thaw frozen meat balls before cooking.*) Heat butter in a large skillet and brown the meat balls over high heat, a few at a time, first on one side, then the other. (Mixture is loose and balls will flatten, like patties.) As they brown, remove balls from skillet and set aside; they will cook through later, in the sauce.

To make sauce, pour off all but a thin film of fat from skillet, pour in brandy, and ignite it. When flames die, scrape up the brown bits. Add butter, melt it, and then add garlic and shallots; cook for a minute or two. Add mushrooms, tomato paste, meat glaze, and potato starch and stir to make a paste. Remove from heat, change to a whisk, and add Madeira and chicken stock, whisking vigorously. Return to heat and bring to a boil. Stir in currant jelly and orange marmalade. Add lemon juice, celery, and anchovies. If sauce is too thick, thin it with more Madeira or chicken stock. Return meat balls to skillet and baste with the sauce. (*Recipe can be made ahead to this point and refrigerated or frozen. Bring to room temperature before reheating.*) Cook for about 5 minutes. For buffet service, transfer to a chafing dish and keep warm.

Teas

Invite neighbors, little girls, great-aunts, and grandmothers to tea—not to mention your best friends. It's a delightful way to entertain, a gentle way to encourage good manners, a pleasant meeting ground for the generations.

I remember my mother setting out her silver tea service a couple of times a week. When her friends stopped in, she'd bring out the thinnest sandwiches, the tiniest cookies. I was enchanted, and to this day I love the plain bread-and-butter sandwiches I first discovered then, their round edges dipped in parsley. It was one of my earliest experiences of being "grown up."

I hope our world never gets too busy for afternoon tea. Even if you drink it alone in a department store after a long day of shopping, it's a revitalizing and comforting ritual. When you dress up for it at home, it's truly civilizing.

Here is a chance to use your fine English bone china. Tea always seems to taste better in fragile cups. Everything on your table or tray or tea cart—the food included—should be dainty in appearance. For small parties, put your tea service and sandwiches on a large tray or low table and serve in the living room. You'll want to arrange a more elaborate tea in the dining room, inviting a friend to pour for you. For a very large group, serve the tea buffet-style and ask several friends to take turns pouring. And, if the weather is nice, don't forget the possibility of serving tea in the garden or on your terrace.

Everyone has his or her own ideas about making tea, and of course you'll want to accommodate individual preferences for lemon or milk. The British way to make tea is precise: water should be freshly drawn and brought to a full boil. Rinse the pot with some boiling water, to warm it. Pour this water out, measure in the tea (1 teaspoon per cup), and pour in fresh boiling water. Steep it for five minutes and stir. The tea is now ready to serve. For a large group, it's often best to make very strong tea and have a second pot of hot water on your tray, to dilute it to everyone's taste—and to refill the teapot for second cups.

Think of the coffee drinkers among your guests, too. There's no reason to offer *only* tea. And if you have very little girls at your party, pour their tea and milk into demitasse cups or doll's china—or make them a pot of cocoa.

Substantial Tea
for 12

Sandwiches of sliced cold roast turkey
on Sandy Ainsworth's white bread
Cheese puffs
Toasted English muffins and strawberry jam
Alice Peterson's chocolate cheesecake
(see p. 71)

SANDY AINSWORTH'S WHITE BREAD

The cooking time for this delicious bread is shorter than usual. People always question it, but it is correct. Not only can this bread be put together very quickly, it will stay fresh for a long time.

1 cup warm water (105° to 115°)
1 teaspoon plus ½ cup sugar
2 packages active dry yeast
2 cups lukewarm water
1 tablespoon salt
½ cup vegetable oil
9 cups lightly spooned flour, about

Put warm water into a large warm bowl and dissolve 1 teaspoon sugar in it. Sprinkle with yeast; stir until blended and let stand 10 minutes. Stir in lukewarm water, ½ cup sugar, salt, and vegetable oil. Beat in flour, 1 cupful at a time, adding enough so that the mixture hangs together and is easy to handle, but still sticky. Scrape the dough out on a well-floured board and knead it for several minutes, until smooth and elastic; if too sticky to knead, add more flour. Form the kneaded dough into a ball, and put it into a lightly greased bowl, turning the ball over to grease the top lightly. Cover with a cloth and let dough rise in a warm place (about 85°), free from drafts, until doubled. This will take from 1 to 2 hours. Punch the dough down, turn it out on the board, and divide it into 3 equal parts. Shape the dough into loaves and place them in greased 8 x 4 x 2¾-inch loaf pans, cover with a towel, and let rise again, in a warm place, free from drafts, until doubled, about 1 hour. Put loaves into a preheated 400°

oven and bake for 20 minutes. Turn out at once and let cool on cake racks, away from draft. Bread will stay fresh for a week, and it freezes well, for up to 1 month.

SANDWICHES OF SLICED COLD ROAST TURKEY ON SANDY AINSWORTH'S WHITE BREAD

Chill 1 loaf of Sandy Ainsworth's white bread so that you can slice it in very thin slices—use a serrated knife. Keep slices in order so that each pair will fit together neatly when you assemble sandwiches. Butter slices with softened butter. Arrange thin slices of freshly roasted turkey breast meat on half the slices; sprinkle with salt and pepper and top with a lettuce leaf, if you wish. Spread remaining slices with homemade mayonnaise (see p. 283) and lay over turkey. Cut each sandwich into 4 triangles. *Can be made up to 2 to 3 hours ahead and covered with a damp towel.*

CHEESE PUFFS

4 ounces sharp cheese, grated coarsely	1 teaspoon Dijon mustard
	¾ cup lightly spooned flour
1 generous teaspoon Worcestershire sauce	¼ teaspoon salt
	4 tablespoons melted butter
3 or 4 drops Tabasco sauce	¼ cup sesame seeds

Mix all ingredients except sesame seeds together, adding the butter last, and shape dough into marble-size balls. Dip each ball into sesame seeds and place, seed side up, on baking sheets. Bake in a preheated 375° oven for 20 minutes or until lightly browned. Makes 30 puffs. Serve warm or at room temperature. *Can be made ahead and reheated if desired. Can be frozen for up to 1 month.*

TOASTED ENGLISH MUFFINS AND STRAWBERRY JAM

Never slice English muffins. Jab them around the edge with a fork, then split them in half. Put them in a 300° oven for about 20 minutes to get hot and crisp, like Melba toast. Butter them and serve with a pot of strawberry jam.

An Elegant Tea
for 8

Sandy Ainsworth's bread-and-butter sandwiches
Rum babas
Strawberry roll
Florentines
Pignolia cookies
Chocolate leaves

SANDY AINSWORTH'S
BREAD-AND-BUTTER SANDWICHES

Chill 1 loaf of Sandy Ainsworth's white bread (see p. 245) so that you can slice it in very thin slices. Butter the slices with softened butter and press together to make sandwiches. With 1½-inch cookie cutter, cut 2 round sandwiches from each big sandwich. Dip edges of each round in mayonnaise and roll in finely chopped parsley. *Can be made 3 to 4 hours ahead and covered with a damp towel.*

RUM BABAS

1 package active dry yeast	½ teaspoon salt
¼ cup lukewarm water	2 tablespoons dried currants
1¼ cups lightly spooned flour	½ cup light rum
3 large eggs at room temperature	¼ cup water
1 tablespoon softened butter	Apricot glaze, optional
1 tablespoon plus 1¼ cups sugar	

Brush 8 or 10 *baba au rhum* molds with oil and set aside. Sprinkle yeast into lukewarm water and stir to dissolve. Add yeast mixture to flour in a bowl and mix together with your hand. Beat eggs well and add to flour mixture, beating with your hand or a wooden spatula until the mixture is very light and shiny. Cover bowl with a cloth and set in a warm place, free from drafts, to rise until double, about 1 to 1½ hours. When risen, mix in softened butter, 1 tablespoon sugar, the salt, and currants. Half-fill the prepared baba molds; cover molds with a cloth and let rise again until dough almost reaches tops of molds. Place molds on a baking sheet and bake in a preheated 375° oven for about 25 minutes, or until nicely browned. Turn them out at once and soak them in rum syrup for ½ hour. To make syrup, put rum, 1¼ cups sugar, and ¼ cup water in a saucepan over high heat. Stir until sugar dissolves; then simmer 10 minutes.

After their soaking, babas may be brushed with apricot glaze: mix 1 cup apricot jam with ¼ cup light rum and stir over high heat until jam dissolves. Rub it through a strainer and brush on babas. *Babas may be completely prepared 2 to 3 days in advance.*

STRAWBERRY ROLL

5 eggs, separated
¾ cup sugar
1 teaspoon vanilla extract
3 tablespoons flour
1½ cups heavy cream

2 tablespoons confectioners' sugar
1½ cups sliced strawberries
Whole strawberries, for garnish

Oil an 11 x 17-inch jelly-roll pan, line it with waxed paper, oil the waxed paper, and set aside. Beat egg yolks, add ¼ cup of the sugar, and beat until very thick and pale yellow. Beat egg whites until stiff peaks form. Add vanilla to egg yolks and carefully fold in flour and then egg whites. Spread batter in prepared pan and bake in a preheated 350° oven for 12 minutes. Loosen the edges of the cake, sprinkle it with ¼ cup of the sugar, and turn cake out, sugar side down, on 2 overlapping sheets of waxed paper. Carefully remove waxed paper liner from bottom of cake and sprinkle bottom with remaining ¼ cup sugar. Whip 1 cup of the heavy cream and sweeten it with confectioners' sugar. Fold in sliced strawberries. Spread on cake and roll up. (Cake should be rolled at room temperature.) Decorate cake roll with remaining ½ cup heavy cream, whipped and piped in rosettes down the length of the cake. Put a whole strawberry on each rosette. *May be made earlier the same day and refrigerated.*

FLORENTINES

½ pound candied orange peel
1 cup blanched slivered
  almonds
½ cup heavy cream
3 tablespoons sugar

¼ cup flour
¼ teaspoon salt
2 ounces (2 squares) semisweet chocolate, optional

Finely chop the orange peel. Toast the almonds in a 350° oven for 15 to 20 minutes. Stir cream and sugar together; add orange peel, almonds, flour, and salt. Line 2 baking sheets with baking parchment. Drop batter by scant teaspoonfuls about 2 inches apart (batter will spread). Bake in a preheated 350° oven for about 35 minutes—but watch them closely, cookies burn easily. Remove from baking sheet with spatula and cool on racks. When cold, bottoms of cookies may be brushed with melted semisweet chocolate (this takes about 5 minutes to set). *May be made ahead and stored in tightly closed plastic bag or airtight tins for up to 1 month.* Makes 30 to 40 cookies.

PIGNOLIA COOKIES

½ pound almond paste
1 cup sugar

2 lightly beaten egg whites
¼ pound pignolia (pine) nuts

Beat almond paste and sugar together to mix thoroughly. Add egg whites and beat until blended. With wet hands, form dough, 1 teaspoonful at a time, into crescents. Dip tops of cookies in pignolia nuts and place on a baking sheet lined with baking parchment or brown paper. Place in a preheated 350° oven and bake for 15 minutes. Cool completely before removing from baking sheet. *Can be made ahead and stored in an airtight tin for up to 1 month.* Makes about 2 dozen cookies.

CHOCOLATE LEAVES

Wash and dry fresh-picked leaves of various sizes and shapes, such as grape ivy, small grape or magnolia leaves. Leaves must be absolutely dry. Melt 2 ounces semisweet or flavored sweet chocolate with 1 teaspoon vegetable shortening. With a brush (not nylon), brush chocolate on the backs of the leaves, just to the edges and about ⅛ inch thick. Chill until firm. Carefully peel leaves off chocolate—this takes patience—and keep the chocolate chilled until needed. *Make at least 1 week ahead and refrigerate.*

Outdoor Entertaining

Where in all outdoors will you eat? The choices—and the food possibilities—are limitless. An outdoor menu can be anything from a snack packed in a cardboard box, to an elaborate picnic, to a black-tie dinner on the terrace next to your pool. When you do move your meal outdoors, count on heartier appetites. If you think the menus in this section look longer than those in the other chapters, you're correct. Fresh air is such a stimulant it even makes up for indifferent food.

If your husband enjoys cooking on an outdoor grill, support him with dishes prepared in the kitchen. His help, plus all the backyard to move around in, makes it possible to entertain more guests than you have room for inside. My husband has made a specialty of London broil, and it really is excellent cooked over coals. (You'll find a recipe on p. 102 for cooking it either way—in the oven or on the grill.) Most food, however, is better cooked indoors, on a heat-controlled stove. That's where I like to do it—ahead of time whenever possible. Thus, most of the recipes in this section are for food fixed in the kitchen and either carried out-doors or packed into picnic hampers. Besides these menus, there are many others among the luncheons and dinners—even the breakfasts—that you might want to carry out on a beautiful day. Don't feel that everything you eat outdoors has to sizzle on a backyard barbecue!

I love picnicking—whatever the excuse or season. There are only a few sensible things you need remember. Always bring along plenty of ice in a cooler, both for drinks and for keeping foods properly chilled. As for plates and glasses, be guided by the occasion and your own mood. Plastic and paper ware are always easy, but at least once consider a formal picnic in a natural setting. It's about as grand a way to eat as I can imagine. For this, pack linen, china, and stemware—and spread a tablecloth on the ground or on one or more card tables. The contrast between sophisticated food and service and a simple setting—a clearing in the woods or a meadow beside a stream—is worth savoring. Try it—and you may be hooked forever.

Formal Dinner
on the Terrace for 6

Cold sorrel soup
Beef birds
Pommes Parisienne
Salad of Bibb lettuce and cucumber
White chocolate roll

Sorrel, a wild plant with a slightly lemony flavor, goes by other names: sour grass or dock and, in Jewish cooking, *shav*. It's an easy-to-grow plant—in fact, much of what I use grows wild—and you'll also find its green, sometimes reddish leaves in many ethnic markets in big cities from spring through fall. If you see it, snap it up. The French cultivate sorrel and serve it as a vegetable, leaves cooked tender-crisp, or as a salad. Sorrel makes a marvelous sour-tasting soup, a sophisticated beginning for this menu. The salad of Bibb lettuce and cucumber on page 49 should be halved to serve 6.

COLD SORREL SOUP

2 tablespoons butter
¾ cup chopped onion
2 tablespoons flour
5 cups chicken stock (see
    p. 278)

2 cups finely chopped sorrel
    leaves
1 cup sour cream
2 teaspoons salt
1 teaspoon freshly cracked
    white pepper

Melt the butter in a large saucepan and stir in onion. Cook over high heat for 3 to 5 minutes, or until onion is transparent. Stir in flour. Add chicken stock and sorrel leaves, bring to a boil, and simmer until sorrel is tender, about 10 minutes. Puree the soup through a food mill, using the fine disk, or in a blender, and chill. Just before serving, stir in sour cream and season with salt and pepper. *May be made the previous day and refrigerated.*

BEEF BIRDS

8 slices beef, ¼ inch thick,
    about 3 by 5 inches
6 tablespoons brandy
2 teaspoons salt
1 teaspoon freshly cracked
    black pepper
    Stuffing (recipe follows)
6 tablespoons butter
2 tablespoons chopped shallots

1 teaspoon chopped garlic
1½ cups dry red wine
1 cup basic brown sauce
    (see p. 281)
2 tablespoons chopped
    parsley
1 bunch watercress

Put beef slices between 2 sheets of waxed paper and pound thin. Brush beef with 2 tablespoons brandy, sprinkle with the salt and pepper, and put a heaping tablespoonful of stuffing on each, dividing stuffing evenly among the 8 pieces of beef. Roll up loosely and tie with string at both ends. Heat 4 tablespoons of the butter in a heavy skillet and brown beef rolls over high heat. Remove from pan, pour off fat, and flame pan with remaining 4 tablespoons brandy. Add remaining 2 tablespoons butter to pan and cook chopped shallots and garlic for a minute or two. Add wine and boil to reduce by one third. Stir in basic brown sauce and simmer 5 minutes. Rectify seasoning. Return beef birds to skillet. (*Can be made ahead to this point the day before, covered with plastic wrap, and refrigerated.*) Cover skillet with aluminum foil and a heavy lid and simmer for 20 to 25 minutes. Turn birds once while cooking. When ready to serve, arrange birds in an au gratin dish, remove strings, pour sauce over, and sprinkle with chopped parsley. Garnish with watercress.

STUFFING

4 tablespoons butter
2 tablespoons chopped shallots
1 teaspoon chopped garlic
½ pound ground smoked
    tongue

½ teaspoon thyme
½ cup bread crumbs
½ cup grated Gruyère cheese
2 tablespoons chopped parsley

Heat butter in a skillet and cook shallots and garlic over medium heat for 3 minutes—do not let them brown. Remove from heat and add remaining ingredients. Mix thoroughly.

POMMES PARISIENNE

4 large baking potatoes
6 tablespoons butter
1 teaspoon salt

½ teaspoon freshly cracked
   white pepper
2 tablespoons chopped parsley

Peel the potatoes and dig out potato balls with a melon baller; drop them into cold water to keep them from turning dark. (*Can be made 2 hours ahead to this point and held in water at room temperature.*) When ready to cook, drop potato balls into boiling water and parboil for 5 minutes. Drain. Melt butter in a large skillet. Add potatoes, salt, and pepper, cover, and shake over high heat until potatoes are tender-crisp, about 15 minutes. Sprinkle with chopped parsley.

WHITE CHOCOLATE ROLL

The use of white chocolate in this recipe produces a beautiful cake—the pale yellow color contrasting with the satiny brown filling.

½ pound white chocolate
5 tablespoons strong coffee
7 eggs, separated
1 cup sugar
2 tablespoons dark crème de
   cacao or Kahlúa

FILLING:
1½ cups heavy cream
½ cup unsweetened cocoa,
   less if desired
¼ cup confectioners' sugar,
   more if desired
2 tablespoons dark crème de
   cacao or Kahlúa

Melt white chocolate in coffee over low heat and set aside to cool. Oil an 11 x 17-inch jelly-roll pan, line with waxed paper, and oil the waxed paper. Set aside. Beat egg yolks in electric mixer bowl; gradually add sugar and beat until mixture is very light and creamy. Add chocolate mixture and blend well. Flavor with crème de cacao. In another bowl, beat egg whites until stiff. Fold into egg yolk mixture and spread in prepared jelly-roll pan. Place in a preheated 350° oven and bake for 15 minutes. Turn oven off and leave pan in oven 5 minutes longer. Remove from oven and turn cake out onto 2 overlapping strips of waxed paper; carefully remove lining paper and cover cake with a double thickness of paper towels wrung out in cold water. Let cool.

Prepare filling: whip the heavy cream, flavoring it with ¼

cup of the cocoa, the confectioners' sugar, and crème de cacao. Spread on cake and roll up. Just before serving, dust cake with remaining ¼ cup cocoa, or with an equivalent amount of confectioners' sugar. *May be made earlier the same day.*

A Picnic in the Woods
for 8

Antipasto
Pâté en croûte (see p. 229)
Oak-leaf lettuce with sour cream dressing
Melon wedges, crystallized ginger

ANTIPASTO

Pack a picnic basket with an assortment of the following ingredients. The vegetables should be washed, trimmed, wrapped in individual plastic bags, and kept icy cold. When you reach your picnic site, spread everything out on a big platter or tray and serve with Italian olive oil, red wine vinegar, a basket of *grissini*—Italian breadsticks—and lots of fresh Italian bread. Don't forget salt and a pepper grinder.

Sardines
Tuna, garnished with mayonnaise and capers
Mortadella (Italian garlic sausage), sliced thin
Salami, sliced thin
Artichoke hearts
Pimento slices
Caponata (Italian-style eggplant salad, available canned)

Prosciutto, sliced thin
Provolone
Black and green olives
Fennel
Radishes
Celery
Tomatoes, sliced
Scallions
Small raw mushrooms

OAK-LEAF LETTUCE
WITH SOUR CREAM DRESSING

This is a very tender, buttery leaf lettuce with leaves shaped like those of an oak tree. Many gardeners grow it, but it's a rarity in markets. You can substitute the ruffly garden lettuce, or Bibb or Boston. To serve 8, you'll need about 2 quarts of the leaf or garden lettuce, or 2 large heads of Boston, or 6 heads of Bibb. The sour cream dressing on page 176 is light, just right for delicate greens. Rinse the lettuce at home, roll it in paper towels, put it in a plastic bag, and bring it to the picnic in a cooler to keep it crisp.

MELON WEDGES, CRYSTALLIZED GINGER

Cut slices or wedges of ripe, juicy cantaloupe or honeydew melon and sprinkle them with finely chopped crystallized ginger. The ginger adds enough of a lively, piquant taste to point up the melon, but if you wish, you can squeeze a little lime or lemon juice over each serving, too.

A Tailgate Picnic
for 8

Fish chowder
Cold fillet of beef
on horseradish-buttered white bread
Jo Klein's baked ham in paper
on mustard-buttered French bread
Cornichons and watermelon rind pickles
Walnuts in the shell and dried fruits
or apples and Cheddar cheese

This is a perfect picnic feast to spread on the tailgate of a station wagon before a football game. Chowder, packed in Thermos bottles, will ward off the chills, and the cold meats with condiments are excellent in any weather. In fact, if it's sunny, picnicking on a brisk fall day is one of the pleasantest of experiences, not to be missed.

FISH CHOWDER

3 pounds haddock or sea bass
2½ cups water
¼ pound diced bacon
1½ cups chopped onions
1 cup chopped celery
4 potatoes, peeled and diced
1 bay leaf

1 teaspoon salt
½ teaspoon freshly cracked white pepper
1 quart light cream
2 tablespoons butter
Dry sherry, optional
2 tablespoons chopped parsley

Buy fish steaks with bone in, or have fishmonger bone them for you and save the bones. Cut fish into bite-size pieces and set aside. Put bones in a saucepan and cover with 2½ cups water, bring to a boil, and simmer, covered, for 15 minutes. Strain and reserve stock. Fry the bacon dice in a large saucepan over high heat. Add onions, celery, and potatoes; cook over high heat until the onions are transparent, stirring with a wooden spatula. Add fish and cook for another 2 minutes. Add strained fish stock. Crumble and add bay leaf, then add salt, pepper, cream, and butter. Bring the chowder almost to the boil, cover it, adjust heat to simmer, and simmer 30 minutes. (*Can be made a day ahead and reheated.*) Add 1 tablespoon sherry for each serving, if you wish. Stir parsley into chowder just before pouring it into Thermos bottles. (If serving fish chowder in bowls at the table, sprinkle each serving with chopped parsley.)

COLD FILLET OF BEEF
ON HORSERADISH-BUTTERED WHITE BREAD

Tie a well-trimmed 5- to 6-pound fillet of beef every 2 inches. Bring it to room temperature, rub it all over with 1 tablespoon coarse salt and 1 teaspoon freshly cracked black pepper, and place it on a rack in a shallow roasting pan. Roast in a preheated 425° oven for about 35 minutes, or until meat thermometer registers 125°. Remove from oven and let cool. Wrap and refrigerate, but bring to room temperature for serving. Slice thinly and serve with Sandy Ainsworth's white bread (see p. 245) and horseradish butter, made by adding 2 tablespoons prepared horseradish to ½ cup of butter.

JO KLEIN'S BAKED HAM IN PAPER ON MUSTARD-BUTTERED FRENCH BREAD

Wrap a 5- to 6-pound half-ham, precooked and smoked, in white butcher paper. Paper should be long enough so that you can bring the ends together over the ham and fold them over two or three times—this is called a drugstore wrap, or lock-seal. Then fold or twist the open sides of your package to enclose the ham securely. Lay it on a baking sheet and put it in a preheated 325° oven to bake, for 25 minutes per pound, or 2 to 2½ hours. Remove from oven and let cool. Wrap and refrigerate, but bring to room temperature for serving. Serve with French bread and mustard butter, made by adding 2 tablespoons of Dijon mustard to ½ cup of butter.

Back Porch Supper for 8

Gazpacho
Jellied chicken
Cold London broil (see p. 102)
Apple and potato salad
Fresh garden lettuce, served plain
French bread with herb butter
Homemade vanilla ice cream, served
from the freezer (see p. 176)
Pound cake

When I was a kid, supper on the back porch meant a trestle table laden with food and a very informal mood. Serving dishes were passed, family-style; everyone helped himself, and second helpings were encouraged. (Many times the menu included leftovers, but my mother made the platters look so attractive we seldom realized it.) Your porch may be a patio, and you may want to serve the food buffet-style. But I think your guests will enjoy this generous country kind of meal with its choice of entrées as well as salads. Top it off with ice cream dipped from the freezer canister, and old-fashioned pound cake.

GAZPACHO

¼ cup red wine vinegar
¼ cup olive oil
2 finely chopped cloves garlic
1 cucumber, peeled, seeded, and diced
1 green pepper, seeded and diced
¾ cup chopped onion
1 teaspoon salt
1 cup dry bread crumbs
2 pounds tomatoes
    Ice water

3 or 4 drops Tabasco sauce, optional

FOR GARNISH:
1 cucumber, peeled, seeded, and diced
1 green pepper, seeded and diced
1 tomato, peeled, seeded, and cut into fine shreds
1 cup garlic croutons
    Ice cubes

Put vinegar, olive oil, garlic, cucumber, green pepper, onion, salt, and bread crumbs into a blender and puree; mixture should be the consistency of heavy cream. Pour it into a serving bowl and taste it; add up to 2 tablespoons more vinegar if needed. Rub the tomatoes through a strainer and add them to the bread crumb mixture, along with enough ice water to thin the mixture to the consistency of light cream. It should look mushy but thin. Chill thoroughly. (*Gazpacho is best if made the day before. Taste for seasoning when soup is cold, adding Tabasco if desired.*) Prepare the garnish vegetables and chill. When ready to serve, add the garnish vegetables to the gazpacho in the serving bowl and sprinkle garlic croutons on top. Or place vegetables and croutons, as well as ice cubes (for thinning soup, if needed), in separate bowls for guests to serve themselves as desired.

JELLIED CHICKEN

1 5-pound stewing chicken	1 teaspoon freshly cracked
½ cup chopped carrot	black pepper
¾ cup chopped onion	Juice of 1 lemon
½ cup chopped celery	1 egg white
2 cups chicken stock (see	2 tablespoons (2 envelopes)
p. 278)	unflavored gelatine
1½ cups dry white wine or	8 deviled eggs (see p. 70)
dry vermouth	Olives and lettuce, to garnish
1 tablespoon dried tarragon	platter
2 teaspoons salt	

Put the chicken in a pot or large saucepan with the carrot, onion, celery, chicken stock, and 1 cup of the dry white wine. Add tarragon, salt, pepper, and lemon juice. Bring to a boil, turn heat to simmer, half-cover the pot, and simmer until chicken is very tender, about 1 to 1½ hours. Cool chicken in broth. When cool, remove chicken and strip meat from the bones, keeping it in good-size (1-inch) pieces. Set aside. Strain the broth (do not mash the vegetables) and measure it; add water or additional chicken stock to make 3½ cups. Put it over low heat and beat in the egg white with a whisk. Whisk and simmer for 2 minutes. Remove from heat and set aside. Sprinkle gelatine over remaining ½ cup white wine, and set aside. Line a sieve with a double thickness of cheesecloth wrung out in cold water. Strain broth, letting it drain through the cheesecloth-lined sieve without stirring or forcing it in any way. Combine with gelatine mixture, stirring and reheating, if necessary, to dissolve gelatine. Cool. Arrange chicken pieces in an oiled mold (a bread pan is a good size and shape). Pour cooled gelatine over chicken. (Pour any extra gelatine into a shallow pan.) Chill mold until set. (*Recipe may be prepared ahead to this point and stored overnight.*) When ready to serve, unmold the chicken on a serving platter. Chop extra gelatine and sprinkle it around the mold. Decorate platter with lettuce leaves, olives, and deviled eggs.

APPLE AND POTATO SALAD

4 cups sliced boiled potatoes
3 cups diced unpeeled apple
½ cup chopped onion
1 seeded, sliced cucumber
¼ cup red wine vinegar
1 teaspoon salt
½ teaspoon freshly cracked
    white pepper

1 to 2 tablespoons chopped
    fresh chives
2 cups sour cream *or* 1 cup sour
    cream and 1 cup mayon-
    naise
Romaine lettuce

Combine all ingredients except lettuce and chill. If the cucumber is heavily waxed, peel before slicing. When ready to serve, turn salad into a bowl lined with the lettuce leaves.

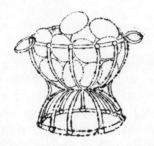

POUND CAKE

4½ cups sifted flour
 ½ teaspoon salt
 ¼ teaspoon mace, optional
 2 cups butter

 2 cups sugar
10 eggs, separated
 1 tablespoon vanilla extract

Sift the flour with salt and mace; set aside. Put the butter in electric mixer bowl and cream it. Gradually beat in sugar and beat until mixture is very light and fluffy. Beat egg yolks well and beat them into butter-sugar mixture, again beating until very light. Gradually beat in flour. When well mixed, flavor with vanilla. Beat egg whites until stiff and fold them into batter. Pour batter into 2 9 x 5 x 3-inch loaf pans that have been greased and lined with silicone paper (KVP baking parchment). Bake in a preheated 300° oven for 70 to 85 minutes, or until cake tester or toothpick comes out clean when pushed into center of cake. Cool on racks for 10 minutes; then remove cake from pans and cool completely. Wrap one of the cakes for the freezer—it freezes beautifully.

Formal Picnic
for 8

Vichyssoise
Breast of veal stuffed with pâté
Cherry tomatoes and fava beans
with coarse salt
Cold glazed squabs (see p. 127)
Hearts of palm salad (see p. 171)
Assorted cheeses, crackers, and breads
Ladyfingers and whole fresh peaches

When you move a feast into a perfect picnic setting, do what you can to make it even more memorable—a study in contrasts. Unpack white linen, stemmed wineglasses, and china to match the elegant food. Elegant as it is, the menu may be enjoyed picnic fashion, using fingers instead of forks. Every bite packs and travels well, but do choose the semisoft or harder cheeses, such as Muenster, Cheddar, Port Salut, Roquefort. Serve with whatever crackers and breads you like best: unsalted water biscuits, stone-ground thin crackers, breadsticks, homemade white bread, pumpernickel, or French bread.

VICHYSSOISE

4 leeks
4 large baking potatoes,
    peeled and cubed
½ cup sliced celery
1½ cups sliced onions
1 tablespoon salt
1 teaspoon freshly cracked
    white pepper

1 cup strong chicken stock
    (see p. 278)
2 cups heavy cream
2 tablespoons chopped fresh
    chives

Clean leeks carefully by splitting them lengthwise and holding them under running water, separating the layers to rinse out all the sand and dirt. Slice them, using all the white part plus about 1 inch of the green. Put leeks, potatoes, celery, onions, salt, and pepper into a saucepan with just enough water to cover—use as little water as possible. Bring to a boil, turn heat to simmer, cover pan, and cook until vegetables are mushy. Add chicken stock and bring to a boil, stirring. Puree the mixture through a food mill, using the finest disk. Chill thoroughly. (*Can be made the day before to this point.*) Immediately before serving or packing in Thermoses for the picnic, whip cream just past the foaming stage and stir it into the soup. Serve icy cold in chilled cups with chopped chives sprinkled on.

BREAST OF VEAL STUFFED WITH PÂTÉ

1 breast of veal, about
    4 pounds
¾ pound ground veal
¾ pound ground pork
2 tablespoons chopped
    shallots
1 teaspoon finely chopped
    garlic
2 eggs
2 teaspoons salt
1½ teaspoons freshly cracked
    black pepper

½ cup chopped natural
    pistachio nuts
½ truffle, chopped
2 tablespoons finely chopped
    parsley
6 tablespoons brandy
4 tablespoons melted butter
1 tablespoon coarse salt
2 tablespoons chicken stock
    (see p. 278) or veal stock
    (see p. 279)

Have the veal breast boned. Or bone breast yourself: place the meat on the counter, rib side up, with the breast bone hanging over the edge of the counter. Lean on it to break breast bone loose from rib bones, and cut around breast bone to separate it from the flesh. Then cut alongside each rib bone, and slide your knife under each rib, cutting against the bone to free the flesh. *Or,* after cutting alongside rib bones stand the breast up and lean on it—bones will pop out.

To make stuffing, mix together ground veal and pork (both ground twice—you can use all veal, if you wish), shallots garlic, eggs, salt, ½ teaspoon pepper, the pistachio nuts, truffle, and parsley. Warm ¼ cup of the brandy in a small, long handled pan, ignite, and pour, flaming, over stuffing mixture. To test stuffing for seasoning, sauté a bit of it in a small skillet until thoroughly cooked and taste. Cut a pocket in the meat, pack with stuffing, and sew up ends.

Brush stuffed veal with melted butter and sprinkle with 1 tablespoon coarse salt and 1 teaspoon pepper. Place in a roasting pan in a preheated 350° oven and roast for 2 to 2½ hours, or until well done. During roasting, baste after 15 minutes with remaining 2 tablespoons brandy, remaining melted butter, and chicken or veal stock, and then baste every 15 minutes with juices in pan. When done, cool and store in refrigerator. Bring to room temperature before carving in thin slices.

CHERRY TOMATOES AND FAVA BEANS WITH COARSE SALT

Wash 1 quart cherry tomatoes, rinse 1 quart shelled fava beans, and pack each in a plastic freezer container, adding a few chips of ice to keep them damp. Serve with a bowl of coarse salt to dip them in. Another nice dip for cherry tomatoes is vodka.

LADYFINGERS

3 eggs, separated
⅓ cup plus 1 tablespoon sugar

1 teaspoon vanilla extract
¾ cup sifted flour

Line baking sheets with baking parchment. In electric mixer bowl, beat egg yolks and sugar at high speed. Add vanilla and continue to beat until mixture is very thick, about 5 minutes. In a separate bowl and with clean beaters, beat egg whites until stiff. Fold one third of the flour and half of the egg whites alternately into egg yolk mixture, beginning and ending with the flour. Do this carefully, with a light touch. Put batter into a large pastry bag fitted with a plain round tube and pipe batter out onto lined baking sheets, making straight lines about 3 inches long. Space them 2 inches apart. Place baking sheets on the middle shelf of preheated 350° oven and bake until set, about 7 to 8 minutes. Do not brown. Remove from oven. With a spatula lift ladyfingers from baking sheets, to cool on wire cake racks. Makes 24 ladyfingers.

A Lobster Party
for 6

Clams on the half shell
Boiled lobsters
Hot buttered French bread
Platter of baked potato skins
Iced cucumber sticks
Melon with port wine (see p. 30)
Florentines (see p. 249)

It's easier to boil lobsters on your kitchen stove, but if you have a big grill, you could do it outside. Start the water in the house and bring it out when it's near the boiling point. If you move the party to the beach, cook the lobster in seawater, and skip the potato skins—they need an oven. To prepare hot buttered French bread, slice it diagonally every 1½ inches, not quite through the bottom. Cream ½ cup butter and spread between each 2 slices. Wrap the loaf in aluminum foil and heat in a preheated 350° oven or on the edge of the grill for about 10 to 15 minutes.

CLAMS ON THE HALF SHELL

Count 6 clams per person. Open them or have them opened as close to serving time as possible. Arrange on plates, preferably on cracked ice, and serve with lemon wedges. Pass the pepper mill. *No red sauce.*

BOILED LOBSTERS

6 live lobsters, about 1¾ pounds   1½ cups melted butter, for
   each   serving hot, *or* mustard
1 tablespoon salt   mayonnaise
                                        Lemon wedges

Put lobsters in a big, 18-quart lobster pot, cover with cold water, and add salt. Cover and place over high heat; bring the water to a boil. Let boil about 5 minutes; then reduce heat to simmer gently and cook, covered, for another 15 to 20 minutes, depending on size of lobsters. Drain off water and serve lobsters hot with individual bowls of melted butter and plenty of lemon wedges. If serving cold, drain lobsters and cover immediately with cold water to stop the cooking. Serve cold lobster with mustard mayonnaise, made by adding ½ cup Dijon mustard to 1 cup mayonnaise (see p. 283).

PLATTER OF BAKED POTATO SKINS

Scrub 6 large baking potatoes. Bake them in a preheated 375° oven for 1 hour, or until very well done, with crisp skins. Cut potatoes in half, lengthwise, and scoop out interior; reserve for another use—Roesti Potatoes, for example (see p. 15). With kitchen shears, cut potato skins crosswise into strips about ½ inch wide. Flatten them and dip into melted butter (you'll need about ¾ cup). Place on baking sheet and sprinkle with coarse salt and freshly cracked black pepper. (*May be prepared ahead to this point.*) Bake in a preheated 350° oven until you can't see the butter running off them and the skins are very crisp, about 10 to 15 minutes. Serve hot.

ICED CUCUMBER STICKS

Peel 3 large cucumbers with a vegetable peeler, cut them in half lengthwise, and scoop out the seeds with the top of a spoon. Cut crosswise into 3-inch pieces, then into sticks. Cover with water, adding 1 tablespoon salt, and soak for 1 hour in the refrigerator. Drain on paper towels and serve—they will be very crisp.

A Fourth of July Picnic
for 16

Tomatoes stuffed with crab-meat salad
Meat loaf en croûte
or Peppered veal loaf en croûte
Baked lima beans
Cucumbers in sour cream and chives
Walnut cake
Bowl of assorted fruits

If you have ever lived in a town that has band concerts in the park on the Fourth of July, this is the kind of food you'd remember, spread out on picnic tables covered with red-checkered table-cloths. It's good backyard fare, too, homespun and hearty.

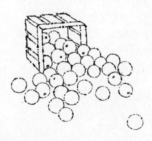

TOMATOES STUFFED
WITH CRAB-MEAT SALAD

16 large tomatoes   16 sprigs parsley or watercress
 2 recipes crab-meat salad
    (see p. 52)

Cut the tops off tomatoes and set aside to make lids. Scoop out seeds and turn tomatoes upside down to drain. Chill. Fill with crab-meat salad. Cut a slit in each lid and insert a sprig of parsley or watercress; place on top of salads.

MEAT LOAF EN CROÛTE

1 recipe sour cream pastry (see p. 288)

2 tablespoons butter

¾ cup chopped onion

1 chopped clove garlic

3 pounds ground beef

2 beaten eggs

½ cup sour cream

½ cup chili sauce

2 teaspoons salt

1 teaspoon freshly cracked black pepper

¼ cup soft bread crumbs

4 strips bacon

1 egg yolk

1 tablespoon water

1 cup sour cream, optional

1 tablespoon chopped fresh dill, optional

Make pastry and put it in the refrigerator to chill for 1½ hours. Melt butter in a small pan and stir in chopped onion and garlic. Cook over high heat, stirring with a wooden spatula, until onion is transparent—do not let it burn. Put ground beef into a large bowl, add onion and garlic, eggs, ½ cup sour cream, the chili sauce, salt, pepper (1 teaspoon is correct), and soft bread crumbs. Mix together and shape into a loaf on a baking tray. Lay bacon strips over loaf and put it into a preheated 350° oven to bake for 35 minutes. Remove partly baked loaf from oven, discard bacon, and chill in refrigerator. Roll out three quarters of the sour cream pastry on a lightly floured board. Wrap it around the chilled meat loaf to enclose it completely. Do not wrap tightly. Seal the seam at bottom and ends with egg wash—egg yolk beaten with 1 tablespoon water—and place, seam side down, on baking tray. Roll out remaining pastry and cut leaves or flowers to decorate top. Stick the decorations on with egg wash and brush the crust all over with it. Prick pastry in 3 places with fork tines. (*Can be made ahead to this point and refrigerated or frozen.*) Place in a preheated 375° oven to bake for 45 minutes, or until pastry is done. Serve plain or topped with 1 cup sour cream mixed with the fresh chopped dill. May be served hot, at room temperature, or chilled.

PEPPERED VEAL LOAF EN CROÛTE

Follow recipe for Meat Loaf en Croûte, substituting ground veal for ground beef, and adding 2 teaspoons (this is correct—3 teaspoons altogether) freshly cracked black pepper.

BAKED LIMA BEANS

4 cups dried lima beans
1 tablespoon plus 1 teaspoon
  salt
1 cup cubed salt pork

½ cup dark molasses
1 teaspoon dry mustard
2 tablespoons butter

Rinse beans in cold water; then place in a bowl, cover with cold water, and soak overnight or for at least 12 hours. Drain, put in a saucepan, add 1 tablespoon salt, and cover with boiling water. Simmer, uncovered, for 1½ hours. Drain beans and place in a 2-quart buttered bean pot or casserole along with cubed salt pork. Mix molasses, mustard, and 1 teaspoon salt in 2 cups hot water and pour over beans. Dot with butter. Cover and bake in a preheated 350° oven until beans are soft, about 3 hours. Uncover the beans during last 30 minutes of cooking to brown them. *Can be baked ahead and reheated.*

CUCUMBERS IN SOUR CREAM AND CHIVES

4 cucumbers
1 tablespoon plus ½ teaspoon
  salt
2 tablespoons finely chopped
  parsley

¾ cup sour cream
3 tablespoons finely chopped
  chives
½ teaspoon freshly cracked
  white pepper

Peel cucumbers and cut them in half lengthwise, scooping out seeds with the tip of a spoon. Slice crosswise as thin as possible, using a vegetable cutter or *mandoline*. Sprinkle with 1 tablespoon salt and place in refrigerator with a plate on top of them, to weight them; the salt and weight will work together to release moisture, which can be bitter. After 2 hours, put in a sieve and rinse off salt. Squeeze to release excess liquid. Put in a bowl, add remaining ingredients, and stir with 2 forks to mix. Chill until ready to serve.

WALNUT CAKE

½ cup butter, plus butter to
    grease pan
1¼ cups confectioners' sugar
½ cup milk
2 teaspoons vanilla extract
½ teaspoon almond extract

2 cups lightly spooned flour
2 teaspoons baking powder
¼ teaspoon salt
5 egg whites
½ cup broken walnuts
    Frosting (recipe follows)

Butter an 11 x 7 x 1½-inch cake pan and set aside. In electric mixer bowl, cream the butter, gradually adding confectioners' sugar, and beat until very light. Add the milk and vanilla and almond extracts. Sift the flour 3 times with the baking powder and add to butter mixture, stirring until blended. Add the salt to the egg whites and beat until stiff but not dry. Fold them into the batter carefully; then very lightly fold in broken walnuts. Pour batter into prepared cake pan and bake in a preheated 350° oven for about 25 minutes, or until cake tests done. Cool in the pan, on a rack. Spread with Frosting, or, for a less rich effect, sift confectioners' sugar over the cake just before serving.

FROSTING FOR WALNUT CAKE

1½ cups sugar
2 egg whites

¼ teaspoon cream of tartar
2 teaspoons vanilla extract

Combine ½ cup water and the sugar in a small saucepan and bring to a boil, stirring until sugar dissolves. Cook until syrup forms a soft ball in cold water (234° to 238° on the candy thermometer), about 15 minutes. When syrup is almost ready, beat egg whites until stiff but not dry; then slowly add the cooked syrup to the whites in a thin stream, beating constantly. Beat in cream of tartar and vanilla and continue beating until smooth and thick. Then place the bowl in a pan of boiling water and beat frosting with a wooden spatula until you feel the spatula grating slightly against the bottom of the bowl. Remove from heat immediately and spread over cooled cake.

A Pool Party
for 12

Crudités with coarse salt
Pissaladière
Stuffed eggplant
Sesame breadsticks
Melon wedges, crystallized ginger
(see p. 257)

CRUDITÉS WITH COARSE SALT

Arrange raw vegetables on a tray or platter of ice and serve with a bowl of coarse salt. For vegetable suggestions, see p. 234.

PISSALADIÈRE

1 package active dry yeast
¼ cup warm water (105° to 115°)
1½ tablespoons olive oil *or* melted butter
1 teaspoon sugar
1 teaspoon salt
⅔ cup warm water
3 cups lightly spooned flour

FILLING:
6 cups sliced onions
½ cup olive oil, plus oil for pan
1 1-pound, 4-ounce can Italian tomatoes
¾ cup freshly grated Parmesan cheese
1 tablespoon rosemary
2 2-ounce cans flat anchovy fillets
16 black olives, pitted and cut in half lengthwise

Sprinkle yeast into ¼ cup warm water, stir to dissolve, and let stand 5 minutes. Put 1½ tablespoons olive oil, the sugar, salt, and ⅔ cup warm water in mixer bowl; add yeast mixture. Beat in flour, 1 cupful at a time. Mixture will be very stiff. Turn dough out on a floured board and knead about 5 minutes, adding a little flour if dough sticks to the board. Put the dough in a plastic bag or a bowl to rest for precisely 30 minutes. In a saucepan, cook onions in ½ cup olive oil over high heat until they are very soft, almost a puree, and brownish yellow. In another saucepan, mash and cook tomatoes until mixture looks like a puree, about 20 to 30 minutes.

Brush a 12-inch pizza pan with olive oil (or substitute 2 6-inch flat, round pans with 1-inch-high sides). Roll out dough and fit it into the oiled pan, rolling the edge to make it thick and crusty. Prick dough all over the bottom, all the way through. Let rest at least 10 minutes. (*May be prepared ahead to this point.*) Then place in a preheated 400° oven for 10 minutes—this prebaking will ensure a crust that's completely baked. Remove from oven and sprinkle the shell with grated Parmesan. Spoon the onion mixture around the edge, the tomato mixture in the center. Sprinkle with rosemary. Arrange anchovy fillets over the filling, like wheel spokes, and place olive halves around the edge, plus 1 in the center. Return to the oven to bake for 15 to 20 minutes, or until crust is brown. Make, bake, and serve in sequence; this gets soggy if made ahead.

STUFFED EGGPLANT

3 large (or 6 small) eggplants
¾ cup olive oil, about
3 cups finely chopped onion
1½ teaspoons finely chopped garlic
1 tablespoon salt

1½ teaspoons freshly cracked white pepper
3 tablespoons chopped parsley
6 tablespoons grated Parmesan cheese

Cut eggplants in half; cut a thin slice from the resulting bottom of each half, so it won't roll around. Dig out centers, leaving shells about ½ inch thick. Parboil the shells for 5 minutes. Chop centers roughly. Heat ½ cup of olive oil in a heavy skillet. Add onion, garlic, and chopped eggplant; stir and cook over high heat until onion is transparent. Season with salt and pepper. Spoon this mixture into parboiled shells. Drizzle with olive oil (use about 2 teaspoons per large half); sprinkle with parsley and Parmesan cheese and another drizzle of olive oil. (*Can be prepared ahead, ready to bake. Or you can bake eggplant and reheat, or serve cold.*) Place in a preheated 375° oven to bake until shells are tender, about 35 to 45 minutes.

A Beach Picnic
for 6

Cold cream of onion soup
Deviled eggs (see p. 70)
Pain bagna
Chick-pea salad
Pears and Gorgonzola cheese
Sangría

COLD CREAM OF ONION SOUP

½ cup butter
6 cups sliced onion
1 chopped clove garlic
1 cup chopped celery
3 cups diced raw potato
2 cups chicken stock (see p. 278)
6 cups light cream

1 teaspoon salt
½ teaspoon freshly cracked white pepper
¼ teaspoon freshly grated nutmeg
2 tablespoons finely chopped parsley

Melt the butter in a large saucepan. When it is hot and foamy, stir in onion, garlic, celery, and potato. Cook slowly for about 15 minutes, stirring frequently—do not let them brown. Heat stock, pour onto vegetable mixture, and cook slowly for about 30 minutes; half-cover the pan. Add light cream, salt, and pepper and heat through. Check the seasoning. Puree the mixture in a blender and chill. (*Can be made the day before.*) Pack it in Thermos bottles, and just before serving flavor each portion with nutmeg and a sprinkle of chopped parsley.

PAIN BAGNA

2 10-inch round loaves of
    French bread
½ cup French olive oil, more
    if necessary
16 lettuce leaves
6 thinly sliced tomatoes
1 cup chopped black olives
2 2-ounce cans flat anchovy
    fillets

1 large red onion, thinly sliced
½ teaspoon crushed rosemary
½ teaspoon basil
½ teaspoon salt
¼ teaspoon freshly cracked
    black pepper

Cut each loaf of bread in half, horizontally, and pull out some of the soft interior from each piece. Drizzle olive oil over the 4 hollowed-out pieces and let it soak in; you may need a little more oil. Cover the hollow of each bottom half with overlapping lettuce leaves. Then arrange tomato slices, black olives, drained anchovy fillets, and onion in circles on top of the lettuce. Sprinkle with rosemary, basil, salt, and pepper and cover each bottom half with a top half of bread. Wrap each loaf in aluminum foil and carry it anywhere. To serve, cut in wedges; have plenty of paper napkins available. *Make this the morning of your picnic, not the day before.*

CHICK-PEA SALAD

1 15½-ounce can chick-peas
½ cup tarragon vinegar
½ cup olive oil
1 chopped clove garlic
1 teaspoon salt
½ teaspoon freshly cracked
    black pepper
¼ pound hard salami, cut in
    strips
½ cup pimento-stuffed olives,
    sliced

¼ cup finely chopped celery
¼ cup finely chopped green
    pepper
    Romaine lettuce leaves to
    line salad bowl
3 tablespoons finely chopped
    scallions
2 tomatoes, peeled, seeded,
    and diced
2 tablespoons finely chopped
    parsley

Rinse the chick-peas in cold water, dry thoroughly, and set aside. Mix vinegar, olive oil, garlic, salt, and pepper in a bowl. Add chick-peas, salami, olives, celery, and green pepper and toss to coat with the dressing. Put in a salad bowl lined with romaine

Stir vegetables occasionally to prevent scorching; remove vegetables when browned. Put the browned vegetables and meat and bones into a deep kettle or stock pot. Pour 1 cup water into the roasting pan and scrape up the brown bits. Pour into kettle, adding more water, enough to make 4 quarts in all. Add wine, garlic, thyme, bay leaf, parsley, tomato paste, salt, and pepper and bring slowly to a boil. Skim. Reduce heat, half-cover the kettle, and simmer gently for 4 hours.

Strain through a sieve lined with a double thickness of cheesecloth wrung out in cold water. Stock may be stored in the refrigerator for up to 1 week, if boiled every day, or frozen for up to 2 months. If recipe calls for extra strength stock, boil ordinary stock, uncovered, over moderately high heat until it is reduced by one third. Makes 2 to 3 quarts.

CHICKEN STOCK

4 pounds chicken backs, wings, necks, and giblets, or a 4-pound whole chicken
1 cup sliced carrots
1 cup sliced celery, with leaves
4 medium-size peeled onions
4 whole cloves
1 cup dry white wine

1 mashed clove garlic
½ teaspoon dried thyme
1 bay leaf
3 sprigs parsley
2 tablespoons tomato paste
1 tablespoon salt
½ teaspoon freshly cracked black pepper

Place all ingredients (stick the whole cloves into the onions) and 4 quarts of cold water in a deep kettle or stock pot. Bring to a boil slowly. Skim. Reduce heat, half-cover the kettle, and simmer gently for 1½ hours. Remove the chicken, strip the meat from the bones, return the bones to the kettle, and simmer for another 2½ hours. (Use the meat in any recipe calling for cooked chicken.) Strain the stock through a sieve lined with a double thickness of cheesecloth wrung out in cold water. Stock may be stored in the refrigerator for up to 1 week, if boiled every day, or frozen for up to 2 months. If recipe calls for extra strong stock, boil, uncovered, over moderately high heat, to reduce by one third. Makes 2 to 3 quarts.

VEAL STOCK

To make veal stock, follow the recipe for chicken stock, substituting veal and veal bones for the chicken.

FISH STOCK

1 cup sliced onion
½ cup sliced celery rib
½ cup sliced carrot
2 pounds fish bones and trimmings, all from lean fish

1 cup dry white wine
   Bouquet garni (see p. 283)
1 teaspoon salt
½ teaspoon freshly cracked white pepper

Put all ingredients and 1 quart cold water into a kettle or stock pot and bring to a boil. Skim. Reduce heat, partially cover the pot, and simmer ½ hour. Strain through a fine sieve. Makes 3 to 4 cups.

COURT BOUILLON

Court bouillon can be used for poaching or boiling any fish or shellfish, but never, never drop fish or shellfish into *boiling* court bouillon—it will toughen the fish.

2 cups dry vermouth or other dry white wine *or* 2 cups cider vinegar
½ cup chopped onion
½ cup chopped carrot
½ cup chopped celery

2 teaspoons salt
8 peppercorns
3 sprigs parsley
1 bay leaf
1 clove
½ teaspoon dried thyme

Put all ingredients and 2 quarts cold water into a large saucepan or kettle, bring to a boil, and boil rapidly for 30 minutes. Strain bouillon and cool. Makes 9 to 10 cups.

ASPIC

2 cups strong chicken stock (see p. 278)
½ cup tomato juice
2 tablespoons (2 envelopes) unflavored gelatine
1 crushed eggshell

2 lightly beaten egg whites
2 tablespoons Cognac, brandy, Madeira, or white wine
1 teaspoon salt
½ teaspoon freshly cracked black pepper

Combine all ingredients in a saucepan and bring slowly to a boil, whisking constantly. Remove from heat and let stand 5 minutes. Strain into a bowl through a strainer lined with a double thickness of cheesecloth wrung out in cold water. Do not force liquid through; just let it drip through by itself. Hold strainer well above liquid in bowl. If not clear, pour it through the strainer again. Place in the refrigerator for 1 hour to set or make a day ahead and refrigerate. Do not freeze. Makes about 2 cups.

MEAT GLAZE

Meat glaze is nothing more than strained beef stock reduced to a syrup. Use it whenever a concentrated beef flavor is called for.

Boil 3 quarts beef stock (see p. 277) in a large kettle for 30 minutes, or until reduced to 1 quart. Strain the reduced stock into a small saucepan and boil 30 minutes more, or until reduced to about 1½ cups. Watch carefully near the end, so it doesn't scorch. Cool about 1 hour; store in a covered jar in the refrigerator for up to 2 months. Always use a clean spoon to dip into meat glaze. Makes about 1½ cups.

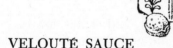

VELOUTÉ SAUCE

¼ cup butter
¼ cup flour

2½ cups chicken stock or veal stock (see p. 278 and p. 279)

Melt butter in a saucepan and stir in flour with a wooden spatula. Cook over high heat, stirring constantly, for 2 minutes. Do not let it brown. Remove from heat, change to a whisk, and add stock, whisking vigorously for 3 minutes. Return pan to high heat and cook, stirring, until sauce thickens and comes to a boil. Boil 1 minute. Makes 2 cups.

BASIC BROWN SAUCE

3 tablespoons butter
¾ cup finely minced onion
½ cup diced carrot
4½ teaspoons flour
2 cups beef stock (see p. 277)
1 tablespoon minced shallot

2 minced cloves garlic
Bouquet garni (see p. 283)
2 teaspoons tomato paste
¼ teaspoon freshly cracked black pepper
½ teaspoon meat glaze (see p. 280)

Melt butter in a small pan; add onion and carrot and cook over high heat for 5 minutes, stirring with a wooden spatula. Blend in flour with wooden spatula and cook, stirring constantly, about 10 minutes, or until nicely browned. Remove pan from heat, change to a wire whisk, and add the beef stock, beating vigorously. Add shallot, garlic, bouquet garni, tomato paste, pepper, and meat glaze. Return pan to heat, bring to a boil, reduce heat, cover the pan, and cook *very* slowly for 30 minutes or up to 2 hours, to intensify flavor. Strain through a fine sieve; taste, and adjust seasoning. Store in refrigerator up to 1 week, or freeze for up to 2 months. Makes 1 cup.

HOLLANDAISE SAUCE

½ cup butter
3 egg yolks
2 tablespoons lemon juice

¼ teaspoon salt
¼ teaspoon freshly cracked white pepper

Melt butter, which should be very hot when you are ready for it. Put egg yolks and 3 tablespoons cold water in a small non-aluminum pan. Whisk them together over high heat, raising and lowering the pan to control heat—the pan must not get too hot. Whisk continuously until mixture starts to mound and is the consistency of heavy cream. Remove from heat and whisk in ¼ cup of the hot melted butter, 1 tablespoon at a time. Return pan to heat and add remaining butter in a thin stream, whisking continuously. Whisk about 5 minutes or until the mixture is thick and creamy; remove the pan from the heat if it starts to get too hot, but don't stop whisking. Add lemon juice, salt, and pepper. Hold sauce in a pan of warm water until serving time. Makes ¾ to 1 cup.

BÉARNAISE SAUCE

½ cup butter
1 tablespoon chopped shallot
½ cup tarragon vinegar
1 tablespoon dried tarragon or
3 tablespoons finely chopped
   fresh tarragon

3 egg yolks
¼ teaspoon salt
¼ teaspoon freshly cracked
   white pepper
2 tablespoons chopped parsley,
   optional

Melt butter, which should be very hot when you are ready for it. Put shallot, vinegar, and tarragon in a small nonaluminum pan. Cook, stirring with a wooden spatula, over medium-high heat, until all liquid evaporates, about 5 minutes. Do not let the mixture burn. Take the pan off heat, add egg yolks and 2 table-spoons cold water, and whisk together until well blended. Return pan to heat and whisk over high heat, raising and lowering the pan to control heat—the pan must not get too hot. Whisk continuously until mixture starts to mound and is the consistency of heavy cream. Remove from heat and whisk in ¼ cup of the hot melted butter, 1 tablespoon at a time. Return pan to heat and, still whisking, add remaining butter in a thin stream. Whisk, raising and lowering the pan over heat, until mixture is thick. Strain sauce, if desired, before adding parsley. Season with salt and pepper. Hold sauce in a pan of warm water until serving time. Makes ¾ to 1 cup.

FRENCH VINAIGRETTE DRESSING

2 tablespoons vinegar
¼ cup oil
1 teaspoon coarse salt

½ teaspoon freshly cracked
   black pepper

Beat ingredients together with a fork, or shake in a jar. You can use red or white wine vinegar, tarragon vinegar, or cider vinegar, and French peanut oil, vegetable oil, or French, Italian, Spanish, or Greek olive oil.

MAYONNAISE

Prepared mustard
½ teaspoon salt
1 tablespoon vinegar or lemon
    juice

¼ teaspoon freshly cracked
    white pepper
1 egg yolk
1 cup olive oil or vegetable
    oil or a mixture of the two

In a small bowl, whisk together mustard, salt, vinegar or lemon juice, pepper, and egg yolk. Whisk in ¼ cup of the oil, 1 tablespoon at a time, whisking thoroughly after adding each spoonful. Then pour in remaining oil in a thin stream, whisking constantly until mixture is thick and smooth, about 5 minutes. Makes 1 cup.

BOUQUET GARNI

1 rib celery
1 bay leaf

¼ teaspoon dried thyme
3 or 4 sprigs parsley

Make a celery sandwich by laying herbs on half the celery rib, folding the other half over, and tying with a string. Leave one end of the string long and tie it to the handle of your pot or casserole so the bouquet garni will be easy to remove.

MUSHROOM DUXELLES

¼ pound very finely chopped
    mushrooms
¼ cup butter
¼ cup finely chopped shallots

1 tablespoon lemon juice
½ teaspoon salt
¼ teaspoon freshly cracked
    black pepper

Put the mushrooms in the corner of a tea towel and wring them out to get rid of excess moisture. (This step is not essential, but it will shorten cooking time.) Melt the butter in a skillet, add the chopped shallots, and cook over high heat for a few minutes, stirring with a wooden spatula, until shallots are transparent. Do not let them brown. Add mushrooms, sprinkle with lemon juice, and cook, stirring constantly with a wooden spatula, until the mushrooms look dry. This may take 15 to 20 minutes. Season with salt and pepper and cool. Can be stored in the refrigerator up to 10 days, or frozen for up to 1 month. Makes 1 cup.

SAUTÉED MUSHROOMS

Wipe mushrooms clean with paper towels dipped in acidulated water (1 tablespoon lemon juice to 1 quart water). Trim stems and slice mushrooms vertically. Melt butter (1 tablespoon butter for each ¼ pound mushrooms) in a heavy skillet over high heat. When it's hot and foaming, add mushrooms, squeeze on a few drops of lemon juice, sprinkle with salt and freshly cracked black pepper, and toss over high heat for about 3 minutes.

SAUTÉED FLUTED MUSHROOM CAPS

Follow directions for sautéed mushrooms, but leave mushrooms whole. To flute mushroom caps, cut off the stems even with the caps—don't twist the stems out, or the caps will collapse—then use a small curved knife or lemon stripper to cut grooves that spiral out from the center of each cap to the edges, all around.

TOMATO ROSES

For each tomato rose, choose a large, red tomato. At the stem end, cut a slice *only two thirds* of the way across—this will be the base of the rose. Then place your knife so as to peel the tomato, starting from this base, in a continuous spiral ¾ inch wide and ⅛ inch thick. If you break the spiral, start over with a fresh tomato. To form the rose, start at the free end of the spiral and coil it up toward the stem base. Secure with a toothpick if necessary.

TURNIP ROSES

For a turnip rose, cut turnip into a rose shape with a paring knife.

BEER BATTER

Make beer batter at least 1 to 2 hours before you want to use it and let stand at room temperature. If you make it further ahead, refrigerate it—can be kept in the refrigerator for up to 3 to 4 days.

1 12-ounce can beer
1 to 1¼ cups lightly spooned
   flour

1 tablespoon salt
1 teaspoon paprika
½ teaspoon baking powder

Pour beer into a bowl, then flour into beer. It will foam; it thickens as it stands. Stir in salt, paprika, and baking powder. Makes about 2½ cups.

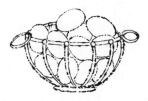

BASIC CRÊPES

½ cup lightly spooned flour
¼ teaspoon salt
2 eggs
2 egg yolks

¼ cup vegetable oil, plus oil
   to film crêpe pan
½ cup milk

Put all ingredients (except oil to film pan) into a blender and blend at top speed, or whisk until smooth. Strain the batter if lumps or flour specks remain. Refrigerate batter for at least 1 hour. Before frying crêpes, thin batter, if too thick, with a little cold milk or water. Batter should be the consistency of heavy cream. Fry crêpes one at a time in a seasoned iron crêpe pan over high heat. Use a 5-inch pan for dessert crêpes, a 7-inch pan for entrée crêpes. Film pan with oil, heat it almost to the point of smoking, and, for a 5-inch pan, pour in 2 to 3 tablespoons of butter, and for a 7-inch pan, a scant ¼ of a cup of butter; quickly tilt pan in all directions to spread batter all over bottom of pan. The crêpe should be very thin. Fry 1 minute, or until the edges brown; then turn crêpe and fry on the other side for about 30 seconds. Film the pan lightly with oil before frying each crêpe. Makes 8 7-inch or 12 5-inch crêpes. Recipe can be doubled or quadrupled.

Note: When you fold or roll crêpes, always put the 30-second side inside.

PÂTE À CHOUX (Cream Puff Paste)

6 tablespoons butter, at room   1 cup lightly spooned flour
   temperature   4 eggs

Cut up the butter and add to 1 cup water in a saucepan. Bring slowly to a boil. As soon as butter melts, dump in the flour all at once and beat it with a wooden spatula until the mixture looks like mashed potatoes. Continue beating over high heat until mixture begins to coat the bottom of the pan, about 2 minutes. Remove from heat. Make a well in the mixture and have the first egg cracked and ready; drop it into the well and quickly beat it in before it scrambles. Beat in remaining 3 eggs, one at a time, beating to mix thoroughly before adding the next. Continue beating the mixture until it is shiny (do this by hand unless you have a mixer with a flat whip—mixture will clog rotary beaters). Use as directed in recipes.

HOMEMADE PASTA

Roll and cut noodles at least 2 hours before cooking them— they need drying time. You can mix the dough the day before and store in the refrigerator. You can freeze uncooked noodles for up to 1 month or store them for 2 to 3 days in the refrigerator. This recipe makes just under 1½ pounds of noodles, or enough pasta to cut 24 cannelloni pieces.

3 cups lightly spooned flour   1 tablespoon olive or
½ teaspoon salt   vegetable oil
3 eggs   2 to 3 tablespoons water

Put flour in a bowl and stir in salt. Make a well and drop in eggs and oil. Mix with your fingers. Sprinkle on water, 1 table-spoonful at a time, and mix with your hands, using a squeezing motion. Use as little water as possible; dough should hold together when it's squeezed, but it will look raggedy. Turn it out on a floured board and knead for 10 minutes; it will not get really smooth—it should still look raggedy, with cracks in it. If you got too much water in the dough, put some flour on your board and knead it into the dough. Cover dough and let it rest for 15 minutes, or wrap and refrigerate overnight.

To roll by hand: divide dough into 4 pieces and roll out each piece, in turn, like pie pastry, on a lightly floured surface. Roll it very, very thin—as thin as possible—and in a rectangular shape. Sift a little flour over the surface, spreading it with your hands to coat lightly; this will keep dough from sticking to itself. Roll it up like a jelly roll—but from the long side. Cut noodles by slicing the roll with a knife, whatever width you want noodles to be. Toss the slices high in the air to unroll the noodles, letting them fall to a floured tea towel. Spread them out loosely to dry, about 2 hours. Cook as directed, or wrap tightly in freezer wrap and freeze.

To use pasta machine: shape dough into a sausage and cut it into 8 equal-size pieces. Flatten each piece. Set machine rollers at widest setting (no. 10 on most machines) and crank dough through to flatten it. Fold dough and crank it through again. Repeat with remaining pieces. Reset rollers to no. 8 and put each piece through again—just once this time, and do not fold. Continue through settings 6, 4, 2, and 0. Pasta gets longer and thinner with each rolling. To cut noodles, remove handle from roller position to cutter position for thin or wide noodles, whichever you want to make. Roll pasta through cutters and toss the resulting noodles high in the air onto a floured tea towel. Spread them out loosely to dry, about 2 hours.

Variation: To make cannelloni, with a knife, cut rolled pasta into rectangles about 4 x 6 inches (or smaller if you wish).

SANDY'S PIECRUST

3 cups lightly spooned flour	1 cup lard
1 teaspoon salt	1 egg
1 tablespoon sugar	2 tablespoons ice water
¼ teaspoon baking soda	2 tablespoons lemon juice

Stir together flour, salt, sugar, and baking soda. With a pastry blender or two knives, cut in lard until mixture looks like small peas. Lightly beat the egg with ice water and lemon juice. Add to flour mixture and toss with a fork to moisten evenly. Gather dough into a ball and wrap in waxed paper; refrigerate for ½ hour or until ready to roll out. (*May be made 2 to 3 days ahead and refrigerated.*) Makes 2 9-inch piecrusts.

PÂTE BRISÉE SHELL

2 cups lightly spooned flour	¼ cup vegetable shortening
½ teaspoon salt	3 to 4 tablespoons ice water
½ cup chilled butter	

Put flour in a bowl and stir in salt. (If you use unsalted butter, increase salt to 1 teaspoon.) With a pastry blender, two knives, or your fingertips, cut or rub in butter and shortening until mixture looks like small peas. Add ice water, 1 tablespoon at a time, sprinkling it on the flour mixture while tossing mixture with a fork. Use just enough water to make dough hold together. Gather it into a ball, wrap in waxed paper, and chill for at least 30 minutes. Roll out on a lightly floured board and fit into a 9- or 10-inch flan ring (whatever your recipe calls for). Prick dough all over the bottom with a fork and chill it again in the refrigerator for at least 20 minutes. Before baking, line the shell with waxed paper and fill it with dried beans or rice. Bake in a preheated 350° oven 30 minutes. Remove beans, waxed paper, and flan ring, reduce heat to 325°, and bake another 20 to 25 minutes, or until pastry is a pale gold color. Remove from oven and cool on a wire rack.

For a partly baked shell, bake in a preheated 375° oven for 20 to 25 minutes, or until pastry is set; then remove beans, waxed paper, and flan ring. Add the filling and continue baking as recipe directs.

Pâte brisée dough can be stored in the refrigerator for up to 2 days, wrapped in foil or plastic wrap. It can be frozen for up to 1 month. Defrost frozen dough in the refrigerator before using. The shell can be frozen unbaked for up to 1 month; defrost it in the refrigerator before baking. Partly baked or wholly baked shells can be refrigerated for 2 days or frozen for up to 1 month.

SOUR CREAM PASTRY

1½ cups lightly spooned flour	¾ cup chilled unsalted butter
½ teaspoon salt	½ cup dairy sour cream

Put flour in a bowl and stir in salt. Cut or rub butter into flour with a pastry blender, two knives, or your fingers; mixture should look like coarse cornmeal. Add sour cream and mix with a fork. Gather mixture together (it will be soft) and knead it a few times on a lightly floured board; then form it into a ball, sprinkle it with a little flour, wrap in waxed paper, and chill in the refrigerator for at least 1½ hours. Dough can be refrigerated for 2 days or frozen for up to 1 month.

Index

Afternoon Tea Menus, 245–249
  Elegant (8), 247
  Substantial (12), 245
Ainsworth, Sandy, Bread-and-Butter Sandwiches, 247
Ainsworth, Sandy, White Bread, 245
Alice Peterson's Chocolate Cheesecake, 71
Almond
  Apricot Marzipan Tart, 43
  Cake, Swedish, 100
  Chocolate Almond Soufflé, Cold, 171
  Orange Almond Torte, 209
  Torte, 167

Alpine Logs, 236
Alsatian cooking, 4, 95
Anchovies and Roasted Peppers, 235
Anchovy Sauce (Salsa di Alici), 238
Antipasto, 256
Apple, Apples
  and Bananas, Glacéed, 145
  Chausson, 97
  Cinnamon, Baked, 14
  Poached, with Meringue, 18
  and Potato Salad, 262
  Tart Tatin, 137
Apricot Glaze, 26
Apricot Marzipan Tart, 43

291

Artichokes, Stuffed, 224
Asparagus
    Roman, 131
    Soup, 101
    White, Vinaigrette, 115
Aspic Dishes
    Aspic (basic), 48, 279
    Aspic for pâté, 230
    Chaudfroid Chicken, 47; on Cold
        Capered Rice, 89
    Chaudfroid Coating, 48
    Chicken, Jellied, 261
    Mustard Ring, 154
    Pâté en Croûte, 229
    Trout, Poached, Glazed, on As-
        pic, 124
Avocado, Cherry Tomatoes Stuffed
    with Guacamole, 158
Avocado with Crab Meat, 73

Bacon
    Breakfast, 14
    Canadian, Baked, 22
    Canadian, Slices, Sautéed, 30
Baked Alaska, 200
Bananas and Apples, Glacéed, 145
Bananas (with) Meringue, 109
Barley Pilaf, 178
Basic Recipes, 278–289
Batter, Beer, 285
Bavarian Cream, 208
Bavarian Cream, Pistachio, 185
Bean, Beans
    Black, Soup with Garnishes, 85
    Fava, with Coarse Salt, 90, 265
    Lima (dried), Baked, 270
    Lima (fresh), with Black Butter,
        212
    Yellow and Green, Mixed, with
        Shallots and Butter, 86
Beard, James, 3
Béarnaise Sauce, 282
Beck, Simone, 3
Beef
    Alpine Logs, 236
    Birds, 254
    Burgundy, 178
    Coulibiac of, with Mustard Hol-
        landaise, 183

Beef (*Cont.*)
    Fillet of, Cold, on Horseradish-
        Buttered White Bread, 258
    Hamburgers with Green Pepper-
        corns, 66
    London Broil, 102
    Meat Loaf en Croûte, 269
    à la Mode, 187
    Roast Beef Hash, 25
    Sirloin Strip, Roast, 114
    Steak Tartare, 221
    Stir-Fried, 144
    Stock, 277
    Zucchini, Stuffed, 201
Beer Batter, 285
Beet Salad, 189
Berries (raspberries or strawber-
    ries) with Cold Zabaglione,
    134
Beverages
    for Brunch, 10
    Café au Lait, 14
    for Luncheon, 40
    Sangría, 276
    Tea, 244
    Viennese Coffee, 27
Bibb Lettuce Salad, 111; and Cu-
    cumber, 49
Biscuits, Baking Powder, Hot, 74
Blowfish, Sautéed, 197
Bouquet Garni, 283
Brandade of Trout, 234
Brandy Curls, 82
Breads, Quick Breads
    Baking Powder Biscuits, Hot, 74
    Carrot Bread, 35
    Cheese Puffs, 246
    Popovers, 20
Breads, Yeast Breads
    Brioche, 11
    Coffee Cake, Easy, 15
    Croissants, 13
    Danish Pastry, 25
    Kugelhopf, 17
    Panettone, 23
    White Bread, Sandy Ainsworth's,
        245
Breakfast Menus, 11–36
    in Bed (2), 29
    Champagne (6), 36

Breakfast Menus (*Cont.*)
  childhood memories, 9–10
  Classic Continental (any number), 11
  Country (6 to 8), 14
  Hunt (10), 34
  Morning After a Late Party (8), 28
  Weekend Guests (4), 21
  Winter, Hearty (6 to 8), 17
Brioche, 11
  Giant, 12; Stuffed with Scrambled Eggs, 32
  Individual, 12
  Kielbasa in Brioche, 69
  Slices with Mustard Butter, 28
Broccoli
  Puree, 108
  Timbales, 173
  with White Wine, 225
Brown Sauce, Basic, 281
Brunch Menus, 24–28, 31–33
  drinks, 10
  by the fireplace (6), 24
  Holiday Buffet (16), 31
  Summer, Light (4), 27
Buffet Menus, 183–213
  "Cook-in" (6 to 8), 197
  Holiday Brunch (16), 31
  Italian (8), 201
  Just Desserts (25), 203
  Lap (12), 183
  Make-Your-Own-Salad (24), 191
  New Year's Eve Sit-down (16), 193
  planning, 181–182
  Sit-down (12), 186
  Summertime Seafood (8), 210
Butter, Maître d'Hôtel, 114
Butter, Olive, 68
Buttercream, *see* Icings and Fillings, Dessert
Butterfish en Papillote with Tartar Sauce, 54

Cabbage
  Red, 96
  Red (with apples), 140
  (sauerkraut) Choucroute Garni, 136

Café au Lait, 14
Cakes and Tortes
  Almond Cake, Swedish, 100
  Almond Torte, 167
  Carlsbad Oblaten Cake, 204
  Cheesecake, Chocolate, Alice Peterson's, 71
  Ginger Roll, 65
  Gold Cake, 200
  Jelly Roll, 208
  Kugelhopf, 17
  Meringue Cake with Peaches, 74
  Meringue Torte with Chocolate Buttercream, 195
  Orange Almond Torte, 209
  Panettone, 23
  Paskha, 154
  Pound Cake, 262
  Rum Babas, 247
  Savarin, 207
  Strawberry Roll, 248
  Tourinoise, La, 206
  Walnut Cake, 271
  White Chocolate Roll, 255
Canadian Bacon, *see* Bacon
Canapés, 232
Cannelloni, 287
Capered Rice, Cold, 90
Capon with Tarragon Butter, Roast, 147
Caramel, 180
Caramel Soufflé, Cold, 226
Carlsbad Oblaten Cake, 204
Carrot, Carrots
  Bread, 35
  Chinese, 46
  and Onions, Braised, 105
  Salad, 179
  Soufflé, 198
Cauliflower and Black Olive Salad, 100
Cauliflower Covered with Broccoli Puree, 108
Caviar Barquettes, 110
Celeriac and Potatoes, Mashed, 97
Celeriac Sticks, 111
Celery, Braised, 83
Celery Victor, 128
Chaudfroid Chicken, 47; on Cold Capered Rice, 89

Cheese-Flavored Dishes
Alpine Logs, 236
Cheesecake, Chocolate, Alice Peterson's, 71
Cheese Croquettes with Tomato Sauce, 64
Cheese Puffs, 246
Cheese Roll, Four Ways, 44
Cheeses, Assorted, 192
Coeur à la Crème, 58
Eggs à la Princesse Caramon, 41
Gnocchi à la Parisienne, 162
Gnocchi, Russian, 188
Gougère, 75
Green Salad with Roquefort Cheese, 125
Noodle Ring, 61
Onion Crêpes, 194
Paskha, 154
Passatelli Soup, 78
Pears Stuffed with Roquefort Cheese, 67
Roman Asparagus, 131
Roquefort Salad Dressing, 192
Tyropita, 153
Cherry Tomatoes, see Tomato, Tomatoes
Chestnut
Buttercream, 189
Mont Blanc, 189
Mousse, 207
Tart, 141
Tourinoise, La, 206
Chicken, see also Capon; Cornish Hens; Squabs
with Almonds, 161
Chaudfroid, 47; on Cold Capered Rice, 89
Jellied, 261
Livers en Brochette, 27
Pancakes, Curried, with Chutney, 217
Paper-Wrapped, 142
Périgourdine, 60
Pie, 93
Stock, 278
Suprêmes with Champagne Sauce, 120
with Tarragon Butter, Roast, 99
Wings, Barbecued, Cold, 70

Chick-Pea Salad, 275
Chicory Salad, 59
Chinese Carrots, 46
Chinese 5-spice powder, 143
Chocolate
Almond Soufflé, Cold, 171
Buttercream, 196
Carlsbad Oblaten Cake, 204
Cheesecake, Alice Peterson's, 71
Leaves, 249
Mint Soufflé, Hot, 95
Mousse, 77
Pastry Cream, 204
Pudding, Steamed, with Hard Sauce, 79
Soufflé, Cold, 205
White, Roll, 255
Choucroute Garni, 136
Cinnamon Apples, Baked, 14
Clams on the Half Shell, 266
Cocktail Party Menus, 229–240
Large (50), 229
planning menu and drinks, 227–228
Small (12), 237
Coeur à la Crème, 58
Coffee
Café au Lait, 14
Coffeehouse Mousse, 223
Praline Ice Cream, 122
Viennese, 27
Coffee Cake, Easy, 15
Confection, Chocolate Leaves, 249
Consommé Normande, 119
Cookies and Small Cakes
Brandy Curls, 82
Florentines, 249
Ladyfingers, 265
Pignolia Cookies, 249
Sand Tarts, 62
Corn on the Cob, 176
Cornish Hens
Glazed, 127
à l'Orange, 166
with Tangerines, 159
Coulibiac of Beef with Mustard Hollandaise, 183
Court Bouillon, 279

Crab Meat, 34
  Avocado with, 73
  Salad, 52
  Sautéed, 88; on Virginia Ham, 34
  Seafood Mélange, 132
Cream Puff Paste (Pâté à Choux), 286
Cream, whipped, for desserts made ahead, 7
Crème Anglaise, 213
Crème Caramel, 206
Crêpes, *see* Pancakes and Crêpes
Croissants, 13
Croquettes, Cheese, with Tomato Sauce, 64
Croquettes, Polenta, 20
Crostini, Salsa di Alici, 238
Crudités with Coarse Salt, 272
Cucumber, Cucumbers
  Balls, Marinated, 109
  and Bibb Lettuce Salad, 49
  (and) Endive, and Mushroom Salad, 185
  in Sour Cream and Chives, 270
  Sticks, Iced, 267
Curried Chicken Pancakes with Chutney, 217
Custards
  Bavarian Cream, 208; Pistachio, 185
  Crème Anglaise, 213
  Crème Caramel, 206
  Riz à l'Impératrice, 115

Danish Open-face Sandwiches, Assorted, 80–82
Danish Pastry, 25
Dessert Omelette, 87
Desserts, *see* Cakes and Tortes; Coeur; Cookies and Small Cakes; Custards; Frozen Desserts; Icings and Fillings; Meringue Desserts; Mousse; Pastry Desserts; Pies and Tarts, Dessert; Pudding; Sauce, Dessert; Soufflé; *see also* names of fruits

Dinner Menus, 93–180
  Adult Birthday (4 to 6), 177
  Alsatian, Informal (6), 135
  with an American Flavor (8), 158
  Autumn, with an Alsatian Touch (6), 95
  Chinese (6 to 8), 141
  Christmas, Hearty (8), 149
  Cooking Lesson Show-off (8), 168
  Duckling (6), 104
  Early, Before a Gala (8), 161
  Easter, Unusual (8), 151
  Formal (6), 116
  Formal, Rich and Delicious (8), 113
  Formal, on the Terrace (6), 129, 253
  Formal, on a Winter's Evening (8), 110
  for Frogs' Legs Lovers (6), 163
  Game (6), 138
  Informal (8), 101; (6), 107
  Old-Fashioned Shore (8), 174
  Potluck (4), 93
  for Special Friends (6), 155
  Spring, Chic (8), 165
  Summer (8), 132
  Summer, Elegant (6), 123
  Summer, Formal (8), 126
  Sunday Night, Relaxed (6), 98
  for Sweetbread Lovers (6), 172
  Thanksgiving (8), 146
  Winter (6), 119
Dinner party planning, 91–92
Duckling, Broiled, 104
Duck Pâté, 239
Duxelles, Mushroom, 284

Eggplant, Stuffed, 273
Eggs
  Hard-Cooked
    Andalouse, 152
    Deviled, 70
    à la Princesse Caramon, 41
  Omelette, Dessert, 87
  Scrambled, 32

Endive, Belgian
  à la Crème, 114
  (and) Mushroom, and Cucumber Salad, 185
  and Watercress Salad, 42
English Muffins, Toasted, and Strawberry Jam, 246

Fava Beans, *see* Bean, Beans
Fennel, Braised, 102
Fettuccine with Pesto Sauce, 202
Field, Michael, 3
Fillings, Dessert, *see* Icings and Fillings
Fillings, Entrée, *see* Stuffings and Fillings
Fish, *see also* names of fish
  Chowder, 258
  en Croûte, 45
  Stock, 169, 279
  Stuffed, Baked, 174
Florentines, 249
Flounder Paupiettes Stuffed with Fish Mousse, Poached, 210
Flour, measuring, 5
Forcemeat for pâté, 230
Freezer use, 6
French Dressing, 192
French Onion Soup, Gratiné, 29
French Toast, Double-Dipped, 22
French Vinaigrette Dressing, 282
Frill for bone of Gigot, 194
Fritters, Mushroom, 33
Frogs' Legs Provençale, 164
Frozen Desserts
  Ice, Raspberry, with Cassis, 56
  Ice Cream, Coffee Praline, 122
  Ice Cream, Vanilla, Homemade (with Strawberries), 176
  Oranges, Stuffed, 218
Fruit, *see also* names of fruit
  and Champagne, 89
  Fresh, Bowl, 28
  Glazed, 31
  Macédoine of, 61

Garnishes
  Mushroom Caps, Fluted Sautéed, 284

Garnishes (*Cont.*)
  Tomato Roses, 284
  Turnip Roses, 285
Garniture Bourgeoise, 188
Gâteau Saint-Honoré, 179
Gazpacho, 260
Giblet Sauce, 150
Gigot Provençale, 193
Ginger Roll, 65
Ginger Sauce, 22
Gnocchi à la Parisienne, 162
Gnocchi, Russian, 188
Gold Cake, 200
Goose, Roast, with Giblet Sauce, 149
Gougère, 75
Grand Marnier Soufflé, Cold, 112
Grape Tart, 205
Green Mayonnaise, 53
Green Salad with Roquefort Dressing, 125
Green Salad, Tossed, 195

Ham
  Baked in Paper, Jo Klein's, 259
  Melon and Prosciutto, 47
  Mushroom-Ham Stuffing, 121
  Rolls, Individual, 32
  Roulade with Lemon Butter Sauce, 77
  Roulade with Mustard Sour Cream, 36
  Scallops and Prosciutto, 210
  and Turkey-Breast Paupiettes, 107
Hamburgers with Green Peppercorns, 66
Hard Sauce, 79
Hash, Roast Beef, 25
Herbs, dried and fresh, 6
Holiday Menus
  Christmas, Hearty (8), 149
  Easter, Unusual (8), 151
  Fourth of July Picnic (16), 268
  New Year's Eve Sit-down Buffet (16), 193
  Thanksgiving (8), 146
Hollandaise Sauce, 281
Hominy, 34
Hominy Soufflé, 35

Hors d'Oeuvres
Alpine Logs, 236
Antipasto, 256
Artichokes, Stuffed, 224
Brandade of Trout, 234
Canapés, 232
Caviar Barquettes, 110
Cheese Roll, Four Ways, 44
Cherry Tomatoes Stuffed with Crab Meat, 234
Cherry Tomatoes Stuffed with Guacamole, 158, 234
Clams on the Half Shell, 266
Crostini, Salsa di Alici, 238
Crudités with Coarse Salt, 272
Duck Pâté, 239
Eggs Andalouse, 152
Lentil Salad, 135
Meat Balls, 240
Melon and Prosciutto, 47
Mushroom Flan, 53
Mushroom, Onion, and Sausage Flan, 163
Mussels en Brochette, Béarnaise, 155
Mussels Marinière, 186
Olive Butter, 68
Oysters, Fried, 237
Oysters Rockefeller, 117
Pâté en Croûte, 229
Peppers, Roasted, and Anchovies, 235
Quenelles de Brochet, 168
Radishes with Olive Butter, 84
Salami Cornucopias on Pumpernickel, 63
Scallops and Prosciutto, 210
Seafood in Strudel, 238
Shad Roe, Poached, Hollandaise, 165
Shrimp Maison, 235
Shrimp, Puffed, 142
Smoked Salmon with Caviar, 149
Tomatoes Stuffed with Crab-Meat Salad, 268
Trout Amandine, 138
Trout, Poached, Glazed, on Aspic, 124
Vegetables, Raw, with Olive Butter, 234

Icings and Fillings, Dessert
Apricot Glaze, 26
Caramel, 180
Chestnut Buttercream, 189
Chocolate Buttercream, 196
Chocolate Pastry Cream, 204
Filling for Coffee Cake, 16
Frosting for Walnut Cake, 271
Pastry Cream, 180
Praline Powder, 123
Vanilla Water Icing, 27

Jelly Crêpes, 30
Jelly Roll, 208
Jerusalem Artichoke Soup, 146
Jo Klein's Baked Ham in Paper, 259

Kartoffelklösse, 140
Kielbasa in Brioche with Assorted Mustards, 69
Klein, Jo, Baked Ham in Paper, 259
Kugelhopf, 17

Ladyfingers, 265
Lamb
Crown of, Béarnaise, 110
(leg) Gigot Provençale, 193
Leg of, Orange, en Croûte, 170
(leg) Roast, with Soubise, 130
Noisettes with Veal Mousse, 118
Rack of, with Green Peppercorns, 198
Leeks Mornay, 199
Leeks Vinaigrette, 94
Lemon Butter Sauce, 77
Lemon Tart, 103
Lentil Salad, 135
Lettuce
Bibb, and Cucumber Salad, 49
Bibb, Salad, 111
Lemon-Dressed, 88
Oak-Leaf, with Sour Cream Dressing, 257
Romaine, Salad, 58
Lima Beans, *see* Bean, Beans
Livers, Chicken, en Brochette, 27

Lucas, Dione, 2, 3
Luncheon Menus, 39–90
  Celebration (12), 59
  Country-Kitchen (6), 83
  Danish Open-face Sandwich (12), 80
  Elegant (8), 44
  Formal (8), 53
  Holiday Season (6), 77
  Informal (8), 66
  Ladies' (8), 41
  Late, on a Wintry Day (8), 75
  Light and Delicate (6), 51
  Light, Easy-to-Prepare (4), 86
  Low-Calorie (4), 88
  Pleasant and Inexpensive (12 to 16), 63
  Quick and Tasty (8), 56
  Robust, After Tennis or Golf (8), 68
  Summer, Formal (12), 47
  Summer, for Ladies and Children (4 and 8), 70
  Summer, Refreshing (6), 72
  Summer, at Tables under a Shade Tree (8), 89
  Winter (12), 84
Lobster, Lobsters
  Boiled, 266
  Halves, Truffled, Cold, Vinaigrette, 129
  Thermidor, 219
London Broil, 102

Macédoine of Fruit, 61
Maître d'Hôtel Butter, 114
Marzipan, Apricot Marzipan Tart, 43
Mayonnaise, 283
Mayonnaise, Green, 53
Meat Balls, 240
Meat Glaze, 280
Meat Loaf en Croûte, 269
Meats, see Bacon; Beef; Ham; Lamb; Pork; Sausage; Veal; Venison
Melba Rounds, Toasted, 42
Melba Toast Fingers, 236

Melon
  with Port Wine, 30
  and Prosciutto, 47
  Wedges, Crystallized Ginger, 257
Meringue Desserts
  Apples, Poached, with Meringue, 18
  Baked Alaska, 200
  Lemon Tart, 103
  Meringue Bananas, 109
  Meringue Cake with Peaches, 74
  Meringue Torte with Chocolate Buttercream, 195
  Mont Blanc, 189
  Salzburger Nockerln, 106
Mincemeat Roll with Hard Sauce, 150
Mont Blanc, 189
Mornay Sauce, 157
Mostarda, 68
Mousse, Cold
  Chestnut, 207
  Chocolate, 77
  Coffeehouse, 223
  Spinach, 51
Mushroom, Mushrooms
  Broth Garnished with Mushroom Rounds, 51
  Caps, Fluted Sautéed, 284
  Duxelles, 283
  (and) Endive, and Cucumber Salad, 185
  Flan, 53
  Fritters, 33
  -Ham Stuffing, 121
  (and) Onion, and Sausage Flan, 163
  Salad, Raw, with a Dressing of Sour Cream, Caraway, and Chives, 78
  Sauce, 175
  Sautéed, 284
  Soup, Cream of, 99
Mussels
  en Brochette, Béarnaise, 155
  Marinière, 186
  (and) Oysters, and Shrimp, Fried, with Tartar Sauce, 225

Mustard
  Hollandaise, 183
  Mayonnaise, 267
  Ring, 154
  Sour Cream, 36

Noodle Ring, 61

Olive, Black
  Butter, 68
  and Cauliflower Salad, 100
  and Red Onion Salad, 67
Olney, Richard, 3
Onion, Onions
  and Carrots, Braised, 105
  Crêpes, 194
  (and) Mushroom, and Sausage
    Flan, 163
  Pie, 85
  Red, and Black Olive Salad, 67
  Rings, Deep-Fried, 85
  Soubise, 130; Filling, 157
  Soup, Cream of, Cold, 274
  Soup, French, Gratiné, 29
  Stuffed with Onions, 69
Orange, Oranges
  Almond Torte, 209
  Grand Marnier, 84
  Leg of Lamb en Croûte, 170
  Stuffed, 218
Outdoor Menus, 253–276
  Back Porch Supper (8), 259
  Beach Picnic (6), 274
  Formal Dinner on the Terrace
    (6), 129, 253
  Formal Picnic (8), 263
  Fourth of July Picnic (16), 268
  Lobster Party (6), 266
  Picnic in the Woods (8), 256
  Pool Party (12), 272
  Summer Luncheon at Tables un-
    der a Shade Tree (8), 89
  Tailgate Picnic (8), 257
Oyster, Oysters
  Fried, 237
  Rockefeller, 117
  (and) Shrimp, and Mussels,
    Fried, with Tartar Sauce, 225
  Stew, Hot, 75

Pain Bagna, 275
Palm, Hearts of, Salad, 171
Pancakes and Crêpes
  Chicken Pancakes, Curried, with
    Chutney, 217
  Crêpes, Basic, 285
  Jelly Crêpes, 30
  Onion Crêpes, 194
Panettone, 23
Paskha, 154
Passatelli Soup, 78
Pasta
  Cannelloni, 287
  Fettuccine with Pesto Sauce, 202
  Homemade, 286
  Noodle Ring, 61
Pastry, Basic
  Barquettes, 49
  for Orange Leg of Lamb, 171
  Pâte Brisée Shell, 288
  Pâte à Choux (Cream Puff
    Paste), 286
  for pâté molds, 230
  Piecrust, Sandy's, 287
  Sour Cream Pastry, 289
Pastry Desserts
  Gâteau Saint-Honoré, 179
  Mincemeat Roll with Hard
    Sauce, 150
  Strawberry Barquettes, 49
Pastry Entrées and Hors d'Oeuvres
  Alpine Logs, 236
  Caviar Barquettes, 110
  Coulibiac of Beef with Mustard
    Hollandaise, 183
  Duck Pâté, 239
  Fish en Croûte, 45
  Gougère, 75
  Meat Loaf en Croûte, 269
  Orange Leg of Lamb en Croûte,
    170
  Pâté en Croûte, 229
  Seafood in Strudel, 238
  Tyropita, 153
  Veal Loaf en Croûte, Peppered,
    269
Pastry Cream, *see* Icings and Fill-
  ings
Pâte Brisée Shell, 288

Pâte à Choux (Cream Puff Paste), 286

Pâté en Croûte, 229

Pea
  Pod Soup, 216
  Potage Saint-Germain, 221
  Roulade, 55

Peaches, Fresh, with Champagne, 36

Peaches in Port, 46

Pear, Pears
  Baked, with Heavy Cream, 21
  Poached, in Cassis, 162
  Poached in White Wine, 165
  Stuffed with Roquefort Cheese, 67
  Tart, Fresh, 132

Pecan Pie, 161

Pennsylvania Scrapple, 19

Peppercorns, green, 66, 198

Peppered Veal Loaf en Croûte, 269

Pepper, Green, Salad, 65

Peppers, Red, Roasted, and Anchovies, 235

Pesto alla Genovese, 202

Peterson, Alice, Chocolate Cheesecake, 71

Picknicking, packing up, 251–252

Picnics, *see* Outdoor Menus

Piecrust, Sandy's, 287

Pies and Tarts, Dessert
  Apple Chausson, 97
  Apricot Marzipan Tart, 43
  Chestnut Tart, 141
  Grape Tart, 205
  Lemon Tart, 103
  Pear Tart, Fresh, 132
  Pecan Pie, 161
  Raspberry Tart, 128
  Tart Tatin, 137

Pies and Tarts, Entrées and Hors d'Oeuvres
  Chicken Pie, 93
  Mushroom Flan, 53
  Mushroom, Onion, and Sausage Flan, 163
  Onion Pie, 85
  Pissaladière, 272

Pignolia Cookies, 249

Pike, Quenelles de Brochet, 168

Pilaf, *see* Barley; Rice

Pineapple, Glazed, in Kirsch, 24

Pissaladière, 272

Pistachio Bavarian Cream, 185

Polenta, 19
  Croquettes, 20
  Ring Mold with Sautéed Fluted Mushroom Caps, 83

Pommes Parisienne, 255

Popovers, 20

Pork, *see also* Bacon; Ham; Sausage
  Choucroute Garni, 136
  Fresh Ham, Roast, 152
  Rack of, 95
  Scrapple, Pennsylvania, 19
  Spareribs, Barbecued, 143

Potage Saint-Germain, 221

Potato, Potatoes
  and Apple Salad, 262
  and Celeriac, Mashed, 97
  Kartoffelklösse, 140
  Pommes Parisienne, 255
  Roesti, 15
  Skins, Baked, 267
  Soufflé, 119
  Steamed, with Caraway and Melted Butter, 137
  Straw, 127
  Sweet, Whipped, 160

Poultry, *see* Capon; Chicken; Cornish Hens; Duck, Duckling; Goose; Squabs; Turkey

Pound Cake, 262

Praline Powder, 123

Provençale Sauce, 164

Pudding, Chocolate, Steamed, with Hard Sauce, 79

Quenelles de Brochet, 168

Radish, Radishes
  Black, Salad, 222
  Black, Slices, Vinaigrette, 76
  with Olive Butter, 84

Raspberry, Raspberries
  with Chilled Framboise, 90
  Ice with Cassis, 56
  Tart, 128

Reheating, 6
Rice, *see also* Wild Rice
    Brown, Pilaf; 167; with Almond
        Slivers, 111; with Pine Nuts,
        105
    Capered, Cold, 90
    Fried, 144
    Risotto, 57
    Riz à l'Impératrice, 115
Ris de Veau, Velouté Sauce, 172
Risotto, 57
Riz à l'Impératrice, 115
Robbins, Ann Roe, 3
Roesti Potatoes, 15
Romaine Salad, 58
Roman Asparagus, 131
Roquefort Dressing, 192
Rum Babas, 247
Russian Dressing, 192
Russian Gnocchi, 188

Salad
    Apple and Potato, 262
    Asparagus, White, Vinaigrette,
        115
    Avocado with Crab Meat, 73
    Beefsteak Tomatoes and Chives
        Marinated in Sour Cream
        Dressing, 176
    Beet, 189
    Bibb Lettuce, 111; and Cucum-
        ber, 49
    Black Radish, 222; Slices Vinai-
        grette, 76
    Broccoli with White Wine, 225
    Carrot, 179
    Cauliflower and Black Olive, 100
    Celery Victor, 128
    Cherry Tomatoes Vinaigrette,
        173
    Chick-Pea, 275
    Chicory, 59
    Crab-Meat, 52
    Cucumber Balls, Marinated, 109
    Cucumbers in Sour Cream and
        Chives, 270
    Cucumber Sticks, Iced, 267
    Endive, Mushroom, and Cucum-
        ber, 185

Salad (*Cont.*)
    Green Pepper, 65
    Green, with Roquefort Cheese,
        125
    Green, Tossed, 195
    Hearts of Palm, 171
    ingredients, 192
    Leeks Vinaigrette, 94
    Lentil, 135
    Lettuce, Lemon-Dressed, 88
    Mushroom, Raw, with a Dressing
        of Sour Cream, Caraway, and
        Chives, 78
    Oak-Leaf Lettuce with Sour
        Cream Dressing, 257
    Red Onion and Black Olive, 67
    Romaine, 58
    Tomato, 87
    Tomatoes with Chives, 73
    Tomatoes Stuffed with Crab-
        Meat Salad, 268
    Watercress, 122; and Belgian
        Endive, 42; with Cherry To-
        matoes and Chives, 162
Salad Dressing
    French, 192
    Mayonnaise, 283
    Mayonnaise, Green, 53
    Roquefort, 192
    Russian, 192
    Tartar Sauce, 55
    Vinaigrette, French, 283
Salami Cornucopias on Pumper-
    nickel, 63
Salmon, Smoked, with Caviar, 149
Salzburger Nockerln, 106
Sand Tarts, 62
Sandwiches
    Bread-and-Butter, Sandy Ains-
        worth's, 247
    Fillet of Beef, Cold, on Horse-
        radish-Buttered White Bread,
        258
    Ham, Baked, in Paper, Jo Klein's,
        on Mustard-Buttered French
        Bread, 259
    Open-face, Danish, Assorted, 80–
        82
    Pain Bagna, 275

Sandwiches (*Cont.*)
  Turkey, Cold Roast, on Sandy Ainsworth's White Bread, 246
Sandy Ainsworth's Bread-and-Butter Sandwiches, 247
Sandy Ainsworth's White Bread, 245
Sandy's Piecrust, 287
Sangría, 276
Sauce, *see also* Sauce, Dessert; Salad Dressing
  Anchovy (Salsa di Alici), 238
  Béarnaise, 282
  Brown, Basic, 281
  Giblet, 150
  Hollandaise, 282
  Lemon Butter, 77
  Maître d'Hôtel Butter, 114
  Meat Glaze, 280
  Mornay, 157
  Mushroom, 175
  Mustard Hollandaise, 183
  Mustard Mayonnaise, 267
  Mustard Sour Cream, 36
  Pesto alla Genovese, 202
  Provençale, 164
  for Quenelles de Brochet, 169
  Shrimp, 211
  Soy Dipping, 142
  Tartar, 55
  Tomato, 64
  Velouté, 281
Sauce, Dessert
  Crème Anglaise, 213
  Ginger, 22
  Hard, 79
  Strawberry, 106
  Zabaglione, 203; Cold, 134
Saucepans, heavy, for high-heat cooking, 6
Sausage
  Kielbasa in Brioche with Assorted Mustards, 69
  (and) Mushroom, and Onion Flan, 163
  Salami Cornucopias on Pumpernickel, 63
Savarin, 207
Scallops, Bay, Sautéed, 86
Scallops (sea) and Prosciutto, 210

Scrapple, Pennsylvania, 19
Seafood Mélange, 132
Seafood in Strudel, 238
Shad Roe, Poached, Hollandaise, 165
Shrimp
  en Brochette, 57
  Maison, 235
  (and) Oysters, and Mussels, Fried, with Tartar Sauce, 225
  Puffed, 142
  Sauce, 211
  Seafood Mélange, 132
Sirloin Strip, Roast, 114
Skewered Dishes
  Chicken Livers en Brochette, 27
  Crostini, Salsa di Alici, 238
  Mussels en Brochette, Béarnaise, 155
  Shrimp en Brochette, 57
Sorrel Soup, Cold, 253
Soubise, 130; Filling, 157
Soufflé, Cold
  Caramel, 226
  Chocolate, 205
  Chocolate Almond, 171
  Grand Marnier, 112
Soufflé, Hot
  Carrot, 198
  Chocolate Mint, 95
  Hominy, 35
  Salzburger Nockerln, 100
  Violet, 212
Soup, Cold
  Gazpacho, 260
  Onion, Cream of, 274
  Sorrel, 253
  Tomato and Dill, 126
  Vichyssoise, 263
  Watercress, 191
Soup, Hot
  Asparagus, 101
  Black Bean, with Garnishes, 85
  Consommé Normande, 119
  Fish Chowder, 258
  Jerusalem Artichoke, 146
  Mushroom Broth Garnished with Mushroom Rounds, 51
  Mushroom, Cream of, 99
  Onion, French, Gratiné, 29

Soup, Hot (*Cont.*)
  Oyster Stew, 75
  Passatelli, 78
  Pea Pod, 216
  Potage Saint-Germain, 221
  Watercress, 191
Sour Cream
  Dressing, 176
  Pastry, 288
Soy Dipping Sauce, 142
Spareribs, Barbecued, 143
Spatula, wooden, 6
Spinach Mousse, Cold, 51
Spinach Timbales, 121
Squabs, Glazed, 127
Squabs à l'Orange, 166
Starch for thickening, 6
Steak Tartare, 221
Stew, Oyster, Hot, 75
Stock
  Beef, 278
  Chicken, 278
  Fish, 169, 279
  Veal, 279
Strawberry, Strawberries
  Barquettes, 49
  in Fresh Orange Juice, 27
  over Homemade Vanilla Ice
    Cream, 176
  Roll, 248
  Sauce, 106
Straw Potatoes, 127
Stuffings and Fillings
  Forcemeat for Pâté, 230
  Mushroom Duxelles, 284
  Mushroom-Ham Stuffing, 121
  Soubise Filling, 157
  Stuffing for Beef Birds, 254
Supper Menus, 216–226
  After Theater, Ballet, or Opera
    (8), 216
  Election Night (10), 224
  Late Night Champagne (6), 218
  Robust, for Poker Players (12),
    220
Swedish Almond Cake, 100
Sweetbreads, Ris de Veau, Velouté
    Sauce, 172
Sweet Potatoes, Whipped, 160

Tartar Sauce, 55
Tea, 244
Toasts
  English Muffins, Toasted, and
    Strawberry Jam, 246
  French Toast, Double-Dipped,
    22
  Melba Rounds, 42
  Melba Toast Fingers, 236
Tomato, Tomatoes
  Beefsteak, and Chives Marinated
    in Sour Cream Dressing, 176
  Cherry Tomatoes
    with Coarse Salt, 265
    Stuffed with Crab Meat, 234
    Stuffed with Guacamole, 158,
      234
    Vinaigrette, 173
  with Chives, 73
  and Dill Soup, Cold, 126
  Grilled, 33, 35
  Roses, 284
  Salad, 87
  Sauce, 64
  with Soubise, Baked, 184
  Stuffed with Crab-Meat Salad,
    268
Tortes, *see* Cakes and Tortes
Tourinoise, La, 206
Trifle, 208
Trout
  Amandine, 138
  Brandade of, 234
  Poached, Glazed, on Aspic, 124
  Poached, with Hollandaise Sauce,
    113
Turkey
  Breast and Ham Paupiettes, 107
  Roast, Cold, Sandwiches, 246
  with Tarragon Butter, Roast, 147
Turnip Roses, 284
Turnips, Braised, 150
Tyropita, 153

Vanilla Ice Cream, Homemade
  (with Strawberries), 176
Vanilla Water Icing, 27

Veal
  Birds with Brown Sauce, 133
  Breast of, Stuffed with Pâté, 264
  Loaf en Croûte, Peppered, 269
  Orloff, 156
  Rack of, Béarnaise, 124
  Stock, 279
  Sweetbreads, Ris de Veau, Ve-
    louté Sauce, 172
Vegetable, Vegetables, *see also*
    names of vegetables
  Crudités with Coarse Salt, 272
  Garniture Bourgeoise, 188
  Raw, with Olive Butter, 234
Velouté Sauce, 280
Venison Bourguignonne, 139
Vichyssoise, 263
Viennese Coffee, 27
Vinaigrette Dressing, French, 283
Violet Soufflé, Hot, 212

Walnut Cake, 271
Watercress
  and Belgian Endive Salad, 42

Watercress (*Cont.*)
  Salad, 122; with Cherry Toma-
    toes and Chives, 162
  Soup, 191
Whisk, 6
Wild Rice Ring, 148
Wine-Flavored Dishes
  Beef Birds, 254
  Beef Burgundy, 178
  Beef à la Mode, 187
  Broccoli with White Wine, 225
  Chicken Suprêmes with Cham-
    pagne Sauce, 120
  Fruit and Champagne, 89
  Melon with Port Wine, 30
  Peaches in Port, 46
  Pears Poached in White Wine,
    165
  Sangría, 276
  Venison Bourguignonne, 139

Zabaglione, 203; Cold, 134
Zucchini, French-Fried, 134
Zucchini, Stuffed, 201